The author realistically examines both the strengths and weaknesses of the French political system in an attempt to assess its ability—or inability—to face and solve its problems. He discusses the sharp cultural and ideological divisions that have always impinged upon the political process and that have made for constant internal disagreement on the very nature of the political regime. And he offers clear insight into the character of a democracy which upholds defiance and suspicion of the state as the best guaranty of individual freedom.

Concise and comprehensive, M. Duverger's book is an honest critical analysis of the French system that no student of French government or of comparative politics should ignore.

About the author . . .

MAURICE DUVERGER is one of France's most astute political economists, and his earlier book, *Political Parties,* is well known to American political scientists. He is professor of law and political science at the University of Paris and vice-president of the International Political Science Association.

THE FRENCH POLITICAL
SYSTEM

THE CHICAGO LIBRARY OF COMPARATIVE POLITICS

ROY C. MACRIDIS, EDITOR

The Soviet System of Government

JOHN N. HAZARD

The Administrative State

FRITZ MORSTEIN MARX

The French Political System

MAURICE DUVERGER

THE FRENCH POLITICAL SYSTEM

By Maurice Duverger

Translated by Barbara and Robert North

THE UNIVERSITY OF CHICAGO PRESS

Library of Congress Catalog Number: 58-5538

THE UNIVERSITY OF CHICAGO PRESS, CHICAGO 37
Cambridge University Press, London, N.W. 1, England
The University of Toronto Press, Toronto 5, Canada

© *1958 by The University of Chicago*
Published 1958
Composed and printed by
THE UNIVERSITY OF CHICAGO PRESS
Chicago, Illinois, U.S.A.

FOREWORD

To the student of comparative politics the French political system is a challenge, for it seems to defy generalization or explanation except as it testifies to the uniqueness of the French mind, culture, history, and politics. No other country bedevils the student more if he tries to apply a systematic theory in terms of which similarities among systems may be identified or differences explained. Why is the country of Descartes and of the Revolution of 1789 one where history and tradition in politics play a far more important role than do discussion and deliberation? Why is a country with a deep and pervasive sense of nationhood so much divided and its people so suspicious of the French state itself and of its political regime? Why is the idea of the Republic associated with this posture of hostility and defiance to public authority? Why is the very heart of politics—ongoing and decisive compromise of interests—so grossly distorted in France, where the various social, political, and ideological forces, barricaded behind old slogans and symbols, are unable to reach any decisions?

Since 1918 the same, recurring problems have faced the Republic, and never since 1918 have solutions been found. The need to strengthen the executive and establish genuine parliamentary institutions; the need to treat public and parochial schools consistently; the need for fiscal reform; the need for an electoral system to satisfy the majority of the political groups; the need to assimilate or to free the French colonies; the need for industrial expansion and with it an equitable wage policy; the need to modernize the country, especially its agriculture and the agricultural sections where the wine lobby reigns; the need for decentralization in order to inject some life into local government; the need to define France's position in the world, particularly in Europe—all these are talked about, and none are dealt with. Have these problems been candidly faced by the French political leadership and in the French political system? Have the political parties attempted to clarify the issues for the electorate? Has the average voter, so articulate and astute in private conversation, understood his country's problems? If not, why?

It is to these questions that Professor Duverger addresses himself in this volume, which he has written expressly for American students. Perhaps it would be more accurate to say that he keeps these questions constantly in mind as he describes the political institutions of his country. He briefly analyzes the political regimes France has known since 1789—without being able to avoid a wistful glance across the Atlantic, where a single regime has not only existed for a long time but has also gained a remarkable ascendancy over the minds and hearts of its citizens. Such a state of "legitimacy" is unknown in France, where there are many "legitimacies," he points out. Then he discusses in detail the institutions of the Fourth Republic and compares them with the institutions of the Third. Though, as he mentions, the Republic is widely accepted today, conflict over its institutions continues, and the weight of the past is beginning to reassert itself. Slowly the Fourth Republic is beginning to look more and more like the Third. Slowly the old quarrels have reappeared. Slowly the right-wing forces, representing the backward sections of the country, have been gaining political strength. To explain why this has occurred, Professor Duverger undertakes in the second part of this book to discuss political parties and pressure groups, to examine their tactics and analyze their ideology. For many readers, this will seem the most original part of the study, and Duverger brings to it his unique knowledge of French politics. Part III is a logical projection of Part II. Theories and conceptions of French democracy are discussed, the mechanisms for the protection of personal rights are analyzed, and current problems facing the country—especially that of the French Union—are studied.

Finally, the author returns to the basic problems that have preoccupied him, and he gives us a "balance sheet" of the regime. He finds it deficient but not hopelessly so. There are new forces at work in France, and perhaps the unrest the country is experiencing indicates that they are making headway. Economic expansion and modernization have been moving rapidly; men like Mendès-France, despite their failure thus far, herald a new type of political leadership that seeks to educate the electorate; and the Poujadist movement, now in decline, might be considered as the last revolt of what is old and static. The new demographic factor must be seriously considered, for France by 1975 will have the youngest population in western Europe. "A nation that is being rejuvenated will burst the confines of the shell," Duverger writes. What form this outburst will take the author is reluctant to predict except to reassure us that republican traditions are so deeply ingrained as to prevent a totalitarian, revolutionary adventure.

The teacher and student who use this volume, comprehensive in itself, are asked to use it as an instrument for comparative study. The author links political ideology, social and economic structures, and political institutions in such a way that we can study the dynamics of the system. The same scheme of analysis can be projected to the study of other political systems. Like our previous volumes, this book stands by itself, but it is part of a series with the purpose of raising questions that train the student to compare and generalize.

Roy C. Macridis

TABLE OF CONTENTS

GENERAL INTRODUCTION

PART I. THE INSTITUTIONS OF GOVERNMENT

PART II. POLITICAL FORCES

PART III. INDIVIDUAL LIBERTY AND LOCAL AUTONOMY

APPENDIXES

INDEX

GENERAL INTRODUCTION

The political divisions characteristic of the French system of government are not artificial. To a great extent they reflect natural divisions and result from the diversity of France.

Geography

The motorist who travels across France sees in a single day four or five kinds of countryside, an experience quite different from that of the motorist who travels the same distance across the western plains of the United States. It is possible to travel in a day from the northern part of France to the Mediterranean—that is, to cross the frontiers of two worlds. At Lille the traveler is on the edge of the great northern European plain that continues without any natural interruption to Poland and on to Russia as far as the Urals. In Marseilles one is closer in spirit as well as distance to Beirut, Tunis, Athens, Rome, Ankara—to the civilization of the Mediterranean. In a single day's travel, too, one can pass from the last outposts of Alpine Central Europe to the shores of the Atlantic, from mountain life to the life of the seaboard.

The variety of France arises of course from the fact that several kinds of terrain, soil, cultivation, and landscape are to be found side by side in a limited area. But its variety results more fundamentally from the fact that France is at the meeting place of several great and differing civilizations, at the point of intersection of their frontiers. Small wonder then that in France different ways of living, different habits of thought, and different conceptions of life belong to different kinds of civilization. The natural reactions of the people of Strasbourg, of Nice, of Lyons, and of Bordeaux are more than superficially distinct.

Race

The variety of races among the French will not astonish Americans; they are themselves familiar with great racial diversity. Compared with other European countries, however, France is somewhat exceptional in this respect. A comparison of France with Italy, Spain, the Scandinavian countries, Germany, and Great Britain reveals a notable difference. The population of France includes some individuals who belong to the racial type dominant in Italy, others of the type dominant in Spain, and still others of the type dominant in Scandinavia.

Racial diversity corresponds more or less to geographical diversity; in this respect the contrast between northern and southern France is fairly sharp. But it also corresponds to a historical situation. After the Roman conquest the Gauls had adopted the customs and institutions of the conqueror. Then the Germanic invasions brought new tribes, customs, and institutions, which fused only partially with the old. On the basis of these events nineteenth-century historians built up quite a theory to explain the opposition between the supporters of the monarchical *ancien régime* and the supporters of the Revolution of 1789, who were still engaged in bitter conflict in the 1800's. According to Augustin Thierry, for example, the conflict reflected the struggle between the two races, Gallo-Romans and Germans. The nobility was of Germanic origin issuing from the conquest; the Third Estate corresponded to the Gallo-Roman conquered. This accounted, according to Thierry, for the persistence of the opposition between the liberty-loving Gallo-Romans and the Germanic partisans of patriarchal institutions and authoritarian monarchy. Today this hypothesis is discounted, but it is interesting to recall if only to show that the French themselves are conscious of their own racial variety.

The fact that since the beginning of the twentieth century France has possessed a vast colonial empire, at present in process of transformation, increases this diversity. The Parliament in Paris includes a considerable number of colored deputies. The not entirely abandoned doctrine of the Third Republic, which aimed at eventual total assimilation between the people of France and the population of French overseas territories, led to an accentuation of the racial diversity of France. In some cases the assimilation has been quite successful. The President of the upper house of Parliament, the Council of the Republic, is a Negro elected by one of the oldest French departments, Lot, on the border of the *Massif Central*.

Ideology

Differences in ideology stem from the Revolution of 1789 and from the Religious Wars in France. These wars ended in the triumph of the Catholics and the partial elimination of the Protestants, but Protestant minorities still play an important part in politics. Moreover, within the ranks of French Catholics there are traditional divergences. To some extent the present-day opposition between liberal Catholics and those who support a rigid doctrine of Church supremacy reproduces the divisions of previous centuries.

More striking than religious differences are the differences in political ideology in France. The foreigner is at once impressed by the existence of a powerful Communist party, which does not accept the principles of the Western democratic system. On the extreme Right, movements more or less Fascist in type take the same kind of stand. By contrast, in the countries of northern Europe, in Great Britain, and in the United States, disagreement is confined to matters of detail; all parties agree on the essentials and especially on the system itself. They fight within the system, but they accept it. In France, on the other hand, it is the system itself which is questioned, but, as we shall see, this fact must not be overweighted. Indeed, it has been suggested that a distinction should be drawn within the Western political system between "unitary" and "pluralist" democracies.

It must be made clear, however, that this difference of political opinion is not new in France. During the nineteenth century the opposition between liberals who supported the ideas of 1789 and conservatives who supported absolute monarchy was just as intense and just as deep: the coexistence of the two groups appeared to contemporaries as impossible as the coexistence of Communists and non-Communists seems to us today. And before that, in the middle of the eighteenth century, one whole section of public opinion was questioning the monarchical principle. In the seventeenth century, at a time when political power was primarily based upon religious concepts, the Religious Wars produced a similar difference of view. Throughout the greater part of its history, therefore, France presents a picture of a country much divided ideologically. At the same time, it is a country in which all the citizens display a profound desire to live together; for the long history of ideological oppositions coincides, paradoxically, with a sense of nationhood. France is the oldest nation on the Continent.

Economy

A varied economy was viewed with favor by most French writers up to 1939. They expatiated on the theme "France, the land of balance"; indeed, they tried to demonstrate the existence of a balance between agricultural and industrial production, balance within the different sectors of agriculture, balance between mass production and crafts, balance between small shops and large stores, balance between different branches of industry.

All this made manifest the profound variety of France's economy. Today the variety is still noted, but it is viewed differently. Instead of being considered an advantage, it is held to be a disadvantage and a hindrance to the development of the French economy. The variety is based in fact upon the existence of economic sectors at very different stages of development.

Generally speaking, the organization of industry is more up-to-date than that of agriculture. Within each category, however, there exist very different situations. In France a modern mechanized agriculture that is highly productive, like wheat raising in the Paris basin and sugar-beet growing in the North, exists alongside small farms worked by medieval methods and owned by families little different from their twelfth-century ancestors, as in some districts in the *Massif Central*. There are, of course, many intermediate situations. In commerce there is an equally striking contrast between the large modern department store and the old-fashioned small shop. In industry the difference is less obvious at first sight. There is, however, a very modern group, including metals, chemicals, mining, gas, electricity and railways; and it will be noted that this modern group is made up of nationalized industries together with some large private industries. By contrast, there exists a group that is more or less obsolete, in which the firms are frequently family concerns with outdated equipment, and in which productivity is lower and production costs higher. The textile industry offers a good instance, although the severe crisis of the last few years has eliminated many unprofitable firms.

The Myth of "Two Frances"

Contemporary French writers are fond of describing an opposition between two Frances—France north of the Loire as against France south of the Loire. They are somewhat vague about the exact frontier, but it would seem to run roughly from the mouth of the Loire to Geneva.

Primarily this is a historical frontier. South of the Loire the Romans made a deep imprint, and Roman institutions had a profound influence on life. North of the Loire the Romans made less impression, and their institutions consequently had less effect on the way of life. Germanic institutions were much more developed north of the Loire than they were south of it. Thus in the Middle Ages the land north of the Loire was a land of Germanic common law, whereas Roman law applied to the south. The difference is appreciable even in language: local speech and dialects north of the Loire belong to the *langue d'oïl*, whereas those to the south belong to the *langue d'oc, oïl* and *oc* corresponding to modern French *oui*.

The opposition is said to be equally visible in the economy: France north of the Loire is dynamic and demographically progressive, has modern farms, and is the seat of large-scale industry. Southern France is static, demographically in decline. Its departments are losing population, its peasantry is attached to outdated methods, its commerce is largely confined to small shopkeeping, and it has few modern industries.

Finally, a political divergence between these two Frances is said to exist. Communism, for example, is especially strong north of the Loire, while General de Gaulle's RPF party (*Rassemblement du Peuple français*) had its principal strength in the same region. The MRP (*Mouvement républicain populaire*) is a party of the North too. South of the Loire the Radicals (now a Center party), the traditional Right, and also the Poujadists have their greatest strength.

These facts are all true, but there is a tendency to exaggerate them. It is quite untrue that the Loire represents a sharply defined frontier. If we go a little deeper into these oversimplified contrasts, we find that some areas south of the Loire are being fully developed, notably the Maritime Alps, the Southeast, Isère, and Savoy. It has been suggested also that a North-South line rather than an East-West line of demarcation (the former contrasting the Atlantic plains with the rest of France) would be more accurate, since the seaboard plains are in fact the regions in decline. But many distinctions would have to be made. The variety of France is not easily reduced to simple terms. Simple generalizations lead to a caricature. Nevertheless, we shall from time to time make use of the division north and south of the Loire insofar as it is pertinent to some aspects of political problems.

THE WEIGHT OF THE PAST

Mark Twain in one of his stories explains that to understand a speech made by a French politician you must have a history textbook. There is a good deal of truth in the satire. Political life in France often creates the impression that ancestral quarrels are being continued rather than the impression that present-day problems are being tackled. The impression does not correspond exactly with reality, however. Politicians and parties refer frequently to history, but behind the language real opinions on current questions are being defined. French political language has a conventional, an esoteric side to it. There is no misunderstanding, however, on the part of the population and the electorate.

Once this has been said, it remains true that French political life is largely dominated by historical memories. Of all the nations in the world, France has one of the longest political memories, and this is a considerable burden on political life today.

Importance of the Revolution of 1789

The French consider the year 1789 to be a fundamental dividing line. In school syllabuses, for example, history before 1789 is given less attention than subsequent history. The *baccalauréat* syllabus begins with the French Revolution, and though the period prior to 1789 is nonetheless studied, it does not figure on the examination syllabus.

The importance thus accorded to 1789 is justified in fact. During the thousand years prior to 1789 there was no great revolution against the very structure of the political system. The French monarchy did indeed change profoundly in the course of those ten centuries; it evolved from a feudal monarchy, in which the king was almost powerless, to the absolute, centralized monarchy of Louis XIV. But the transformation came slowly, without violent change. By contrast, the Revolution of 1789 represented a break. It did not, however, succeed immediately in setting up a new system. The century following the Revolution was a century of constitutional instability. As we shall see, some fifteen political systems were to succeed one another between 1789 and 1875. Constitutional stability was not recovered until the foundation of the Third Republic; and ministerial instability then to some extent continued the constitutional instability of the preceding century.

In the eyes of the French the Revolutionary epoch does not belong entirely to the pages of history. Discussions between historians over different aspects of the Revolution still have political relevance. When Lamartine wrote his *Histoire des Girondins,* he aimed at rehabilitating the Republic from the bloody memories of the Jacobin Terror: it was a political act. When at the outset of the twentieth century the two great historians Aulard and Mathiez were at odds over the respective roles of Danton and Robespierre (Aulard was a Dantonist, Mathiez a Robespierrist), their views also involved taking a stand on contemporary issues. In the political language of our day there are constant references to the vocabulary of the Revolution and to the great men of the Revolution. But it does not follow that this shows any failure to comprehend present-day problems. What is involved is an attempt to invest current opinions with the prestige of memories of the Revolution.

Political Instability in the Nineteenth Century

Fundamentally, the United States and France both began their modern political history at about the same period, the end of the eighteenth century. The American Constitution dates from 1787, the first French constitutional text—the Declaration of the Rights of Man—from 1789. Since 1787, however, the United States has retained the same constitution, subject to a few amendments, whereas France has had a succession of fifteen different political systems, often greatly contrasting. This explains why the French do not display toward their constitution the veneration with which Americans surround theirs. It also explains why the very structure of the system is attacked by one group of Frenchmen, whereas for Americans their constitution is no longer a matter of discussion.

Let us briefly review the regimes since 1789. The Constitution of 1791 set limits to the old absolute monarchy by establishing a countervailing parliament elected on the basis of a property franchise. It was applied only for a year, however, because the monarchy was overthrown and the First Republic declared on August 10, 1792. During the First Republic a number of regimes rapidly succeeded one another: first came the revolutionary dictatorship; then, after the fall of Robespierre, a period of disorder; next, the Constitution of Year III (1795), known as the Directory Constitution, established a very complicated democratic system in which legislative power lay with two assemblies elected on the basis of a property franchise, while executive power lay with a College of five Directors who were elected by the assemblies but could not be overthrown by them. When the Directory proved ineffective, a second dictatorship, this time military, was set up by the coup d'état of 18 Brumaire (second month in the calendar of the First Republic), after which Bonaparte seized power. The Constitution of Year VIII (1799) established a dictatorship, which was transformed four years later into an imperial monarchy with a false show of democracy (e.g., universal suffrage, meaningless for all practical purposes, and representative assemblies, so numerous as to lack prestige). This regime lasted fifteen years.

The defeat of the imperial armies led to the return of the monarchy. The brother of Louis XVI became king under the title of

Louis XVIII and drew up a new constitution, the Charter of 1814, which marked the first important stage in the introduction of the parliamentary system in France. The other brother of Louis XVIII, who as Charles X succeeded him on his death, did not agree with the parliamentary interpretation of the Charter and attempted a return to authoritarian monarchy. This provoked the Revolution of 1830, which brought no more than a change of dynasty: the cousin of Charles X became king under the title of Louis Philippe I. The Charter of 1830 differed in only a few details from that of 1814. Consequently, from 1814 to 1848 France was governed by parliamentary monarchies, and this gave her a certain political stability. The popular basis of the regime was very limited, however, since deputies were elected on the basis of a very limited suffrage. There were only 100,000 voters from 1814 to 1830 and 200,000 from 1830 to 1848 out of a population of more than 30 million.

The refusal of Louis Philippe to extend the franchise caused the Revolution of 1848, which proclaimed the Second Republic. The revolutionaries, however, were divided into a liberal middle class and a socialist working class. The former, afraid of a social revolution, moved toward the moderates and conservatives. Having quelled in blood a workers' rising (June Days, 1848), they adopted a republican constitution based on the American model. It provided for a president directly elected by universal suffrage, a single assembly elected by universal suffrage, and separation of powers. There was one legislative chamber, not two, for France was a unitary and not a federal country. This constitution remained in force for three years, during which the legislative majority was composed of monarchist deputies and the President was the pretender to the imperial throne. This "Republic without republicans" could not last. In fact, on December 2, 1851, the President by a coup d'état transformed it into a dictatorship. The Constitution of 1852, then enacted, was very similar to that of Year VIII.

The new emperor, Napoleon III, was to some extent a liberal. He gradually attenuated the dictatorship by a series of important reforms until in 1870 a new constitution re-established a parliamentary system somewhat similar to Louis Philippe's. But the defeat of the French armies at Sedan a few weeks later overthrew the empire, and a republic was proclaimed for the third time.

The Third Republic and the New "Legitimacy"

The proclamation of the Third Republic opened a new era in French constitutional history. The lapse of time from 1789 to 1875 is approximately the same as that from 1875 to the present, but the earlier period was much less stable politically than the later period has been. About fifteen constitutions were declared during the first period, but in the second period a single system has functioned except during the German Occupation (1940–44).

On the surface, the new regime instituted by the Third Republic did not differ markedly from that of Louis Philippe, despite the fact that it ended the era of revolutions and constitutional instability. A parliamentary republic was created instead of a parliamentary monarchy, but the Constitution of 1875 was drawn up by an assembly with a monarchist majority. Basically, however, the Third Republic incorporated two important differences: male suffrage was made universal, and Parliament became the sovereign institution in the state.

Military defeat led to the collapse of the regime in 1940, when the aged Marshal Pétain was temporarily invested with dictatorial powers. But the new constitution drawn up in 1946, after the Liberation, closely resembles that of 1875.

Throughout the nineteenth century, there was intense opposition to the very nature of every regime. For some, the only truly "legitimate" regime was the traditional monarchy; for others, the only possible "legitimacy" lay in the sovereignty of the people, and this implied a republic. The two Napoleons and Louis Philippe attempted to fuse the two legitimacies. Napoleon I sought both popular investiture, by means of elections and the plebiscite, and divine investiture, on which traditional monarchy was based, by papal consecration. Louis Philippe was king both by the will of the Chamber of Deputies which had called him to the throne and by virtue of belonging to the royal family. These attempts to reconcile such contradictory systems could not of course succeed in practice.

In 1875 the parliamentary republic was also contested, but little by little this opposition disappeared. Opinion polls have shown that the majority even of Communist voters are today attached to the regime. It is a striking fact that the draft constitution left among his papers by Marshal Pétain strongly resembled the Constitution of 1875, despite amendments of a conservative tendency. In the same way, after the announcement on the morrow of Liberation of a "revolution," a constitution was drawn up closely resembling that of 1875, though modified in the direction of greater democracy. Herein lies the proof that the parliamentary republic has become a "legitimate" regime, that is, has become very widely accepted by public opinion. Few dare declare a desire to overthrow the parliamentary republic.

There is some contradiction between these considerations and previous remarks about French Communists and Fascists who disagree with their countrymen over the value of Western democracy. But this contradiction exists in the French mentality itself. The majority of Communist voters are not ready to overthrow the parliamentary regime; typically, the Communists make little reference in their propaganda to the "dictatorship of the proletariat." Nor does anyone dare call himself a Fascist. Certainly the present regime does not arouse much enthusiasm; it is even despised, somewhat unjustly, by a certain section of opinion. But no other system is considered.

This does not prevent many Frenchmen from saying—and even believing—that they are "revolutionaries." Such verbal violence makes up for great conservatism in practice. If we are really to understand French political life, we must never forget that its principal defect is not instability, as is too often thought, but an excess of stability—a defect that has been called "immobility."

PART I

THE INSTITUTIONS OF GOVERNMENT

INTRODUCTION

A parliamentary regime, in the technical sense of the term, is a political system in which the executive is divided into two organs: a head of state who performs ceremonial functions but does not directly share in the exercise of power; a cabinet led by a head of government who in fact exercises governmental authority. In Great Britain, where parliamentary government was first introduced, the form of monarchy was preserved. In fact, until France became a parliamentary republic in 1875—through a compromise between moderate royalists and moderate republicans—only parliamentary monarchies were known.

Though the French parliamentary regime established in 1875 was suppressed by the German invasion of 1940 and though in referendums held after the Liberation voters declined to restore the Third Republic, the Constitution of 1946 is very similar to its predecessor of 1875. The former Chamber of Deputies is now called the National Assembly, and the former Senate is now known as the Council of the Republic, under which title it has less power than did the second chamber in the Third Republic. Procedural changes have affected the method of choosing and dismissing the head of government and his ministers, and proportional representation with list voting by departments has replaced the old single-member majority system. But these differences are relatively slight.

Similarities between the Third Republic and the Fourth Republic have become more pronounced over the last ten years. In the first place, political figures of the Third Republic who were at first barred from office in the Fourth Republic because of their supposed support of Marshal Pétain and collaboration with the Germans have returned to political life. Meanwhile the dynamic young leaders of the Resistance movement during the Occupation, who held power immediately after the war, have been losing control. The return to power of President Queuille was highly symptomatic of this trend, for he was a noted prewar leader. In the second place, the habits and practices of the Third Republic are being reintroduced into the

Fourth Republic. The constitutional reform of December 7, 1954, emphasized this development by re-establishing, as we shall see, some of the powers of the second chamber, the Council of the Republic. It is noteworthy that these developments parallel a swing to the right in political power. In 1945 and 1946 the left-wing parties wanted a republic more progressive than the 1875 model, while the right-wing parties wanted to return to it. From 1947 on, power has shifted toward the center, and the right-wing trend has been more marked.

CHAPTER 1

PARLIAMENT

The French Parliament is made up of two chambers: the National Assembly, which sits in the Palais Bourbon on the bank of the Seine opposite the Place de la Concorde, and the Council of the Republic, which meets in Luxembourg Palace near the Latin Quarter and adjoining the magnificent Luxembourg Gardens. The two chambers differ greatly in size, electoral composition, and powers. Ordinarily the National Assembly is composed of 626 members (627 before the French Indian territories, which used to elect a deputy, were returned to India). The Assembly elected on January 2, 1956, however, consists of only 596 members, because it was impossible to hold elections in the Algerian departments, which used to send 30 deputies. The Council of the Republic consists of 320 members. Delegates to the National Assembly are elected by direct universal suffrage, whereas those of the Council of the Republic are elected indirectly by a method that gives preponderance to the rural districts.

Members of the National Assembly are called "deputies"; members of the Council of the Republic are called *conseillers de la République* or "senators." The "conseillers" decided in 1948 to revert to the old title of "sénateurs" to demonstrate their nostalgia for the power and prestige of the second chamber under the Third Republic. Article 5 of the Constitution of 1946 declares, "Parliament is composed of the National Assembly and the Council of the Republic," but in fact only the Assembly has real power.

The importance of Parliament, despite the weakening of the second chamber, is greater today than it was under the Third Republic. The majority of those responsible for the regime of 1875 were monarchists, who naturally restricted Parliament by institutional counterweights. Today the sovereignty of Parliament—a traditional and fundamental republican idea in France—is strongly established, although a gradual increase in the importance of the Cabinet has caused some discrepancy between theory and practice.

QUALIFICATIONS OF MEMBERSHIP

Eligibility

In order to qualify for election to Parliament, one must be a voter, but not all voters are eligible. Deputies must be at least twenty-three years old and "senators" at least thirty-five years old, as compared with twenty-one years old for voters. Naturalized citizens are eligible to vote five years after naturalization but may not be elected to Parliament until ten years after naturalization unless they receive a decree of dispensation for exceptional services.

Individuals may be ineligible because of legal restraints, as in the case of owners whose business is going through voluntary liquidation (a mitigated form of bankruptcy) and in the case of persons who have been convicted of electoral fraud or bribery. Certain important officials may not present themselves for election in the constituency in which they held office until six months have elapsed since their resignation or transfer. Prefects, subprefects, general secretaries of prefectures, generals commanding military regions, judges, public prosecutors, and some directors of public technical services are constrained in this way to avoid the possibility of their using undue influence in their constituency. From 1944 to 1953, persons convicted of collaboration with the Germans or with Marshal Pétain's Vichy regime or of wartime profiteering were disqualified for election to Parliament.

Conflict of Interests

The successful candidate is obliged to choose between his parliamentary mandate and his office or professional position where the law declares them incompatible. To avoid the faults of the July monarchy (1830–48), under which deputies could at the same time be civil servants and therefore easily influenced by the government, all civil and military offices are held to be incompatible with the parliamentary mandate. This rule of incompatibility applies likewise to those in managerial positions in the nationalized industries, e.g., railways, coal, gas, and electricity. The only exceptions are professors holding chairs in the universities or in the Collège de France, for they are considered to be independent of the government. It is also possible for a deputy to be appointed to a temporary government mission for a period not exceeding six months. This arrangement has led to certain abuses since 1946, through the renewing of missions.

There are other cases of incompatibility in connection with private professions, the aim being to remove members of Parliament from financial influence and to prevent their using their mandate to obtain concessions from the state for the firms to which they belong. It is deemed incompatible with the parliamentary mandate to hold a managerial position in a joint-stock company formed with a purely financial aim (e.g., banks and loan companies) or in a company engaged on state contracts (e.g., public works).

Parliamentary Privileges

Members of Parliament enjoy legal immunity from certain kinds of civil and criminal prosecution. The aim is to protect them in the exercise of their functions.

First, the member of Parliament is protected from any legal action that might be brought against him in connection with the exercise of his duties. For example, if a deputy slanders someone in a speech in the Assembly, that person cannot take legal action against him. This is as much a protection against criminal proceedings as against civil actions for damages, but it is only applicable to acts accomplished by the deputy in the exercise of his functions. It does not cover newspaper articles, speeches at public or private meetings, blows or wounds inflicted on another deputy or a journalist within the precincts of the Assembly, and so on.

Second, the member of Parliament is protected from actions brought against him because of acts committed outside the exercise of his duties, that is to say because of felonies and misdemeanors. If a member of Parliament commits a theft or a murder he cannot be prosecuted. This privilege seems extravagant, but its aim is really to prevent the government from prosecuting members of Parliament for acts they may not have committed and so preventing them from taking their seats. It is a precautionary measure against false arrest and undue pressure.

The protection is not absolute, however. The chamber to which the member belongs may vote to suspend the immunity. Moreover, there are two exceptions in which prosecution is possible without the consent of the chamber: if the member of Parliament is caught in the act or if he is arrested when Parliament is not in session. The second exception had been suppressed by the Constitution of 1946 but was re-established by the reform of December 7, 1954, with certain restrictions. The member arrested while Parliament is not sitting can vote by proxy when a session opens, and he must be freed within thirty days following the opening of the session unless in the meantime the chamber has decided to suspend his immunity. Even when Parliament is not sitting, the deputy can be arrested only if the Bureau of the chamber gives its authorization, except when he is caught in the act. Finally the Assembly can always by vote order the cessation of proceedings against a member.

Salary of Members of Parliament

Members of Parliament receive a salary which is fixed in relation to the remuneration of a category of civil servants (Art. 23 of the Constitution) called Councillors of State. This indirect method of determining the remuneration of deputies was devised in order to avoid demagogy. It is a tradition in France for some sections of the public to protest when deputies' salaries are increased. Nevertheless, a high salary is a means of protecting deputies from temptation and of making it possible for them to perform their duties in a fitting manner. The present parliamentary salary is about $800 a month, which is not sufficient insofar as the member of Parliament has to provide for his own secretarial work. Secretarial expenses come to about $300 a month. Besides his salary the member of Parliament receives a free permit for railway travel throughout France and on the public transport services of metropolitan Paris.

INTERNAL ORGANIZATION

The organization of the French Parliament does not differ much from that of the parliaments of other democratic states. It transacts business through rules of order voted by the chambers themselves. Each chamber has at its head a Bureau elected by itself, the duty of which is to control the debates. The work of Parliament is prepared by committees. One point of organization peculiar to the French system is the official recognition of political parties in the National Assembly under the title of parliamentary "groups."

The Bureau

The Bureau must not be confused with the *bureaux*, which are ephemeral bodies chosen by lot at the beginning of each legislature to verify the credentials of the deputies and to consider the demands for invalidation made by defeated opponents. Neither must the Bureau be confused with the *bureau d'âge* which controls debates in the Assembly at the opening of the legislature or at the beginning of each annual session before the election of the real Bureau. On these occasions the oldest deputy becomes president and the youngest deputies become secretaries.

The real Bureau is a very important body. It is composed in each chamber of a president, 6 vice-presidents, 14 secretaries, and 3 stewards. The Bureau is elected annually by its chamber at the beginning of its session. The Constitution of 1946 laid down that it should be elected by proportional representation of the "groups," but the reform of December 7, 1954, put an end to this requirement. This was done in order to rid the Bureau of Communists. In practice there is even now a certain amount of proportional representation.

The President of the Bureau (and hence of the chamber) is elected by secret ballot. His function consists of presiding over debates with complete impartiality, and according to tradition he does not take part in the voting. The President of the National Assembly, but not the President of the Council of the Republic, has an executive role also. He acts as Provisional President of the Republic when the latter is incapacitated or the post is vacant. He promulgates laws if the President of the Republic does not so do within the time laid down by the Constitution. He must be consulted before any dissolution of the Assembly. He automatically becomes Premier and Minister of the Interior when the dissolution of Parliament is announced after a vote of censure.* He is a member of the Constitutional Committee. The vice-presidents act as deputies for him in presiding over debates. The secretaries are responsible for drawing up the minutes of the chamber and for counting votes, but in practice these duties are carried out by very experienced clerks. The shorthand service of the National Assembly, particularly, is organized in a remarkable fashion. The duties of the stewards consist of the administration of the buildings and materials and the recruiting and supervision of staff ushers, secretaries, typists, librarians, and so on.

The Groups

A rule passed by the Chamber of Deputies in 1910 recognized the existence of political groups in Parliament. The Constitution of 1946 gave official sanction to their existence and accorded them important duties. In order to participate in the duties thus laid down, a group must have at least fourteen members in the National Assembly, and it must be strictly a political group. Forming groups for the protection of particular interests, e.g., those of beetroot growers or

---

* This is to be distinguished from the situation in which a Cabinet crisis and dissolution of Parliament follow a vote of no confidence. In that case the Premier remains in office and calls for a national election.

wine producers, is forbidden. In practice this rule has been circumvented by the formation of study groups which have no official duties but are not without influence. Membership in political groups is optional, but a deputy who wishes to take part in committee work and in the planning of business must belong to or be affiliated with a group. If affiliated, he counts as one of the group, but he is not bound by the obligations the group imposes on its members, nor can he be considered to adopt the political viewpoint of the group.

The internal organization of the groups is most varied, for no rules about it are fixed either by the Constitution or by the chambers. The Communist and Socialist groups on the Left correspond to parties organized throughout the country. They have a very strong

TABLE 1

Party Groups	No. of Members and Affiliates
Communists	144
Progressives (associated with Communists)	5+1 affiliate
Socialists (SFIO)	94
Union of Democratic and Socialist Resistance and African Democratic Rally (UDSR-RDA)	18+1 affiliate
Radical Socialists	54+3 affiliates
Union of Left-Wing Republicans (RGR)	10+4 affiliates
Movement of Popular Republicans (MRP)	70+3 affiliates
Overseas Independents (associated with MRP)	10
Social Republicans	20+1 affiliate
Peasants-Independents	80+3 affiliates
Peasant Action (associated with Peasants-Independents)	13
French Union and Fraternity (UFF-Poujadist)	51+1 affiliate
Unregistered	9

organization, and their deputies must vote as the group dictates. In certain cases the executive committee of a party decides how its group in Parliament must vote. With the Radicals and MRP of the Center, the link with a national party exists, but discipline is less obvious. The Radicals knew no discipline with regard to their voting until 1957, when Mendès-France tried to establish some. The Radical group was to decide how its members should vote in important ballots. Those of its members who were not in agreement had the right to abstain but not to vote against the group. In practice these rules were and are seldom adhered to.

On the Right the groups do not generally correspond to organized parties. They have no discipline and are very fluid. At the beginning of a legislature there is quite often a certain amount of recruiting of adherents in order to swell the representation of the groups in the committees. In January, 1956, the National Assembly contained the groups listed in Table 1.

The Committees

There are two main committee systems in the democratic parliaments of the West: the British system and the Franco-American system. In Great Britain there are no permanent committees specializing in one category of problems (Finance Commitee, Committee of Justice, Foreign Affairs Committee, and so on). Committees are set up *ad hoc* for the study of each bill, or else the bills are passed on to one of the five large permanent and unspecialized committees. In France, as in the United States, permanent committees are set up to specialize in certain categories of problems. France adopted such committees in 1902 to do the work that was formerly done by the *bureaux* of the chambers, which were chosen by lot.

Today in the National Assembly there are 19 committees that have 44 members each. They are elected for a year at the beginning of each session. There are two other committees: one for Parliamentary Immunity, with 29 members, and one for Accounts, with 11 members. At present the list of committees is as follows: Economic Affairs; Foreign Affairs; Agriculture; Liquor; National Defense; National Education; Family, Population, and Public Health; Finance; Interior; Justice and Legislation; Pensions (civil and military); Press, Radio, Cinema, and Television; Industrial Production and Energy; Reconstruction, War Damage, and Housing; Universal Suffrage, Constitutional Laws, and Decrees and Petitions; Overseas Territories; Employment and Social Security; Merchant Marine and Fisheries; Communication and Tourism.

The committees are elected by the Assembly by proportional representation of the groups, and each group is allowed one representative for every fourteen members or affiliated members. Small groups make alliances in order to reach this figure. Groups may exchange committee seats among themselves, but no deputy may be a member of more than two committees. Some committees are more important than others, and the Finance Committee is the most important of all. In practice it is rare to vote the members to their committees. The officers of the groups agree among themselves as to the allocation of committee seats and the appointment of deputies. The proposals they have agreed upon are published in the *Journal Officiel*. If within three days fifty members of the Assembly object to these proposals, voting must take place; but if there is no such opposition, the candidates are considered to be elected. The committees elect a *bureau*. They have at their disposal a staff and a place for meeting, both of which, however, are inadequate. One of the difficulties of the French Parliament is that the accommodation is not sufficient, especially in the case of the National Assembly. As a rule the committees meet on Wednesdays or any weekday morning, since the Assembly meets in the afternoon every weekday except Wednesday.

For voting to be valid, the presence of the majority of committee members is necessary. Attendance at committee meetings, moreover, is obligatory, but it is permissible to send a replacement or to delegate one's vote to another committee member in writing. Three consecutive and unexcused absences or absence from a third of the meetings held in a single month may entail dismissal from the committee but this rule is not often applied.

The function of committees is dual. First, they examine all bills, whether initiated by the government or by a private member, before they are discussed by the Assembly. After an initial exchange of views, one of the members of the committee is appointed to be *rapporteur*. His duty is to make a further examination of the question and prepare a draft. (Only the Finance Committee has a permanent *rapporteur-général*.) The draft is then discussed by the committee. Once adopted, it is printed and distributed to the deputies as the basis of the debate that takes place in public session. Second, committees exercise a strict control over government action. They invite ministers, for example, to come and explain their point of view. Ministers are not obliged to do so, but politically it is in their interest that they should. Under the Third Republic, governments even resigned following a disagreement with an important committee. The Caillaux ministry did so in 1912 and that of Briand in 1922, following disagreements with the Foreign Affairs Committee. Such disagreements with a committee usually presaged a disagreement with the Assembly.

Apart from the permanent committees, the Assembly can always nominate special committees to examine particular questions. In practice this is done mostly in the form of "committees of inquiry," the role of which will be examined subsequently. Such special committees possess legal power, but they are less important than the investigating committees of the United States Congress.

The French committee system has been the subject of much discussion. It has been severely criticized by many writers on constitutional law, notably Joseph Barthélemy, and by many politicians, notably Poincaré, Tardieu, and Blum. The control of the committees over ministers of course weakens the authority of the latter, but above all it causes them a considerable waste of time. Provided they have the consent of the minister whose department is concerned, committees may interrogate high-ranking civil servants. This is a considerable extension of the idea of parliamentary control over the government. Moreover, the fact that parliamentary debate takes place on a bill amended by a committee and not on a bill as proposed by the government weakens the latter's right of initiative. The action of the Finance Committee with regard to budget proposals has been the subject of especially lively criticism from this point of view.

In spite of this criticism the powers of the committees are still developing because of the increase in the legislative work of Parliament. Theoretically, the committees are only screening and deliberative bodies. In fact, the tendency has been to give them real powers of decision and law-making. To a certain extent French committees are becoming in this way more like the committees of the Italian Parliament, to which the Italian Constitution grants a real share in the power to legislate. Here are some examples. The law of December 12, 1945, authorized the Finance Committee to revise the budget estimates of expenditure. The law of December 31, 1953, made it obligatory for the government to obtain the agreement of the Finance Committee before decreeing certain taxes. Finally, and most important of all, the decree of June 19, 1956, determining how the budget should be presented, gave to the Finance Committees of the two chambers a power to veto decisions with regard to the allocation of the credits fixed by the budget. Henceforth, all the budget does is to allocate large blocks of credit to each ministry. The detailed allocation is made by government decrees. A time limit of two months is fixed during which committees of the National Assembly or the Council of the Republic may oppose these decrees. If one of them does so, a debate opens in Parliament and the allocation of credits must be the subject of a law. If there is no opposition from the committees, the allocation by decrees is valid. This novel system was put into practice on several occasions before the decree of June 19, 1956. It has made a profound change in parliamentary procedure.

So far there have been few factual studies of the political orientation of committees. Because their composition is decided by proportional representation, they should in theory reflect the composition of Parliament, but in practice the representatives of groups on the various committees often hold extreme opinions as compared with their groups. For example, the MRP representatives on the Committee for Employment are rather advanced trade unionists standing as a general rule more to the left than their group.

PARLIAMENTARY DEBATES

Each parliament has a character of its own. Debates in the French National Assembly seem very different from those in the American House of Representatives or the British House of Commons. There is even some difference between the two chambers, for debates in the National Assembly are in general more animated and more passionate than those in the Council of the Republic.

Sessions

The word "session" is used to denote the period of time during which a chamber can validly meet and hold its sittings. The Council of the Republic sits at the same time as the National Assembly. It is the latter body, therefore, that makes the decisions with regard to sessions.

Under the Third Republic it was obligatory for the two chambers to have an annual session that opened in January and lasted five months. It became the custom also to convene them for an extraordinary session in the month of October, so as to pass the budget. In 1931–32 it was decided that the financial year should start on April 1, so that the budget could be passed during the ordinary session. Because this would have made the convocation of the extraordinary session superfluous and limited the time during which Parliament functioned, the reform was applied only for a year.

The Constitution of 1946 adopted a system of "permanent session" that made it mandatory for Parliament to convene on the second Tuesday in January. Then the National Assembly was free to make the session last as long as it wanted, althought it could not interrupt the session for more than four months. Any interruption decided on by the National Assembly applied equally to the Council of the Republic.

The constitutional reform of December 7, 1954, adopted a novel system closely related to that of 1875 but with a change of dates. Since then the ordinary session has opened on the first Tuesday in October. It must meet for at least seven months, against which period interruptions of more than a week may not be counted. When the seven months have passed, the President of the Council of Ministers may close the session by a decree of the Council. Therefore the budget is now passed in the ordinary session, so that there is no reason for convening an extraordinary session, and the government's freedom of action is increased. At the same time, Parliament is less restricted than it was by the reform of 1931–32, because the ordinary session has been lengthened by two months.

Should there be a real need, Parliament may be convened for an extraordinary session either by the President of the Council of Ministers or by the Bureau of the National Assembly. The Bureau is obliged to convene the Assembly at the request of half its members. When the session has been so convened by the Bureau, the government cannot declare a closure until the business for which the Assembly was called has been completed. Thus far convening at the request of the deputies has never taken place.

Sittings

When the Assembly (and therefore the Council of the Republic) is in session, it may meet when it likes. The dates are fixed by the Assembly itself. As a general rule, meetings take place at three o'clock in the afternoon on Tuesdays, Thursdays, and Fridays. Meetings can be requested by the President of the Assembly, by the government, by a committee, by the conference of group presidents, by fifty members who are present, or by a single member when the agenda is under discussion. In any case it is the Assembly itself which decides when to hold the meeting that has been requested.

Meetings are public in the sense that a verbatim report of the proceedings is published in the *Journal Officiel*. Deputies are not allowed to touch up the text of their speeches, which are transcribed in correct French by the shorthand service of the Assembly. Such is the independence and reliability of this service that in practice the text issued by it is never questioned. Only factual corrections can be made by deputies.

A limited number of visitors are admitted to meetings of the Assembly. They must not make any kind of manifestation; otherwise the gallery is immediately cleared. These precautions are a result of recollections of the assemblies of the French Revolution, which the public used to attend and at which they made violent manifestations. The deputies of those days used to fear the presence of the public. Today the Assembly prohibits disturbance from the public galleries while it is deliberating.

The Assembly may decide to meet in secret session, in which case the public is not admitted and no report of proceedings is published. Secret sessions are very rare, however. They have been held only in time of war.

The Debate

At the end of each meeting the Assembly itself decides on the business for the next meeting. The agenda is prepared by the group presidents' conference, but the Assembly can always reject the proposals of the presidents' conference and adopt another agenda. Some debates on the agenda are of great practical importance, for discussion of a question can be postponed indefinitely by putting it at the end of the agenda.

At the beginning of each meeting the President of the Assembly puts the minutes of the previous meeting to the vote and gives out various notices. Then he puts to the vote the non-controversial bills and business. These items of minor importance are placed at the head of the agenda on condition that they will be adopted without a debate. Any deputy can ask to be heard on one of these bills, in which case it is sent back to the appropriate committee, and at some later date there will have to be a debate on it. If no one asks to speak, it is passed immediately. After this introduction the debate proper begins.

The general principle is that each deputy may ask to be heard and may speak as long as he likes, but he must speak in turn, the order depending on the time when the request was made. There are deviations from this principle: members of the government can speak at any time, and the presidents and *rapporteurs* of committees have priority over other deputies. Similarly, a deputy can interrupt at any time on a point of order if in the course of the debates someone contravenes a rule of the Assembly. At any time the closing of the debate may be requested. This is decided by a vote of the Assembly. Voting on the closure takes place after one speech in favor and one against. If the closure is adopted, voting immediately takes place on the bill under discussion.

Besides this ordinary procedure, there exist special procedures for which detailed rules obtain. In case of urgency there is a procedure according to which the debate continues without interruption and the general vote on the bill under discussion must take place three full days after the beginning of the discussion. The Assembly decides on a motion of urgency and organizes the debate accordingly. After the maximum time has been decided upon, the presidents' conference divides this time between the government, the committee, and the speakers whose names are on the list. Those speaking officially in the name of their groups are allowed more time than the others. One group, moreover, may yield its allotted time to another.

The reform introduced by the rule of March 27, 1952, tightened up this organization of the debate by introducing the procedure of "limited debate." The only deputies who may speak in a limited debate are members of the government and the president and *rapporteur* of committees, each of whom is allowed to speak for only five minutes to every amendment reported by the committee. Before the vote on the whole bill is taken, a representative of each group is allowed to speak for five minutes.

Disciplinary action can be taken against deputies who disturb the order of debates. Some sanctions are purely moral: the deputy may be called to order by the President of the Assembly and the fact entered in the record, or there may be a simple censure by the Assembly. These simple reprimands, published in the *Journal Officiel,* do not entail any material consequences. A more serious punishment is censure with temporary exclusion. This entails exclusion from the Assembly for a fortnight and loss of half a month's salary. These penalties are doubled if the offense is repeated or if the deputy who is condemned to censure with temporary exclusion refuses to leave the chamber.

Voting

The debate ends in a vote that expresses the decision of the Assembly. Theoretically, voting can only take place when there is a quorum. The quorum is an absolute majority of the members of the Assembly, that is to say, 314 before the North African crisis and 299 in the Assembly elected on January 2, 1956. This rule, however, is applied only if a request signed by 100 deputies is made to the Bureau of the Assembly. If fewer than 100 deputies are present, the request cannot be made, and therefore the quorum rule ceases to function.

There are several kinds of voting. The simplest kind is by the counting of hands or, if the result is doubtful, by the deputies sitting or standing. The votes are counted quickly by very experienced tellers. When these two procedures are followed there is no record of the vote, and it is impossible for the public to discover how the deputies voted. Voting by the counting of hands or by the deputies sitting or standing is the usual procedure, and it is applicable in all cases where Assembly regulations do not specify a public ballot.

The public ballot is carried out with cards on which are printed the deputy's name. The deputies vote from their seats by placing a card in urns carried round the chamber by ushers. The cards are white for a vote in favor of the proposal, blue for one against. Voting by absent members is allowed, contrary to the procedure adopted in most parliaments in the world. Each deputy has a box (*boitier*) in which he keeps his cards and which he may entrust to a colleague. In practice they are given to the president of the parliamentary group. Only a few deputies, therefore, need to be present to vote for all the rest. It is possible for a vote to be changed if the person entrusted with the *boitier* has not voted according to the instructions of the absent deputy, but only the result announced during the sitting counts. By this rule, votes have counted even after they were repudiated by absent deputies. The public ballot is mandatory (*a*) if the results of voting by deputies sitting or standing are doubtful, (*b*) on any question of taxation, (*c*) at the request of the government, (*d*) at the request of a committee, (*e*) at the request of the president of a group of more than twenty-five members or at the request of twenty-five deputies who are present in the chamber.

Finally, there is "public ballot at the tribune," in which only deputies actually present in the chamber may vote. Voting takes place at the tribune (or rostrum) of the Assembly, where each deputy answers to his name and places a voting card in the urn. In order to simplify matters, this kind of voting sometimes takes place in a room near the chamber, so that the meeting may continue. There has been a great deal of discussion about the public ballot at the tribune. Before 1952 it was obligatory on a written request signed by fifty deputies actually present in the chamber. Because voting at the tribune takes more than an hour, the work of the Assembly could be paralyzed by frequent requests for it. The Communists often took advantage of this. To thwart them the Assembly decided in 1952 to limit public ballot at the tribune to occasions on which the elections of deputies were being verified. This, however, gave more strength to the traditional criticism of absentee voting, and the idea of further reform was strongly supported by the Edgar Faure ministry in 1955.

The Assembly modified its rule on July 26, 1955, by making the public ballot at the tribune mandatory in four cases: for the investiture of governments, on a question of confidence, on a motion of censure, and for the verification of elections. It can also be used for the ratification of international treaties if the Assembly so decides. The extension of the public vote at the tribune to four obligatory instances and one optional one is extremely important because the investiture and overthrow of a government can now be brought about only by the deputies present in the chamber.

THE POWERS OF PARLIAMENT

There is a capital difference between the Third Republic and the Fourth in regard to the respective powers of the two chambers. In spite of the amendment of the Constitution on December 7, 1954, the Council of the Republic remains primarily a consultative body. The National Assembly alone has any real power of decision.

The National Assembly

The essential power of the National Assembly is that of making the law, that is, it possesses legislative power. "The National Assembly alone has the right to legislate" (*vote seule la loi*), states Article 13 of the Constitution. It should be noted that *la loi* is not defined by the Constitution, which simply enumerates certain matters that legislative power alone can deal with: the settlement of strikes, amnesty, and organic laws, which supplement the Constitution or concern the organization of Parliament, of the French Union, of the courts, and of the administration. Besides these particular matters the Assembly is more or less free to deal with anything else it pleases. When the Assembly has voted a law, the government must conform to it and has no power to change it. All it can do is to supplement it and define its clauses by executive orders, and such orders must conform strictly with the provisions of the law. The Constitution expressly forbids the Assembly to delegate its legislative power, that is, to authorize the government to act by means of decrees. Nevertheless, since the law of August 17, 1948, there has been a recrudescence of the kind of government decrees that played an important part under the Third Republic. This phenomenon will be studied subsequently in connection with the relations between the Assembly and the government.

The initiative in introducing laws belongs only to the President of the Council of Ministers and to members of the National Assembly, the Council of the Republic, and the Assembly of the French Union. Bills proposed by the President of the Council are called *projets de loi;* those introduced by a deputy or a senator are called *propositions de loi.* This difference of nomenclature does not correspond to any difference in substance or procedure. Government bills have no legal priority, but in practice the Assembly obviously tends chiefly to discuss bills introduced by the government. Nevertheless, this tendency is not as strong as in Great Britain, where in practice only bills introduced by the government are debated and become law. Until the reform of December 7, 1954, bills introduced by a senator had to be referred to the National Assembly first. Since the reform of 1954, the Council of the Republic is allowed to introduce and debate bills.

The discussion of bills takes place first in the appropriate committees, which receive them in printed form for critical examination and possibly modification. It is the bill as modified by the committee that is debated in the Assembly and not the initial text, a fact that many consider regrettable. Before the debate opens at a public sitting, the National Assembly may ask the opinion of the Economic Council or of the Assembly of the French Union if the bill deals with matters within their competence, but it is only obliged to do so in certain cases. The debates themselves take place according to the procedure already described.

Any member may introduce amendments both in committee and on the floor, and therefore amendments tend to be numerous and to change the nature of given bills. If an amendment made on the floor would result in an increase of expenditure or a reduction in revenue, the government, the President of the Finance Committee, or the *rapporteur* of the Finance Committee may ask that it be ruled out of order. In that case the amendment is not discussed but is referred back to the committee.

The Council of the Republic

The Council of the Republic has little power. Its only powers of decision are concerned with the appointment of three members of the Constitutional Committee, of twenty-five members of the Assembly of the French Union, and of members of certain administrative councils. It also shares in the election of the President of the Republic in a joint meeting with the National Assembly. Finally, it has the right to refer matters to the Constitutional Committee, as will be seen later.

The legislative powers of the Council of the Republic were even more limited before the reform of December 7, 1954. Prior to that time, voting on all bills took place first in the National Assembly. Bills were then sent to the Council of the Republic for it to express an opinion within a period of two months. This period was reduced in two cases: for the Finance Bill, the Council of the Republic was allowed only the time taken by the National Assembly to discuss the bill at its first reading; in a case of urgency, the same rule applied, although the Constitutional Committee had decided, in a report dated June 18, 1948, that the Council of the Republic should be allowed at least three full days. If the Council adopted the Assembly's bill as it stood, or if the Council did not finish examining it within the time allowed the bill became law. If the Council, after examining the bill, modified it on certain points, a second reading would follow in the National Assembly, but only of the amendments passed by the Council of the Republic. Whether the Assembly accepted or rejected these amendments, its decision was then final, and the bill was promulgated in the version adopted at the second reading by the National Assembly.

Despite the preponderance of the Assembly, the Council of the Republic had at its disposal what was mistakenly called a "right of veto." If the bill amended by the Council of the Republic had been voted by an absolute majority of its members (161 out of 320), the Assembly could not reject, either totally or in part, the amendments proposed by the Council except by passing the bill with an absolute majority also. In practice the "right of veto" never interfered with the decision of the National Assembly. It even happened, in one exceptional case, that a bill unanimously thrown out by the Council of the Republic was unanimously passed by the National Assembly at the second reading!

The reform of the Constitution on December 7, 1954, made notable changes in the legislative powers of the Council of the Republic. It dealt principally with the re-establishment of the old shuttle system, that is to say, the practice of shuttling a bill from one chamber to another until an identical text was agreed upon. At the same time the "right of veto" through the mechanism of an absolute majority was suppressed.

The Council of the Republic now has the right to introduce and debate bills presented by its members or laid before it by the Premier. He has the right to introduce bills either in the Council of the Republic or in the National Assembly except in the case of bills concerning ratification of treaties and finance bills or bills with financial implications, which must be introduced first in the National Assembly. The senators have no initiative in financial matters, and they cannot propose anything that involves a reduction in revenue or an increase in expenditure.

Bills on which discussion and voting take place first in the National Assembly are sent to the Council of the Republic, which, as in 1946, is allowed a period of two months in which to examine them. In the case of finance laws, the period is equal to the time taken by the National Assembly to discuss them. In the case of bills that the National Assembly has deemed urgent, the period is double the time taken by the National Assembly. If the Council of the Republic has not declared itself within the time allowed by the Constitution, the law may be promulgated, but the National Assembly may decide to extend the period.

After this first reading of the text by the Council of the Republic, the shuttle starts; that is to say, the bill will be sent from the Council of the Republic to the National Assembly, then from the National Assembly to the Council of the Republic, and so on, until the two chambers agree on an identical text. With ordinary bills, the time allowed for shuttling must not exceed a hundred days from the beginning of the second reading of a bill in the Council of the Republic. The limit is a month for budget bills and two weeks for bills deemed urgent by the National Assembly. At the expiration of the time limit the National Assembly takes a definitive vote on whichever version of the text it chooses. The Assembly, therefore, always has the last word.

The members of the Council of the Republic were delighted with the reform of 1954. It does not legally increase the powers of the Council. The latter has even lost its "right of veto," which might in some circumstances have blocked Assembly legislation. Moreover, by adopting the urgency procedure, the Assembly can limit the duration of the shuttle to two weeks, which greatly reduces the Council's power of postponement. But, in spite of this, there can be no doubt that the reform increases the prestige of the Council of the Republic. Moreover, given the French political system and the difficulty of getting together a majority for a bill, the shuttle system might result in paralysis of the initiative of the National Assembly. The Council of the Republic is thus on the road to achieving what constituted the power of the Senate under the Third Republic, that of obstructing legislation. In short, the reform of December 7, 1954, is regrettable, the more so since the Council of the Republic is not really representative in its composition. This reform was an achievement for the parties of the Right and the Radicals, who since 1946 had been demanding an extension of the powers of the Council of the Republic and a return to the Senate of the Third Republic. It is to be noted that the MRP and the Socialists, who are very hostile to the Council, nonetheless voted for this bill. This marks a very important change on their part. The suppression of the "right of veto" was the price they claimed for their support.

Extralegislative Powers

Parliament's financial power is at least as important as the legislative power, and it is the oldest parliamentary prerogative. Parliaments levied taxes and approved the budget before they made laws. In addition to its financial power, Parliament has a voice in foreign policy and in administrative and judicial matters, with the Assembly, of course, predominating over the Council of the Republic. The powers of the Assembly with regard to the government (investiture of the President of the Council of Ministers, inquiries, interpellations, votes of censure, and votes of no confidence) are also of capital importance. They are taken up subsequently in a general examination of the relation between Parliament and the government.

Financial power includes the voting of the budget, the voting and modification of taxes, the settling of the nation's accounts, and the voting of additional and supplementary credits. The initiative with regard to spending officially rests with the deputies, but Paragraph 2 of Article 17 of the Constitution definitely limits the bearing of this principle when it declares: "However, no proposal entailing an increase in the expenditure forecast, or additional expenditure, may be submitted during the discussion of the budget and of anticipated and supplementary credits." The right to initiate expenditure exists therefore only when non-financial bills are being presented, as, for example, the creation or development of services and granting of subsidies, but it no longer exists during debates on the budget or in truly financial matters, which is a considerable limitation. And even when non-financial bills are being presented, the rules of the Assembly limit the deputies' initiative by allowing proposed amendments to be buried in committee. In practice the deputies try to circumvent these limitations. They refuse to discuss the part of the budget in which they deem the estimates to be insufficient, although this is difficult because of the reform in budgetary procedure in 1956. They also introduce token credit reductions; that is to say, they limit by 1,000 francs (equivalent to about $2.50), for example, the budget of a certain ministry in order to demonstrate to the government their wish to see the credits increased. The government is not obliged to yield to this wish, but the rules of the parliamentary system, which oblige it to retain the confidence of the National Assembly, make it very likely that it will do so.

The powers of the Council of the Republic are even more restricted when it comes to passing the budget than in the case of laws. The National Assembly has priority in the examination of the budget proposals, and the duration of the shuttle between the two chambers is reduced to a month instead of a hundred days. The senators do not have the right either to increase the proposed expenditure or to reduce the revenue.

The government alone conducts foreign policy, establishes diplomatic relations, and signs treaties. No important treaty, however—no peace treaty, no treaty concerning international organization or national finance, no treaty modifying a French internal law or involving the cession, exchange, or annexation of territories or property, no treaty concerning the status of individuals or rights, and no treaty concerning the status of the French abroad—may be applied without being ratified by the National Assembly. The Council of the Republic is consulted on ratification just as it is on domestic bills. Sometimes the Assembly does not ratify treaties signed by the government, as on August 30, 1954, when it rejected the treaty organizing a European Defense Community. The Assembly can also pass resolutions which indicate to the government the foreign policy it wishes to pursue. These resolutions are not legally binding, but if the government does not conform to them, it risks being overthrown by the Assembly. Treaties in force, except trade agreements, cannot be abrogated except by a vote of the Assembly. Finally, war cannot be declared except by a vote of the National Assembly, but this rule does not apply either to colonial expeditions, which are not considered as real wars, or to military self-defense, when the army must resist an attack before Parliament has time to vote.

In principle Parliament possesses no administrative or judicial powers. Administration depends on the executive, and judicial powers are the prerogative of the courts. Nevertheless, certain administrative decisions are taken by the chambers. Some are indirect, as, for example the nomination of certain members of administrative councils or the control of public services by the discussion on the budget. Others are direct, Parliament itself making decisions of an administrative nature. The most important prerogative in this respect concerns the declaration of a state of siege, an exceptional measure taken in time of war or internal troubles, which suspends the exercise of certain civil rights and gives certain discretionary powers to the military authorities. Besides these cases, the authorization of Parliament in the form of a law is necessary for certain administrative acts which are considered important because they are concerned with the wealth of the nation: concession of public property to individuals, loans by local governments (communes or departments), or expropriation in the public interest.

As for judicial power, the National Assembly has some extraordinary prerogatives. For one thing, it shares in the appointment of members of the Supreme Council of the Judiciary. Six of the fourteen Supreme Council members are appointed by the Assembly on a two-thirds majority vote on candidates who are not themselves deputies. The Assembly also appoints the president, the vice-presidents, and the other members of the High Court of Justice. Through the usual legislative procedure, both chambers by a law of amnesty can reduce penalties imposed by the courts.

Among the other powers exercised by Parliament, the power of revising the Constitution deserves special study. The procedure for revision is very complex and of such a nature as to insure the preponderance of the National Assembly and to avoid as far as possible recourse to a referendum, for which provision is made nonetheless. There are three stages to any revision.

First, initiative with respect to any revision lies with the National Assembly alone, which must vote by an absolute majority of its members that there is a case for revising the Constitution. The proposal for revision must state its aim precisely. No reform may be undertaken or pursued if France is totally or partially occupied by an enemy. This rule was made to prevent any renewal of what happened in 1940, when the revision of the Constitution was decided on at Vichy at a time when two-thirds of France was occupied by German forces. The Republican form of government cannot be the object of proposed revision.

The proposal for revision is sent to the Council of the Republic, which must give its decision within three months. If it agrees by an absolute majority of its members, discussion of the text of the revision begins. If the Council of the Republic rejects the proposal of the National Assembly or does not accept it by an absolute majority, the proposal returns to the National Assembly. If the latter by an absolute majority of members reaffirms the proposal for revision, discussion on the text of the proposal begins despite the opposition of the Council of the Republic.

The work of revision proper takes place first in the National Assembly, where a text is discussed and put to the vote. Once the bill has been passed by this body, it is sent to the Council of the Republic, which must give its decision within two months. If the Council accepts the Assembly's version, it is adopted. If not accepted by the Council, the bill is again examined by the National Assembly at a second reading, and the decision is this time final. If the opposition of the Council of the Republic has been expressed in a public ballot by an absolute majority of its members, however, the Assembly's decision must be expressed by a vote in the same form and by the same majority.

Once it has been adopted under the conditions just described, the revision bill is in principle subject to a popular referendum. Those who drafted the Constitution of 1946, however, viewed the referendum with suspicion and obviously did their best to limit its use. They decided there would be no need for a referendum if the revision bill were adopted by each of the chambers by a three-fifths majority only, or by the National Assembly alone at the second reading by a two-thirds majority. Whatever the majority, there must always be a referendum if the existence of the Council of the Republic is at stake, lest the National Assembly should decide alone to put an end to the second chamber.

CHAPTER 2

THE GOVERNMENT

In France the executive consists of the President of the Republic, who is the ceremonial head of state, and the President of the Council of Ministers (or Premier), under whose leadership the Council of Ministers (or Cabinet) exercises the effective powers of government. The Constitution of 1946 recognized the office of Premier and modified the procedure for nomination to the office. It also reduced the powers granted to the President of the Republic by the Constitution of 1875, but the present structure is for all practical purposes the same as that of the Third Republic.

THE PRESIDENT OF THE REPUBLIC

During the Constituent Assembly of 1945–46, some opposition toward the office of President of the Republic became evident. The Left (especially the Communists) wanted to do away with the presidency and to retain the provisional system of 1944–45, in which the Premier was also head of state. In the end, the Left accepted the presidency but took steps to limit the powers of the office. This is a traditional play of attitudes: the Right wants to increase the powers of the presidency, while the Left is opposed to it. Generally speaking, the Right misunderstands the very nature of parliamentary government, for executive power should not be separated from responsibility to Parliament, which now falls on the Premier and his Council of Ministers.

Election

The President of the Republic is elected for seven years at a joint session of both chambers of Parliament. This session is known as a Congress, and traditionally it is held at Versailles in an annex to the palace built by Louis XIV.

Under the Third Republic, the election of the head of state was conducted by secret ballot, but the Constitution of 1946 prescribed no form of balloting. There was a long struggle in the Constituent Assembly between supporters of the open ballot, which enables parties to control their members, and those who wanted a secret ballot, which insures independence in voting and makes it impossible for the President-elect (who is supposed to be impartial) to know who supported him and who opposed him. The Left favored open balloting, the Right secret balloting; and when no agreement could be reached, it was decided that the ballot would be secret for the first election (January 6, 1947) and settled by law thereafter. The organic law (that is, a law fundamental to government organization) of December 18, 1953, finally prescribed the secret ballot. Voting takes place at the tribune and continues until a candidate secures an absolute majority of the votes cast. There is no debate prior to balloting.

In theory, any citizen may be a candidate for the presidency, and at every election there are some freak candidates. In practice, every President elected since 1875 has been a member of Parliament. In accordance with the Constitution of 1946, Presidents may succeed themselves only once. Generally, the election is a simple matter. The first President of the Fourth Republic, Vincent Auriol, was elected at the first ballot. The same was true of nine Presidents of the Third Republic, while the other four were elected at the second ballot. By contrast, the present President, René Coty, was elected at the thirteenth ballot after the Congress had been in session for seven days; the insistence of Premier Joseph Laniel on maintaining his candidacy was the cause of the confusion.

Powers

The powers accorded the President by the Constitution of 1875 were nominally very great, for it had been drawn up by the monarchists, who associated the presidency with the throne. Because the President had no responsibility to Parliament, however, he was obliged then as now to submit his decisions for countersigning by a minister, so that the latter could be held responsible. The prerogatives accorded him by the Constitution were in fact exercised by ministers. The Constitution of 1946 withdrew from the President even some of these nominal prerogatives and gave them to the Premier but this represented little substantive change from the Third Republic.

In reality, the President can play no greater part today than before, even though it has been claimed that restricting his powers would make those left to him more effective. The very system that makes him unaccountable to Parliament concentrates real executive authority in the Cabinet. The President is in the first place politically irresponsible: he cannot be overthrown by Parliament or obliged to resign. The rule was violated on two exceptional occasions during the Third Republic: in 1887 both chambers brought pressure to bear upon President Grévy to force his resignation in consequence of a scandal involving his son-in-law; in 1924 the Chamber of Deputies decided that because President Millerand had abused his presidential prerogatives during the preceding legislature it would oust every cabinet he appointed. We have already seen that the political irresponsibility of the President obliges him to obtain the signature of a minister and of the President of the Council to all his acts.

The President is in the second place legally irresponsible. He cannot be prosecuted in the ordinary courts of law for actions committed in the exercise of his duty. Ultimately he is only responsible in the case of high treason, for which he may by resolution of the National Assembly be tried in the High Court of Justice. This is a kind of "impeachment," but high treason as a criminal act or as a fundamental breach of duty is not defined. In fact the "crime" is so vague that the National Assembly has never made use of its prerogative in this matter.

The influence of the presidency varies a great deal according to the personality of the incumbent. There have been unobtrusive Presidents with no real influence in political life; there have been some who played a considerable part in government. In a multiparty regime such as exists in France, several combinations are always possible for the formation of a majority in Parliament, and since the parties are very loosely organized, several leaders stand at the head of every party. When it comes to choosing a Premier, the influence of the President of the Republic is therefore considerable by contrast with what happens in Great Britain, where the nomination of the Prime Minister is almost automatic. Some Presidents, either by ignoring or supporting leaders, have had a decisive influence over political developments. The President of the French Republic is in this respect much more powerful than the Queen of England. The President can also exert his personality on the Council of Ministers, over whose meetings he presides, and on the public if he is popular. Some Presidents, Vincent Auriol, for example, have not hesitated in their public speeches to take a stand on fundamental issues.

The Constitution of 1946 gave to the President two new prerogatives: first, he heads the French Union, which allows him to intervene in the relations between France and her overseas territories; second, he presides over the Supreme Council of the Judiciary, which allows him to play a part in guaranteeing the independence of judges. He is also custodian of the minutes of meetings of the Council of Ministers (drawn up by the General Secretary of the Government), and he is responsible for communicating them to all members of the Cabinet. He is thus in some measure the "memory" of the state, and this strengthens his influence with the Premier and ministers, whose time in office is as a rule short.

Finally, the President has the power to return a law to the National Assembly for a second deliberation, although he may not suspend its application whether there is to be a reconsideration or not. A law must be put into effect within ten days (or five days if the Assembly has voted for "urgent" promulgation), but during that period the President may return the law to the assembly for reexamination. This prerogative was never exercised under the Third Republic, but it has been used under the Fourth Republic on occasions when the letter or the spirit of the Constitution was involved.

The early years of the presidency in the Third Republic were unfortunate: the first President, Marshal MacMahon, was a royalist; the second, Jules Grévy, was self-effacing. With Vincent Auriol, however, the Fourth Republic began with a head of state who played an important part. As President of the Supreme Council of the Judiciary he persevered in his efforts to secure the independence of judges, backing the Council in its fight against the Ministry of Justice; as President of the French Union he intervened personally in the negotiations with Bao-Daï and with the Bey of Tunis, so that it is possible to say that there was a presidential policy on French Union matters. Auriol played a particularly important part during ministerial crises: he refused to accept the resignation of governments that had not been defeated in the manner prescribed by the Constitution (Schuman in 1948, Pleven in 1950, Queuille in 1951). He intervened in ministerial crises by issuing official communiqués that were veritable appeals to public opinion. He instituted the practice of asking political leaders during times of ministerial crises to explore the possiblity of finding a majority on the basis of which a new cabinet could be formed. He nominated some Presidents of the Council of Ministers in an effort to find a new majority. Auriol was a great President of the Republic; no President of the Third Republic participated so directly and so effectively in the life of the state.

With René Coty, elected in 1953, there has been a change of style. President Coty is discreet and unobtrusive, but he remains very popular and commands the respect of public opinion, which was hardly the case throughout most of the period of the Third Republic. There is no doubt, however, that President Coty is less influential politically than his predecessor.

THE PRESIDENT OF THE COUNCIL

There was no mention in the text of the Constitution of 1875 of a President of the Council of Ministers. From the very beginning of the Third Republic, however, one minister in each Cabinet assumed the Premier's duties, though he was obliged to take a particular ministerial post (e.g., Finance, Foreign Affairs, or Interior) in order to have an office and a secretariat. Legally, he had no special powers: in practice, his authority over the other ministers depended on his personality. Some Presidents of the Council—e.g., Waldeck-Rousseau, Caillaux, Clemenceau, Poincaré, Tardieu, Briand, Blum —had great influence, while others were weak and ineffective.

A law was passed in 1934 to strengthen the Premier's position. A special building, the Hôtel Matignon, was assigned to him, and thereafter it was possible to be President of the Council without taking a ministerial post. However, no change was made in the Constitution in order to recognize the office formally; Cabinet leadership remained entirely personal. The Constitution of 1946 changed the situation considerably: the President of the Council is now recognized in the constitutional text, and his appointment and powers are precisely defined.

Election

Under the Third Republic the procedure of appointment was very simple: the President of the Republic chose the President of the Council. The latter chose his own ministers and then had them nominated by the President of the Republic, whose signature (a mere formality) was required on the decrees of appointment. Next the whole ministry presented itself before Parliament to ask for a vote of confidence. Should this be refused, another President of the Council had to be nominated, other ministers chosen, and so on. This procedure was considerably altered by the Constitution of 1946, which set up a very complicated system, but the constitutional revision of December 7, 1954, reintroduced the procedure followed in the Third Republic.

According to the system of 1946, the President of the Republic nominated the Premier who then had to present himself alone before the National Assembly to obtain investiture. This could be accorded only by an absolute majority of the Assembly whether deputies were absent or present, voted or abstained. Thus in an Assembly of 625 members, 314 votes had to be obtained. Only then did the President of the Council choose his ministers and have them appointed by the President of the Republic. Once the ministry was formed, it was not necessary to present it to the assembly. This procedure was intended to strengthen the personal authority of the President of the Council over his ministers; he alone received the investiture of the Assembly. Furthermore, the requirement of a special majority was supposed to make the Assembly think carefully before voting and thus to reduce the instability of ministries.

The 1954 revision made two alterations in this procedure. First, the Premier, once he has been nominated by the President of the Republic, chooses his ministers before presenting himself to the Assembly. Second, a special majority is no longer required. The Premier is now invested by an ordinary majority, that is, by a majority of votes cast.

Powers

The Constitution of 1946 theoretically allocated to the Premier wide powers that he did not possess under the Constitution of 1875. In practice, the difference is not so considerable as a mere comparison of the constitutional texts would suggest. The powers that were ascribed to the President of the Republic under the earlier constitution were in fact exercised by the President of the Council and the other ministers. That they are now attributed personally to the President of the Council simply recognizes what the office has long since become.

Generally speaking, the chief powers of the President of the Council may be summed up as follows: he executes the laws; he leads the Cabinet; and he directs public administration. His power to issue executive orders is the power to complement and supplement laws by decrees and regulations that define their application in detail. It is common in the French system for laws to refer to executive orders that supposedly will define their application, and until the orders have been issued, the laws cannot be put into effect. Sometimes such orders are never issued, and therefore the corresponding laws are never applied. Parliament can avoid this shocking practice by threatening the President of the Council with a vote of no confidence, but if it has passed a given law merely to appease the electorate, it is grateful to the government for suspending its application.

As head of the government, the President of the Council has authority over the ministers: he chooses them, and he can dismiss them.* Dismissal legally must be pronounced by the President of the Republic, but in fact the decision rests with the President of the Council. It is he who summons ministers, presides over ministerial meetings, and pledges the collective responsibility of the government. It is he who speaks in the name of the government before Parliament. His authority of course depends to a great degree on his personality and his political standing. There have been mild, self-effacing Premiers like Laniel, forceful Premiers like Mendès-France (who owed his power to his personal prestige), and forceful Premiers like Guy Mollet (who owed his strength to the backing of a large party without which it was impossible to secure a majority in Parliament).

As the supreme head of the administration, the President of the Council is responsible for all steps necessary to civil and military appointments and for all steps necessary to insure the organization and functioning of public services. He has authority over the armed forces, and he is responsible for the co-ordination of national defense, the general organization of the army, the placement of troops, and so on. Several administrative departments of the highest importance answer directly to him.

Despite these powers, the President of the Council lacks permanent administrative machinery for supervising the various ministries. The Minister of Finance is better able to oversee the government, because his comptrollers of authorized expenditures are placed in every ministry to see to it that disbursements are made in accordance with the provisions of the budget. Since almost any ministerial activity involves expenditure, the Minister of Finance has a power over his colleagues that the President of the Council lacks.

MINISTERS

Ministers have a dual role. Individually, they are the heads of a department of state or of a group of public offices forming what is known as a ministerial department or post, and in this capacity they are administrators. Collectively, under the leadership of the

---

* The power of dismissal was a moot point under the Third Republic, but an effective precedent was set for the Fourth Republic in May, 1947, when the Communist members of Ramadier's coalition voted against their own Cabinet on the question of confidence.

President of the Council, they form the Cabinet, which is the central policy-initiating organ of parliamentary government.

Administration

As we have seen, ministers are chosen by the President of the Council and appointed by the President of the Republic. On paper, no special qualification is laid down for appointment as a minister, and ministers supposedly can be chosen from inside or outside Parliament. Politically, things are different, for ministers must be chosen so as to secure the approval of Parliament. Drawing a "quota" of ministers from the various political parties and, within each party, from the groups of leaders is an extremely delicate matter, on which the future of the Cabinet will frequently depend. The constitutional reform of December, 1954, has increased the difficulties by making it necessary to establish the "quota" before investiture.

Ministers are collectively responsible to Parliament, and they are more or less individually responsible for their actions, but in reality this individual political responsibility rarely comes into play. Ministers are also responsible under the penal law for any offenses committed by them in carrying out their duties; they can be prosecuted in the ordinary civil and penal courts and may be brought before the Hight Court of Justice by resolution of the National Assembly. They theoretically are accountable to the state if they spend more than the sums allocated to them in the budget but no machinery exists to deal with such cases.

Their prime responsibility is political, and the National Assembly may force the resignation of any minister who has lost its confidence. These forced individual resignations are forestalled in the majority of cases by the President of the Council, who backs his minister by raising the question of the collective responsibility of the Cabinet. Yet ministers to whom Parliament has shown hostility have been compelled by the President of the Council to resign. Usually, however, this is a prelude to the fall of the entire Cabinet.

There is a certain hierarchy among ministers. The first distinction to be made is between ministers proper and secretaries of state. Secretaries of state are attached to a minister under whose supervision they are responsible for certain public departments. There are sometimes ministers of state, or ministers without portfolio, who are members of the Council of Ministers but have no administrative departmental duties. Alongside this juridical hierarchy there exists a political hierarchy. Some ministries exercise especially wide political influence, e.g., Foreign Affairs, Interior, Finance, and Education. The Minister of Finance, as we have seen, exercises some supervision over all the other ministries. He is a veritable deputy head of the government.

An interesting feature of the Fourth Republic is the growth of the personal staff, or secretariat, attached to a minister. The minister's private office is staffed by personal assistants working directly with him and maintaining contact between him and the department and between him and the general public. There is a hierarchy within the office: director, "principal," technical adviser, attaché. Such secretariats were less well organized under the Third Republic. They were made up primarily of the minister's friends, often of inexperienced persons, and rarely did they include any first-rate personalities. Since 1945 the tendency has been to bring in high-ranking civil servants, who play a very important part in the formulation of decisions. This alters the nature of the secretariat and is one of the ways in which the higher career civil servants have extended their power.

The Cabinet

The Cabinet is the collective body which, so long as it retains the confidence of Parliament, insures the political direction of the state. Its meetings are of different kinds.

The most important is the Council of Ministers, which makes the main decisions of government. It is attended only by ministers, the President of the Council, and the President of the Republic. The secretaries of state do not attend unless a question within their jurisdiction is to be discussed. The President of the Republic can at these meetings of the Council exercise some influence by the part he takes in discussion. A high-ranking civil servant known as the General Secretary of the Government is present at all Council discussions and draws up the minutes, which are kept by the President of the Council. This is an innovation of the Fourth Republic, for under the Third it was forbidden to draw up minutes of Cabinet meetings. The controversies and accusations that arose as a result of the Cabinet meetings of May–June, 1940, when the French government capitulated to Germany, led the Constituent Assembly of the Fourth Republic to provide for Cabinet minutes.

The Cabinet Council, a second kind of ministerial meeting, is different from the Council of Ministers in two ways: the President of the Republic does not take part, but all secretaries of state attend along with ministers and the President of the Council. It is, in fact, the real meeting of the entire government. Ostensibly, it does no more than prepare the work of the Council of Ministers, but in practice it makes important decisions to which the Council of Ministers simply gives official sanction.

In addition to these two general meetings of the government, there are meetings restricted to certain ministers. As the number of ministers increases (the Bourgès-Maunoury Cabinet of 1957 contained more than forty-five ministers and secretaries of state), there is an attempt, modeled on British practice, to create a kind of supercabinet. Some Presidents of the Council have tried to make these meetings of the most important ministers a regular and permanent feature of government. Restricted meetings, with or without the President of the Council, also take place among ministers who are dealing with a particular problem. Though such functional meetings are concerned primarily with technical matters, their deliberations may influence political decisions.

Ministerial Solidarity

Fundamental decisions on French government policy are taken by the ministers collectively. This differs radically from the American system, in which the secretaries of government departments are no more than aides to the President, in which ultimately he alone decides, and in which therefore there is no true cabinet. In France, the system of parliamentary democracy requires the President of the Council to make decisions as a member of a ministerial body rather than by himself.

From collective action is derived the principle of ministerial solidarity: all ministers are jointly responsible for the decisions taken by the Cabinet. Before a decision is taken, differences of view may be made known; some ministers may champion a policy different from that proposed by others and by the President of the Council. But once the decision has been made by a vote of the Council, all ministers must apply it, even those who voted against it in the Council meeting. Furthermore, they are considered to be equally responsible for the decision with those who approved it. If they wish to escape this responsibility, they must resign.

The principle of ministerial solidarity is not always honored in practice, however. Ministers hostile to a decision taken by the Cabinet often remain with the ministry precisely in order to limit the effects of the decision. The explanation of this anomaly is to be found in the political structure of the French Cabinet. For strict ministerial solidarity to exist, the Cabinet should be "homogeneous," that is, all members should belong to the same party, and that party should be well disciplined. But as a rule homogeneity is possible only in two-party countries, e.g., Great Britain. In the multiparty parliamentary systems of Continental Europe, homogeneity in the government is unusual. Therefore, with exception of the very rare cases when a single party has an absolute majority in Parliament, a minority cabinet drawn from a single party having no majority in Parliament can govern only with the support of other parties. Minority cabinets are common in Scandinavian countries. In France, however, they are exceptional and appear only in the formation of "caretaker" cabinets, which prepare the way for changes in the alliances between parties.

The French Cabinet is normally a coalition of ministers belonging to different parties. Rivals in politics and in Parliament, these ministers find it difficult to unite in the government. In other Continental parliamentary systems where the situation is similar, an attempt is made to remedy this defect by drawing up a government program to which all the parties allied in the ministry subscribe and which they therefore jointly carry out. In France the outlining of such a program is hindered by the absence of internal cohesion in the parties; except in the left-wing parties (Socialist and Communist) and in the MRP, ministers and deputies do not feel themselves bound by the decisions of the party. In 1936 with the Popular Front, and in 1945 with the National Resistance Committee, governments carried out a common program, but the circumstances were exceptional.

Weakness in ministerial unity has two main consequences. First, each minister enjoys considerable freedom to carry out his own personal policy within his department. This explains why parties struggle so bitterly for the key ministries when governments are being formed. After a ministerial crisis, many of the members of the former government are to be found in its successor, but they do not always hold the same offices. Such changes are often the essential element in the crisis, its real political significance. Second, ministers often disagree on the general policy of the government. Between 1952 and 1954, for example, every government included opponents and partisans of the European Defense Community, since at that time representation of both views was essential for commanding a parliamentary majority. In this way, one often finds at government level the same cleavages that separate the different sections of Parliament and of the country. This is one of the fundamental causes of the weakness of the executive in France—a more fundamental cause by far than instability.

Similar defects, of course, are to be found in many other countries. In the United States, differences of opinion between federal department heads are common. Even in Great Britain, the homogeneity of the cabinet is often less marked in practice than in theory. But elsewhere there are means of resolving disputes: the constitutional authority and the popularity of the President in the United States, the Prime Minister's authority over his party in Great Britain. Neither the Constitution nor party organization gives the President of Council sufficient authority to secure unity of opinion in the French government.

As it happens, Presidents of the Council fall into roughly four categories with respect to executive unity. First, there is the King Log type (e.g., Laniel and Queuille), who by giving their ministers a free hand produce ineffective government. Parliament prefers this type to all others. Second, there is the party-leader type of Premier (e.g., Blum and Mollet), who is supported by a disciplined party (like the Socialists) that plays a leading role in the parliamentary majority. In such a case the President of the Council holds over his ministers an authority somewhat similar to that enjoyed by a British Prime Minister, though he is still subject to the pressure of coalition. The third type is the forceful Premier (e.g., Gambetta, Clemenceau, and Mendès-France), who by strength of personality and national prestige dominates the government. Parliament detests this type, since he tends to seek support for the government directly from the nation and not from the deputies. The fourth type is the bargaining Premier (e.g., Faure), who are conciliatory on the surface but fundamentally forceful. They seek to create unity within the government by patient negotiation with ministers, by perpetual, tireless, and repeated maneuvering, by a kind of wearing-down process. The way in which the Sultan of Morocco was restored to the throne in 1955 by Premier Faure provides a characteristic example of this type of action. Bargaining has a deplorable effect on the public, which gets the impression of widespread disorganization. The disorganization is greater with the King Log type of Premier, but it is less obvious, for there are no spectacular clashes between Premier and ministers.

The problem of effectiveness in government comes up again when we analyze French political parties and the alliances they contract to form parliamentary majorities. It is the number, structure, and respective size of the parties which explain the defects in the French system of government far more than the nature of the political institutions proper.

CHAPTER 3

RELATIONS BETWEEN PARLIAMENT
AND GOVERNMENT

Democratic theory distinguishes two kinds of relationship between the executive and the legislature: on the one hand, true separation of powers, and, on the other, the parliamentary system. The latter requires co-operation between the executive and the legislature.

Separation of powers in France is limited; Parliament and the Cabinet must collaborate to reach decisions. The legislative disposes of means to bring pressure to bear on the executive, of which the most extreme is the refusal of confidence. The executive can also bring pressure to bear on the legislative, the dissolution of the Assembly being its supreme weapon. Yet the French parliamentary system is unbalanced because of the inequality that exists in the weapons available to each side. The National Assembly has much more effective powers over the Cabinet than the Cabinet over the Assembly. The refusal of confidence can be applied in all or almost all cases, whereas dissolution can occur only in very rare circumstances.

We must not, however, exaggerate the disparity between the two powers. Everyday practice is somewhat different from the narrowly formal relationship. In fact, the government often has at its disposal very effective ways of influencing Parliament, and the march of events is leading to an increase of the powers of the executive relative to those of the legislative. Paradoxically, this development has not mitigated the problem of ministerial instability.

PARLIAMENT'S POWERS OVER GOVERNMENT

We must make a distinction between the powers common to both chambers and those restricted to the Assembly, which are the more significant. Indeed the framers of the Constitution of 1946 sought to reduce to a minimum the role of the Council of the Republic and to prevent it from imperiling the existence of the government. Only the Assembly, by a vote of no confidence, can cause the Cabinet to resign.

Both chambers have two basic means of extralegislative action. One is the committee of inquiry, and the other is the formal questioning of ministers. The first procedure is not so much used in France as in the United States. The National Assembly and the Council of the Republic can, like Congress, set up committees vested with power to investigate any question. The committees can compel witnesses to give evidence before them, but, because French law is very different from American law, especially in the matter of the rules of perjury and the right of witnesses not to speak, there is virtually no risk either in giving evidence or in refusing to give evidence before a committee of inquiry. Furthermore, in France such committees are rarely set up and are not very important. They usually investigate some financial or political scandal, which is then buried.

In Great Britain the questions put by members to ministers at the beginning of each sitting of the House of Commons are quite important politically. This kind of questioning is not so important in France. Questions may be put only at the opening of certain sittings, and they are generally of a technical nature and receive little attention from deputies or the public. Recently an attempt has been made, without much success, to improve the machinery of questioning. In addition to the oral question put at the opening of a sitting by a deputy to a minister, written questions are published in the *Journal Officiel*. Some of these questions on occasion are politically or administratively important, but most of the time members use them only as a way of consulting ministers on some matter of law affecting their constituents. Every ministry has a section to deal with written questions, and it is a veritable claims bureau. Questions therefore remain a very ineffective device for engaging the responsibility of the Cabinet.

The National Assembly alone possesses other and more effective powers over the government. The first is interpellation, which differs from the question in two ways. Questioning is limited to a brief exchange between deputy and minister, whereas the interpellation opens a general debate over a matter of policy, in which all members may take part. The question does not give rise to a vote, whereas the interpellation ends in a vote which may involve disapproval of government action. Interpellations are less common today than under the Third Republic. This is due to the fact that a greater proportion of parliamentary time is taken up by the discussion of bills introduced by the government. The Premier will frequently ask for the interpellations to be deferred to the conclusion of business (*le renvoi à la suite*), and this means putting them at the end of the agenda and virtually burying them. The *renvoi* gives rise to a very brief debate which nonetheless does allow some discussion. It is in this restricted form that the majority of interpellations now occur.

Under the Third Republic the discussion of an interpellation could bring about the fall of a Cabinet, as could the refusal to pass a bill or the estimates put forward by the government if the Cabinet was willing to stake its existence on a vote of confidence in connection with the specific issue. Today the procedure for a vote of confidence is more complicated. The Constitution of 1946 laid down precise rules for it in order to avoid frequent falls of Cabinet on a surprise vote and in order to compel deputies to think before threatening the life of a ministry. Since 1946 no ministry can be defeated except by a vote (taken under certain conditions as to procedure and majority) on a motion of confidence or censure proposed with all due formality. The question of confidence can be put only by the Premier with the authorization of the Council of Ministers. Under the Third Republic no authorization by the Council was required, and any minister could propose a motion of confidence during any sitting. As for the motion of censure, it must be proposed formally by a deputy under the express title of motion of censure and must be signed by him. In the case both of confidence and of censure the vote cannot be taken until twenty-four hours after the motion has been made. In both cases the government is defeated only if it has against it an absolute majority of all members of the Assembly (299 votes).

If a certain number of deputies abstain, it is possible for the government to be defeated by a relative minority without being obliged to resign. The Cabinet, for example, might receive 220 votes for and 280 against and thus according to the Constitution stay in office if it wished. But the government is always free to resign, and as a rule it does so when it is put into any kind of minority. When Vincent Auriol was President of the Republic, he tried to refuse the resignation of Cabinet that had been defeated by less than an absolute majority and thus to compel them to return to the Assembly for another vote on the question of confidence. Governments continue to resign, however, without being constitutionally defeated, and this, as we shall see, has a bearing on the right to dissolve Parliament.

The Constitution of 1946 forbids the putting of the question of confidence to the Council of the Republic, but this restriction has been informally evaded at least once. Premier Queuille, in a peculiar instance, declared that he would resign if the Council of the Republic did not pass a certain measure proposed by the government. This was considered an unofficial way of raising the question of confidence before the second chamber.

GOVERNMENT'S POWERS OVER PARLIAMENT

The question of confidence is Parliament's fundamental method for coercing the Cabinet, but the method may be turned around and used by the Cabinet to influence Parliament. Frequently, indeed, the Cabinet brings pressure to bear by making a particular bill the occasion for a question of confidence. Since it is ridiculous to overturn the Cabinet every time a bill is disputed, this device is politically effective, especially when the Cabinet has just taken office. The public resents chronic ministerial crises, and thus it is politically unwise to defeat ministries at too close intervals. During its initial months in office, the Cabinet enjoys a period of delightful certainty that its existence is unthreatened. It can take advantage of the period to get the Assembly to take important decisions. Quite often, as a matter of fact, decisions would never be taken without the potential threat of crises to break legislative deadlocks.

The Cabinet exercises certain rights in its relations with Parliament. The Premier and his ministers have the right to enter and to speak in the Assembly. Moreover, members of the government may intervene in debate at any time without waiting as deputies must for their turn to speak. Some Premiers have exercised considerable oratorical dominion over the Assembly.

The government, moreover, may at the end of the ordinary session of the Assembly (lasting seven months) declare Parliament adjourned, that is, end its meetings for the year. This device was frequently utilized under the Third Republic. It gives the government a period of respite during which its existence is no longer dependent on the Assembly.

The fundamental weapon, however, is the right to dissolve the Assembly. The Constitution of 1875 gave the President of the Republic the power to dissolve the Chamber of Deputies with the assent of the Senate. It was the President of the Council who could in practice exercise the right. The procedure was used only once: in 1877 the monarchists, with the complicity of Marshal MacMahon, a royalist President of the Republic, attempted to overthrow the regime and to restore the king to the throne. Up to 1940 dissolution was generally considered an antirepublican device, and this explains why it was never used.

The Constitution of 1946 retained the right to dissolve the National Assembly, but it made dissolution contingent on a number of conditions very unlikely to be realized all at the same time. In the first place, dissolution cannot be pronounced during the first eighteen months of a given Parliament's existence. Thereafter, dissolution is possible if two fundamental conditions are fulfilled: first, at least two cabinet crises must have occurred within a period of eighteen consecutive months; second, both crises must have been brought about by a vote of no confidence in the Assembly upon a motion of censure or a motion of confidence, and the government must have been defeated by the constitutionally prescribed absolute majority. If both conditions are fulfilled, the Council of Ministers may decide on dissolution after seeking the advice of the President of the National Assembly, though it is free not to follow that advice. Once the decision has been taken, dissolution is pronounced by a decree of the President of the Republic, whose role is purely formal.

Strict rules have been made to prevent the government from abusing its powers during the period of dissolution. Elections for the new Parliament must take place at least twenty and not more than thirty days after the dissolution; the new Assembly meets on the third Thursday following its election. These periods were made very short to limit the time during which the government is freed from parliamentary control. The Cabinet continues to hold office, but if dissolution follows a vote of censure, the President of the National Assembly takes over the Presidency of the Council and the Ministry of the Interior; thus any attempt at a coup d'état is prevented.

There is no doubt that the Constituent Assembly was very suspicious of the right of dissolution. There is similarly no doubt that the National Assembly is very unfavorably disposed toward it. In consequence the Assembly has taken pains to avoid it by defeating Cabinets by simple and not absolute majorities. Since some politicians know Parliament through and through and are capable of predicting within a few votes the results of a trial of confidence, this is often easy to arrange. It is a striking fact that since 1946 a constitutional majority for the defeat of a ministry has been achieved only five times out of twenty ministerial crises. Furthermore, in almost all cases the power of dissolution did not become operative, since there had not been two ministerial crises within eighteen months by the prescribed constitutional majority.

The only time in eleven years when all the conditions for the exercise of the right of dissolution were fulfilled was in November, 1955, when the politicians made what one might call an error of calculation. It happened to be the first occasion on which the new Assembly ruling of July, 1955, became applicable, requiring all votes on questions of confidence to be made personally and thus excluding the absentee vote by proxy. This upset the calculations of some parliamentary leaders, and the Cabinet was defeated by 319 votes. Premier Edgar Faure seized the opportunity and dissolved the Assembly. Public opinion generally welcomed the step, and in this respect it is true to say that a great advance had been registered, for the memories of 1877 were wiped out and dissolution became respectable in republican eyes. Faure's government, however, was defeated at the elections, and this may well make its successors more prudent in their recourse to dissolution.

It is around the right of dissolution that proposals for constitutional revision generally center. Two basic reforms have been suggested: unconditional dissolution and automatic dissolution. In the first case the Premier would be free to dissolve the Assembly when he wished, without any restrictive conditions. This presupposes the political courage necessary for dissolution. Some skepticism may be entertained on this point if we bear in mind the practice followed for many years by Premiers who have resigned from office without being constitutionally defeated.

The suggested system of automatic dissolution is based on an entirely different idea. It assumes the absence of political courage in Premiers and their natural disinclination to dissolve Parliament. Dissolution would be automatic under certain conditions—for example, if a government were defeated after a certain time in office (say eighteen months). But it would be easy to get round the rule of automatic dissolution, for the government can always resign without being officially put in the minority. The way in which the constitutional safeguards set upon the vote of confidence have been bypassed justifies some skepticism on the matter. In the last resort it may well be asked whether such a purely juridical device would be adequate to solve the problem of governmental stability, for this is fundamentally a problem of political balance, as we shall see later.

CHANGES IN THE SYSTEM

It is certain that the French political system does not correspond to the classical pattern of parliamentary regimes: a system of balance between Parliament and Government. The Right claims that France tends toward the "assembly system," that is, a system in which government is entirely dominated by the Parliament. In reality, the relationships between Parliament and the Cabinet are more subtle and more difficult to define. On the one hand, the instability of ministries and the difficulties of dissolving Parliament weaken the executive; on the other, many practices tend to strengthen the Cabinet. In this connection, the resuscitation of "decree laws" and the new procedure for voting the budget are very important.

Decree Laws

During the Third Republic after 1926 and especially after 1934, there developed what was known as the decree-law system. Parliament used to delegate, as it were, to the government its legislative powers under certain defined conditions. Parliament would pass a law, known as a "plenary powers law," which gave the government (within certain limits of time and subject matter) authority to make decrees having the "force of law," that is, capable of modifying existing laws and of being themselves modified only by laws. In theory, these decrees had subsequently to be ratified by Parliament; in practice, so long as Parliament did not oppose them, they continued to apply. There were in fact few ratifications but similarly few cases of opposition. Although Parliament would protest verbally against the decrees made, it usually allowed them to remain in force.

The Constitution of 1946 sought expressly to prevent the recurrence of such practices, for there were vivid memories of the law of July 9, 1940, which delegated to Marshal Pétain the power to make constitutional changes by executive order. Consequently, Article 13 of the Constitution declares, "The National Assembly alone has the right to legislate. It cannot delegate this right." Most postwar jurists interpreted decree laws as an instance of delegation of legislative power, but the pressure of events has been more powerful than the text of the Constitution. The decree-law procedure was resuscitated at first in disguise and then openly.

The disguise took the form of the so-called "cadre law" or "cadre-clause" procedure. This was initiated by the law of August 17, 1948. The process is as follows: a law orders the government to present by a certain date a bill reforming existing legislation on a particular question; once the bill has been introduced in the Assembly, there is a period set aside for its examination and if at the expiration of the period the Assembly has not rejected it, the bill becomes law. This system has been used for a number of fiscal measures.

The law of August 17, 1948, similarly initiated the technique of "extension of the power to make regulations." Parliament passes a law declaring that in the future a particular question falls within the province of the government's power to make regulations. This means that thereafter the government has the right to modify by simple decree any existing laws covering the question, and the legislation so modified is considered to have lost the status of law and to have become modifiable by other decrees. The Council of State, in an opinion pronounced on February 6, 1953, declared that this procedure was not contrary to Article 13 of the Constitution.

In the period 1953–54 there was a return to the decree-law procedure, pure and simple. Plenary-powers laws are now generally more precise than they were under the Third Republic. Sometimes only the government in office at the time may use the powers, and, should the Cabinet change, its successor may not. Moreover, in some cases a new procedure has been introduced to retain certain rights for Parliament. The decree laws prepared by the government must be submitted to the committees of Parliament, and if they oppose the substance of a decree, it must be presented to the Assembly and voted in the form of an ordinary law.

New Budget Procedure

On June 19, 1956, a decree law established a new procedure for passing the budget, and it considerably increased the powers of the government. Till then Parliament had debated the budget in great detail, taking a separate vote on each heading, and there were some 3,500 headings. So detailed a discussion made close scrutiny of the administration possible, but it wasted a good deal of time, and Parliament always found it difficult to pass the budget by the end of the year. The Finance Act or Budget Law under the new procedure distributes the sums under several block headings for each ministry so that only some 150 items have to be voted by Parliament. Thereafter the credits voted are allocated to the various services within each department by government decrees known as distribution decrees. These decrees are presented to the Finance Committee in each chamber and go into provisional effect within fifteen days. But the committees have up to two months to give their opinions on the decrees. A shuttle procedure between the Finance Committees of the two chambers has been introduced, the Assembly having the power of ultimate decision. Should the opinion of the Finance Committee of the Assembly prove, on final reading, unfavorable to the distribution decree, it must then be put before Parliament as a bill. If the chambers' opinion is favorable or if no opinion is pronounced, the decree remains in force. The new system clearly makes the procedure for passing the budget more flexible and also increases the power of the Cabinet in this field.

Increased Government Influence

Although it is true that the Assembly can always defeat the Cabinet and that it uses its right to do so as often under the Fourth Republic as under the Third, the very developments in administrative or government techniques do in practice give the executive more and more ways of bringing pressure to bear on the Assembly. In particular, the government alone controls the technical machinery for gathering information, especially in the economic and political fields but also in the international field and in some sectors of domestic policy. This gives it great authority in debate. Furthermore, the requirements of economic or international policy may make it necessary for the government to take immediate action and so present the Assembly with a *fait accompli*. Thus government may alter the exchange rate of the franc without consulting Parliament. It embarked upon the Suez military expedition without informing Parliament.

This increase in the authority of the executive, however, does not generally strengthen the Cabinet. As we shall see, it primarily increases the power of the higher civil service. Rivalry between ministers and permanent officials has always existed, in France as in other countries. The increased importance of a minister's personal office under the Fourth Republic apparently adds to his powers; the members of these secretariats have more influence in government departments than did their Third Republic predecessors. Many questions which were formerly decided by high-ranking civil servants are now in fact settled in the minister's personal office. In this sense it might be argued that the minister has scored over the civil service. But we have seen that the personal office tends to be recruited among the higher officials of powerful administrative bodies, which in the last resort seem to be the true victors.

CHAPTER 4

ELECTIONS

UNIVERSAL SUFFRAGE

Universal male suffrage came into operation in France for the first time under the Constitution of 1792 at the elections of the same year, but it disappeared almost immediately. In 1800 it reappeared for the elections under the Consulate and the Empire, which took place, however, at the discretion of a dictatorial regime without real freedom for the voters. The Revolution of 1848 re-established universal male suffrage, but the Second Empire in essence destroyed freedom of elections by a system of official candidates, according to which the government manipulated the electoral machinery to secure the choice of its own candidates. Truly free elections became the rule after the establishment of the Third Republic.

Woman suffrage was withheld until the ordinance of April 21, 1944, which allowed women to vote for the first time in 1945. Woman suffrage had been proposed many times under the Third Republic, especially after World War I, but all the proposals were wrecked by the upper chamber, the Senate. Those who opposed woman suffrage feared an increase in the political influence of the Church and its clergymen.

Restriction of suffrage in the French overseas territories did not end until 1957. For, although the Lamine Gueye Law of May 7, 1946, accorded French citizenship to all inhabitants of the overseas territories, the constitution-makers of 1946 did not want every native to have the right to vote. A very complicated system of restricted suffrage was therefore maintained. The vote was granted only to certain categories of native citizens, some of them defined by law as follows: "notables," the "educated," the holders of certain posts or of a state pension, persons exercising certain professions, persons able to read French or Arabic, former soldiers, the holders of decorations, mothers of two children, heads of families paying a certain minimum of taxation, the holders of a driving license, a hunting license, or a work permit, and so on. Furthermore, there were two electorates in many territories: one consisting of white settlers and the other consisting of the natives. This distinction was truly discriminatory and all the less defensible since the members of the two groups were unequal in numbers.

The important law of June 23, 1956 (known as the *loi-cadre* because it laid down only general principles, a cadre or framework, within which the government carried out individual reforms by executive order), put an end both to restrictions on the right of natives to vote and to the system of double electorates in all overseas territories. Henceforward, for all elections, universal suffrage is established in these territories, without distinction of sex, race, color, or status. The first elections of territorial assemblies based on universal suffrage were held in the overseas territories on March 31, 1957.

Qualifications for Voting

The right to vote is accorded to all French nationals who are over twenty-one years of age and who are not disqualified by legal incapacity or restraints.

Since only French citizens have the right to vote, foreigners living in France may not vote, although under the Conventional Assembly of 1792 they had the right, and an American, Thomas Paine, became a French deputy. Naturalized citizens do not receive the vote until five years after naturalization. Persons suffering from mental disorder have no right to vote, provided that the disorder is certified by a court judgment. Insane persons under detention have no vote even if they have not been the subject of a court order of interdiction. Finally, a certain number of persons are classified as unworthy of the right to vote. The withdrawal of the vote is a kind of supplementary penalty imposed by the courts. This is the case with businessmen declared bankrupt, discharged officers of the law (notaries, attorneys, bailiffs), and especially persons who have suffered certain serious penal sentences. These limitations of the right to vote apply to relatively few individuals.

Under the Third Republic, members of the armed forces on active duty had no right to vote. It was believed undesirable for military men to concern themselves with politics, and it was feared that officers might bring political pressure to bear on their troops. After

1945 the rule was abolished. Today, soldiers on active duty may vote; some even have the right to vote by mail.

Voter Registration

The French system for registering voters is automatic. It is performed by the municipal authorities, who are obliged to establish a list of all persons resident in the commune eligible to vote. The establishment of the list is facilitated by the fact that the "registry offices" are also a municipal responsibility.

Every year the list must be revised so as to remove the names of electors who have died or left the commune and add the names of persons who have attained their majority during the year and persons newly arrived in the commune. The revision is carried out from January 1 to 10 under the control of a committee made up of the mayor, a representative of the municipal council, and a representative of the prefect. Within a period of twenty days, an appeal may be made by any voter or by the prefect. Cases are considered by a municipal committee, and there is a right of appeal to a magistrate. Voter lists are closed on March 31, but any individual who meets the residency requirements and who has not been registered may at any time apply to a magistrate to deal with the case immediately.

This system has the great advantage of making registration as easy as possible, without requiring much initiative on the part of the electorate. Every voter resident in the commune, once registered on the roll, receives a voter's card which he must show when voting. In order to be registered on the electoral roll of a commune, the individual must have resided there for at least six months or else have paid direct taxation in the commune for at least five years. Multiple registration is forbidden.

Rules of Campaigning and Balloting

Many measures are taken to assure the honesty of balloting. To safeguard the voter from any pressure, attempts at electoral corruption are severely dealt with by the law. Electoral propaganda is controlled in order to assure equality between candidates and to prevent the wealthier from conducting campaigns that might stifle the voice of the poorer. Throughout the official period of the election campaign, posters may be affixed only upon sites that are specially reserved for them and equally divided among the candidates. Pamphlets and electoral programs are sent free to all voters through the national postal service. The national radio service puts an equal length of time at the disposal of each candidate. A departmental committee, presided over by a judge and including representatives of all candidates, exercises strict control over the execution of these arrangements.

In France, as in most countries, voting is optional. The number of abstentions, however, is low. At the elections for the National Assembly 17.23 per cent of the electorate abstained in 1956, 19.81 per cent in 1951, and 21.9 per cent in 1946. On the average, less than one elector in five abstains. Proposals have been made to render voting compulsory (Mendès-France came out definitely in favor of compulsion in 1955), but without success.

The secrecy of the ballot is a fundamental feature of the French democratic system. A whole series of detailed technical rules guarantees this secrecy. In particular, voters have to go into separate booths where they put the voting card they choose into an envelope. Before World War II, the desire to insure secrecy of ballot and to prevent any fraud led to the denial of the principle of voting by proxy or voting by mail. The law of August 12, 1946, established some exceptions and facilitated voting for those absent from home. The postal vote is available to men in the armed forces, merchant seamen, women nearing childbirth, hospital patients, civil servants away from home on official duties, and so on. Vote by proxy may be utilized by men in the armed forces and merchant navy who are more than six days away from France by mail.

Finally, the proper conduct of the ballot is assured by constant observation on the part of the public and representatives of the political parties. The public has free access at all times to the polling station. Votes are counted at the polling station itself in the presence of and with the help of the public.

Validating Elections

There are two different systems in France, depending on whether the offices in question are local or national, by which the proper conduct of elections may be safeguarded. In the case of local elections, disputes are referred to administrative courts, from which the participants may appeal to the Council of State and thus secure the maximum impartiality. For parliamentary elections, each chamber acts as judge over the election of its members. This system, which is democratic in principle, leads to abuses if majority parties show any tendency to judge their opponents' breaches more severely than their own. The invalidation in 1956 of eleven out of fifty-two Poujadist deputies aroused violent discussion, although it was justified by a correct reading of the electoral law.

ELECTION TO THE NATIONAL ASSEMBLY

The Old System

The election system for the Assembly, formerly the Chamber of Deputies, has always been the object of keen criticism. In general during the Third Republic, a simple-majority system with a second ballot was in force for each constituency. Because the constituencies elected only one member each, they were small, usually coinciding with the administrative subdivision known as the *arrondissement,* and thus the term *scrutin d'arrondissement* was used to describe the system. To win at the first ballot, it was necessary to

TABLE 2*

FIRST BALLOT
(100,000 Voters)

Party	Votes
Communists	25,000
Socialists	20,000
Radicals	20,000
Moderates	15,000
MRP	10,000
Poujadists	10,000

* Tables 2 and 3 have been added by the editor.

TABLE 3

SECOND BALLOT
(100,000 Voters)

Party	Votes
Communists	28,000
Socialists	37,000
Moderates	23,000
Poujadists	12,000

poll an absolute majority of the votes cast, that is, a least 50 per cent plus one. At the second ballot, assuming no candidate achieved an absolute majority on the first ballot, a plurality was sufficient. The aim of the system was to allow alliances between parties when no one of their candidates was a clear-cut favorite. The great party coalitions of the Third Republic (e.g., the Popular Front of 1936) were essentially electoral alliances for the second ballot. The system was traditionally the object of criticism from the extreme Left and the extreme Right, and there were several campaigns for proportional representation, particularly in the period 1906–10 and after World War I.

To take a purely hypothetical case for the purpose of illustration, the *scrutin d'arrondissement* would operate as shown in Table 2.

Since no party received a majority of 50 per cent plus one of the ballots cast, a second election would have to be held two weeks later. In this election some of the parties would desist in favor of others, and the result might be as shown in Table 3. Thus the combination of votes, in this case of two Center parties, would result in the election of the candidate with the highest number of votes whether he obtained an absolute majority or not. The constituency would send one deputy, a Socialist.

Proportional Representation

After the Liberation a Center party, the MRP, which had acquired a strong following, opposed the *scrutin d'arrondissement*. Traditionally, the system had brought alliances between parties of the Right or parties of the Left, and the issue of parochial schools and "clericalism" had partly served to delineate the Left from the Right. But the MRP was both a Catholic party supporting parochial schools and a democratic party with a fairly progressive social policy. The two-ballot system would have pushed some of its supporters to the Right and some to the Left, so that the party itself would never have been represented. The Communists, for their part, were also hostile to the *scrutin d'arrondissement*, because it tended to isolate them and favor the regrouping of all anti-Communist forces. Faced with this and other opposition to the old system, the provisional government of General de Gaulle established a system of proportional representation, which was maintained by the two Constituent Assemblies until the modification of 1946.

The modification of 1946 set up a system of proportional representation with the distribution of remainders calculated on the highest average (as illustrated in the next paragraph). The department became the constituency, and, since the department elected a number of deputies, each party entered a whole list of departmental candidates. The voters had to choose among the lists and vote for one *in toto*. The first seat was given to the list with the highest number of votes (not necessarily an absolute majority). The second seat was allocated theoretically to each of the lists, and a calculation was made as to the average number of votes that would then have been cast for each seat. The list with the higest average received the second seat, and the same kind of calculation determined which list received the third seat, the fourth seat, and so on.

For the purpose of illustration, consider a hypothetical constituency in which the votes were divided as follows: Right, 27,000; Socialists, 23,000; Communists, 15,000; Radical, 7,600; MRP 7,400. The first seat would go to the Right. Next, after assuming the allocation of the second seat to each list in turn, the average vote cast per seat is calculated. The second seat would go to the Socialists, as shown in Table 4. The third seat would go to the Communists, as shown in Table 5. This system of highest averages favors the large parties on the whole.

TABLE 4

LISTS	VOTES POLLED	SEATS		AVERAGE NO. OF VOTES CAST FOR EACH SEAT
		Actual + Assumed		
Right..........	27,000	1 +	1	13,500
Socialists........	23,000		1	23,000
Communists.....	15,000		1	15,000
Radicals........	7,600		1	7,600
MRP..........	7,400		1	7,400

TABLE 5

LISTS	VOTES POLLED	SEATS		AVERAGE NO. OF VOTES CAST FOR EACH SEAT
		Actual + Assumed		
Right..........	27,000	1 +	1	13,500
Socialists........	23,000	1 +	1	11,500
Communists.....	15,000		1	15,000
Radicals........	7,600		1	7,600
MRP..........	7,400		1	7,400

Parties did and still do present their candidates in a definite order which determines who is elected. If a list wins two seats, candidates 1 and 2 on the list are declared elected. At the 1945 elections voters were forbidden to alter the order of classification, and they had to vote for the whole list without cross-voting, that is, without deleting names and adding others to the lists officially drawn up by the parties. This fixed-list system was very unpopular, but the parties viewed it with great favor since it insured a degree of disciplinary control over candidates by the party committees. The law of May 9, 1951, eventually permitted the modification of party lists by cross-voting or simply by a change in the order of candidates on the list. These alterations are only taken into account, however, if they exceed half the votes cast for the list in question, and in practice the changes never attain this proportion. With generally less than 10 per cent of the voters altering the lists, the law of 1951 remains a dead letter. The parties have had their way; they pretend to give voters the right to modify lists but took precautions to make the modifications ineffective.

Electoral Alliances

In 1951 the Center parties were afraid that the Communists and the rightist RPF of General de Gaulle would between them win more than half the seats in the new Assembly. It would then have been ungovernable like the Weimar parliament in the last years when Communists and extreme Right were able by uniting to overturn any government without replacing it. To avoid this danger, the Center parties altered the electoral law of 1946 and diminished proportional representation by instituting a premium for the majority. This is known as the "alliance system."

Two or more parties wishing to form an alliance must before the election declare their intention officially at the administrative seat of each department, the prefecture, and only parties putting forward lists in thirty or more departments may ally. Allied parties put forward separate lists and campaign separately, although their connection is known. If the total votes polled by the allied lists equals an absolute majority of the votes cast, the *allied parties gain all the seats*. The seats are then distributed proportionately among the "allies" but not at all among the other parties. If one party, not in alliance, obtains an absolute majority, it gains all the seats, but this has happened once only, in some parts of France in 1951. If no allied parties and no single party obtain an absolute majority, the previously described system of proportional representation applies.

In the 1951 elections, the alliance system favored the Center parties (Socialists, MRP, Radicals) at the expense of the RPF and the Communists. In fact, alliances can seldom be used by the extreme Left and the extreme Right, because they are isolated. In the 1956 elections, the same electoral law was used, but few alliances succeeded. In only eleven departments, as compared with thirty-eight in 1951, did allied lists obtain an absolute majority. As a result, proportional representation applied more widely in 1956 than in 1951.

The 1946 electoral system, with its 1951 modification, is still the subject of lively discussion. It is far from commanding unanimity, either in the parties or among the public. In contrast with the practice in some countries, the French electoral system is not fixed and immutable but changing and flexible. The question of electoral reform has been discussed in every postwar legislature.

Public opinion is almost totally opposed to the alliance system, which is very likely to be suppressed. The majority of voters undoubtedly prefer the Third Republic *scrutin d'arrondissement* (single-member majority system with second ballot), but proportional representation has a minority of ardent supporters. The parties are very divided: the Radicals, the Right, and the Socialists officially declare themselves in favor of *scrutin d'arrondissement* though many deputies do not in fact want its return, while the Communists and the MRP are strongly opposed to it and remain faithful to proportional representation.

Special Systems

The electoral system we have described is applicable only to the departments of metropolitan France (except two) and Algeria. Other systems operate in Seine, Seine-et-Oise, and the overseas territories.

The system of alliances and the majority premium does not obtain in the departments of Seine and Seine-et-Oise. Elections there are conducted on proportional representation, pure and simple. It is not, however, the 1956 system of proportional representation, for the distribution of seats is based on highest remainders and not on highest average, and this is unfavorable to the large parties. The system was established because in 1951 the Communists and the RPF were the biggest parties in these departments and would have been favored by P.R. with highest average. The highest remainder system, on the other hand, favors the Center parties.

The system operative in Seine and Seine-et-Oise is also applied in the overseas departments of Guadaloupe, Martinique, and Réunion. In the overseas territories and in the department of Guiana, one of two systems operates according to the number of deputies to be elected in the constituency. In single-member constituencies, the simple-majority, second-ballot method used under the Third Republic applies. Constituencies electing several deputies use the 1946 system of P.R. with distribution of remainders according to the highest average and without alliances. When, on the death of a deputy, a by-election is to be held in constituencies (at home or abroad) functioning normally under the P.R. system, with or without alliances, the single-member majority system with second ballot is used.

ELECTION TO THE COUNCIL OF THE REPUBLIC

Like the Senate, from which it is so proud of descending, the Council of the Republic is elected by indirect suffrage, for in theory it represents local communities. Electors to the Council, known as "senatorial electors," are of three categories: members of the National Assembly; members of the councils of departments, numbering 3,000; representatives of municipal councils, numbering approximately 99,000. Because these three categories of electors are themselves elected by universal suffrage, the Council of the Republic is elected not by restricted suffrage, as is sometimes erroneously stated, but by indirect universal suffrage. The number of delegates from municipal councils varies according to the population of the commune. There is, however, no true proportional representation, and the rural communes are overweighted.

Senatorial electors meet in the capital town of the department. Their expenses are reimbursed, and they are fined if they do not attend. The system of election varies with the department.

Departments electing fewer than 4 senators (79 metropolitan departments) make use of the simple-majority list vote with second ballot and unrestricted cross-voting; that is, the electors make up their own lists. On the first ballot, candidates obtaining an absolute majority are elected even if they belong to different lists. On the second ballot, a plurality only is required. Departments electing 4 or more senators (11 departments) operate the system of P.R. with highest average and fixed lists (cross-voting not allowed). In practice, 5 departments elect one senator, 53 elect 2, 21 elect 3, 5 elect 4, 2 elect 5, Pas-de-Calais elects 6, Seine-et-Oise elects 7, Nord elects 9, and Seine elects 20.

Overseas senators are elected on the majority system with second ballot. Depending upon the area concerned, there is either a single college, including electors both of European origin and of native origin, or else two separate colleges, one for Europeans and one for natives.

DISPARITIES IN REPRESENTATION

In many democratic countries the representation of different sections of the territory is not egalitarian. Rural areas, for example, are generally favored by comparison with urban areas. Considerable disparities in this sense exist in the United States Senate. In Soviet Russia, the Constitution of 1924 created disparities in the other direction, towns being favored against the country. Furthermore the hazards of the electoral regime create disparities in representation as between parties. The average number of votes required per parliamentary seat is not the same for all parties, as shown, for example, in the disadvantage of the British Liberal party in this respect between 1920 and 1939. Similar disparities exist in France; relatively unimportant in the National Assembly, they are very marked in the Council of the Republic and fairly marked in departmental General Councils.

Disparities in representation in the National Assembly are the result of two phenomena. First, the less populated departments, which are generally rural, have proportionately more deputies than the more populated departments, in general predominantly urban and

TABLE 6

RESULTS	PARTIES					
	Commu- nists	Socialists	Right	MRP	Independ- ents and Moderates	RPF
Elected under 1951 system..........	103	104	94	85	121	118
P.R. with highest average..........	181 (+78)	86 (−18)	60 (−34)	57 (−28)	97 (−24)	144 (+26)
P.R. with highest remainder........	160 (+57)	93 (−11)	65 (−29)	71 (−14)	103 (−18)	133 (+15)
Outgoing deputies..	189	99	59	143	106	24

industrial. Industrial France is therefore underrepresented by comparison with agricultural France. The disparity is slight, however— approximately 3 or 4 per cent. Second, proportional representation with highest average works against small parties and sometimes penalizes them harshly. (In the 1945 and 1946 elections, for example, the Radical party was maltreated in this way by the electoral system.) It is the machinery of alliances, however, which produces the serious disparities. When alliances succeed, the allied parties receive a proportion of seats much higher than the proportion of votes polled by them. Table 6 shows the 1951 results as compared with the results that would have been obtained under other systems.

At the elections held on January 2, 1956, the disparities were much less considerable, precisely because the alliances succeeded less frequently. This was a factor that accounted for the electoral success of the Poujade movement. In fact, Poujade took votes particularly from the parties of the Right, and in 1956 the main alliances were between the MRP and the Right. The votes taken from the Right prevented the alliances from succeeding in many departments. As a consequence, the distribution of seats in the National Assembly elected in 1956 is roughly proportional to the distribution of the votes.

Disparities in representation in the Council of the Republic may be traced to its predecessor. The Senate was set up in 1874 under the pressure of right-wing parties who wanted to increase the rep-

TABLE 7

Communes Classified by Population	No. of Senatorial Electors Delegated	Average No. of Inhabitants per Delegate
Under 500............	1	241
501– 1,500.....	3	270
1,501– 2,500.....	5⎫	
2,501– 3,500.....	7⎬	360
3,501– 9,000.....	15⎭	
9,001–10,000.....	23⎫	
10,001–30,000.....	27⎪	540
30,001–40,000.....	31⎬	
40,001–45,000.....	33⎭	
45,001–50,000.....	34	
50,001–55,000.....	36	
55,001–60,000.....	37	
60,001–90,999.....	37+1 delegate per 5,000 inhabitants in excess of 45,000	2,250
100,000............	48	
200,000............	68	
500,000............	128	
Paris (2,725,000)....	625	4,400

resentation of the country districts where they were in the majority. They thus hoped to maintain a conservative policy. The constitutional reform of 1884 lessened the disparity, but it nonetheless remained considerable to the end of the Third Republic. The Fourth Republic began by eliminating the disparity by means of the 1946 electoral law. In 1948, however, there was a return to a system similar to that of the Third Republic. The disparity arises from the fact that, in spite of appearances, the number of senatorial electors representing municipal councils is not proportionate to the population of the communes. The small communes are highly favored, and the large communes are at a great disadvantage, as shown in Table 7.

The result is that 56 per cent of the senatorial electors (that is, an absolute majority) represent the communes with less than 1,500 inhabitants, and these include only 35 per cent of the population. On the other hand, towns with more than 10,000 inhabitants, which include almost 40 per cent of the population, have only 16 per cent of the senatorial electors.

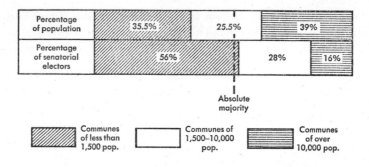

Distribution of Senatorial Electors by Size of Commune

Thus on the whole, the Council of the Republic represents only rural France and especially the traditional country districts which are much less dynamic and up to date than the rest of the country. However, the consequences of this disparity in representation are less serious than under the Third Republic, when the Senate had the same power as the Chamber of Deputies and could paralyze any decision of that body. Today, the Council of the Republic plays a secondary legislative and political role, and the National Assembly always has the last word.

CHAPTER 5

SUBSIDIARY INSTITUTIONS

The Constitution of 1946 set up a series of bodies which play a part subordinate to that of Parliament and the Cabinet but the importance of which must not be overlooked. They can be divided into two distinct categories: those integral to the structure and function of the Fourth Republic itself; those peculiar to the overseas states, territories, and departments that together make up the French Union. The latter are more important insofar as the French Union is really evolving toward federalism. Of the domestic institutions that are subordinate to the legislative and the executive, some are merely technical, such as the Economic Council, and some are politically important, such as the Supreme Council of the Judiciary.

THE ECONOMIC COUNCIL

The idea of special representation for economic interests is not new in France. There were individual representatives of commerce and industry in the Chamber of Deputies set up in 1815 by the "act annexed to the Constitutions of the Empire." The Luxembourg Committee formed during the Revolution of 1848 in a sense presaged the contemporary Economic Council. The idea, moreover, has been adopted by opposing political groups. Fascist systems deduced from it in the 1919–39 period their conception of a corporative assembly designed to restrict or replace the political assembly. Thus the extreme Right distorted an institution which had been originally conceived by the Socialist parties and then adopted by some Christian-Democrat parties.

Under the Third Republic a National Economic Council was set up by governments of the Left. It was created in 1925 by the Left, and in 1936 it was given wider scope by the Popular Front government. Although restricted to a consultative role and not provided for constitutionally, it accomplished useful work. Its example moved the postwar Constituent Assembly to provide expressly in Article 25 of the Constitution of 1946 for the organization of an Economic Council.

Membership

The Fourth Republic Economic Council is rather different in membership from the Third Republic National Economic Council. The latter had fifty occupational sections, in each of which employers and wage earners were equally represented. The General Assembly was composed of sixty delegates from these sections together with representatives of other branches of the national economy, e.g., regional interests, owners of housing property, interprofessional bodies. The fundamental basis was thus occupational.

By contrast, the present Economic Council gives the preponderance of membership to interprofessional bodies to which are added representatives of the family associations, co-operative movements, overseas departments, and so on. The intention was that broad economic views should take precedence over the narrow interests of individual occupations and that the discussions should range widely. Thus the Economic Council has 169 members: 45 represent wage earners and salaried employees; 40 represent industry, commerce, and crafts (of whom 6 are drawn from the nationalized industries, 8 from large firms employing more than 100 workers, 6 from smaller industrial firms employing under 100 workers, 10 from commerce, 10 from the crafts); 35 represent agriculture; 9 represent co-operatives; 15 represent overseas departments and territories; 8 represent "French thought"; 9 represent the family associations; 4 represent savings organizations, real estate, and tourist and export trades; 2 represent the middle classes; and 2 represent war-damage victims' associations.

As a general rule, the members of the Council are appointed by professional trade-union or co-operative organizations. When there is rivalry between different bodies, an effort is made to distribute the seats among them in proportion to their size. In some cases, agreement between two organizations is required. Some members, such as the representatives of "housing" or "French thought," are directly nominated by the Council of Ministers. Members are appointed for three years.

Operation

The Economic Council is not a true parliamentary assembly, but it does its best to resemble one. Its members do not enjoy parliamentary immunity, although they draw a salary equal to two-thirds of the parliamentary salary. The Council sits during the periods when the National Assembly is in session, twice a month as a rule. It sets up special committees among its members, and it has the services of a secretariat. Its meetings are public: the chairmen and rapporteurs of parliamentary committees may be present, and ministers may attend and speak.

Powers

The duties of the Economic Council are, generally speaking, advisory. It has no power to make decisions. In the first place it advises Parliament after examining bills and proposals for legislation of social and economic interest as well as international agreements on financial and economic matters. Yet it has no right to discuss the budget, which is somewhat extraordinary in view of the markedly economic nature of modern budgets. Both the National Assembly and the Council of the Republic request the opinion of the Economic Council, but it may discuss issues on its own initiative. The opinion of the Economic Council is circulated to all members of Parliament and put down for general debate. A representative of the Economic Council may attend parliamentary debates at the request of the minister or chairman of the parliamentary committee involved; he may also speak at the request of the chairman of the committee.

Second, the Council has the duty of giving advice to the government, which is obliged to consult it in four cases: (1) with a view to drawing up a national economic plan; (2) on the formulation of decrees and regulations made in conformity with laws of an economic nature which have been presented for the Council's opinion; (3) on the development of the economic situation; and (4) on the official estimates of national income.

Third, the Council may, on its own initiative, discuss any economic, social, or financial question. In particular, it can carry out investigations as a result of which it may forward suggestions to the President of the Council of Ministers and the President of the National Assembly. Some investigations undertaken by the Council have produced work of great value, as, for example, the 1954 inquiry into wholesale and retail prices and the cost of distribution.

Finally, the Economic Council may be called upon to arbitrate in social or economic disputes. Its intervention must be requested by the parties to the dispute, and the agreement of the ministers concerned is required. This is the only case in which the function of the

Council is not purely advisory and in which it has power to decide. In practice, it rarely exercises this function.

The Economic Council does not play the part that it deserves in the system. Its discussions are generally well conducted. Its publications are always read with interest. It fairly represents the various trades and professions: the representatives of agriculture account for some 23 per cent of the membership, for example, while those of commerce and crafts account for less than 12 per cent. This corresponds to the actual importance of these two branches of national activity, while in Parliament they are overrepresented. The Economic Council is the only body in which the dynamic elements of the French economy are not underrepresented to the advantage of the static elements. The Council's powers and its prestige could usefully be increased. President Émile Roche is making considerable efforts to achieve this, but he is meeting with some opposition in Parliament, which does not greatly care to increase the importance of a rival institution. Furthermore, right-wing opinion is on the whole rather hostile to the Council, because the body is suspected of favoring a "planned" economy, which runs contrary to the liberal principles defended by the Right.

THE CONSTITUTIONAL COMMITTEE

In France there is no judicial review of the constitutionality of laws. The courts cannot consider the question. They do not have the right to declare that a law is contrary to the Constitution and, in consequence, to refuse to apply it, as in the United States. An explanation may be found in the general lack of independence of the French judiciary. Despite this condition, the Constitution of 1946 established in embryo some control over the constitutionality of laws. It is relatively weak and unorganized, but it nonetheless marks an advance on the complete absence of any such institution under the Third Republic. This control is exercised by the Constitutional Committee.

Membership

There are thirteen members of the Committee: the President of the Republic, the President of the National Assembly, the President of the Council of the Republic, and ten elected members, of whom seven are elected by the Assembly and three by the Council of the Republic. The elected members are appointed for the duration of the legislature in direct ratio to the strength of the parliamentary groups, in conformity with the procedure used for the appointment of members to the committees of Parliament. Although chosen by political vote, the elected members of the Constitutional Committee are not politicians; they must, in fact, be chosen from outside Parliament, and the majority are jurists.

Powers

The powers of the Committee are rather curiously defined. The Constitution does not expressly charge it with the duty of examining whether laws passed by the National Assembly are in accordance with the Constitution. It simply declares that the committee examines "whether the laws passed by the National Assembly imply a revision of the Constitution." This means the same thing, for a law which implies the revision of the Constitution is, by definition, contrary to it. In effect, therefore, the Committee judges the constitutionality of laws.

The powers of the Committee to intervene are very limited, however. It may not on its own initiative question the constitutionality of a law. No citizen may call on it to act. Only the Council of the Republic, by a resolution passed by an absolute majority of members, can call upon it to act. This resolution, moreover, must be passed within the very short space of time allowed for the promulgation of a law—ten days normally, five days if the Assembly has voted for urgent promulgation.

Once set in motion, the Committee has a dual role. Before examining the law submitted to it and pronouncing whether or not it involves constitutional revision, the Committee must "endeavor to bring about an agreement between the National Assembly and the Council of the Republic." It thus plays the part of conciliator. It is only if the attempt at conciliation fails that the Committee gives its opinion on the constitutionality of the law referred to it. Should it consider the law unconstitutional, it invites the National Assembly to take steps for the revision of the Constitution. Until this has been effected, the law is not enforceable. The Committee is much more a body designed to resolve conflicts between the two chambers than a body for insuring the constitutionality of laws. To be more precise, it serves to safeguard the Council of the Republic against possible encroachments by the Assembly; that is why only the Council may refer laws to it and why the pre-eminent duty laid on it is to seek to bring about an agreement between the two chambers. It has no power to prevent the implementation of laws that infringe the constitutional rights of citizens, for it was meant to protect the Council of the Republic rather than individuals.

The Committee has met only once, on June 16–18, 1948. It deliberated a difficult question concerning the period of time at the disposal of the Council of the Republic for considering laws referred to it by the Assembly. It overstepped its terms of reference to some extent by venturing to suggest that the National Assembly should modify its standing orders. This the Assembly did, and the solution adopted as a result of this action was confirmed subsequently in the constitutional revision of December 7, 1954.

THE SUPREME COUNCIL OF THE JUDICIARY

Judges in France are not entirely independent of the government, and the Supreme Council of the Judiciary was created to remedy this situation.

The Supreme Council is made up of fourteen members as follows: President of the Republic (chairman), Minister of Justice (vice-chairman), six members elected by the National Assembly, four elected by the judiciary, and two appointed by the President of the Republic. The members nominated by the National Assembly are chosen from outside its ranks and elected by a two-thirds majority. This has caused difficulties: in 1952 the replacement of a single member led to thirteen separate ballots without result. Each of the representatives of the judiciary is elected by a different grade of the four grades in the judicial hierarchy.

The functions of the Supreme Council are twofold, for it deals with the careers of judges and with the exercise of the right to pardon. It has power to appoint and to discipline judges, but this concerns only those who sit in court as judges and does not include examining magistrates, prosecutors, or attorneys who belong to the Public Prosecutor's Office. Though these are all classed as magistrates in France, they remain under the authority of the Minister of Justice. In matters of discipline the Council tries judges accused of malfeasance and decides upon the penalty to be imposed—suspension, transfer, or removal. In the matter of appointments the Council restricts itself legally to putting forward names to the President of the Republic, who makes the appointment; but in practice he is obliged to accept the proposals made by the Council.

The Council also has duties in regard to the right of pardon by which a sentenced man may be excused wholly or partly or may have his sentence commuted. The exercise of the prerogative is in the hands of the President of the Republic, but the case is prepared by the Supreme Council which then makes a recommendation. The final decision rests with the President of the Republic, who makes it alone. This is the only instance in which he has a real power of personal decision. The origin of the prerogative provides the explanation; it is one of the last vestiges of royal power.

THE HIGH COURT OF JUSTICE

In most political systems there exists some institution charged with the duty of judging the leading officials of the state in the event of their committing crimes in the exercise of their office. Sometimes this body is also given the duty of trying any citizen accused of exceptional political crime such as acts endangering the security of the state. The existence of such political courts is controversial both from the point of view of legal principles and from that of the equity of their decision. "Political justice" is rarely just. The ordinary courts, however, lack the prestige to judge the accused of exalted rank. In fact, political justice is in large measure a survival in democratic systems from earlier and less liberal systems. It is something exceptional, a means by which a political system defends itself against enemies in times of stress.

Under the Third Republic, France adopted a system directly inspired by traditional British practice. It was the upper chamber, the Senate, which transformed itself into a High Court of Justice to judge ministers or individuals accused of crimes against the security of the state. At the Liberation a special High Court was set up in 1944 by the provisional government to try the chief of state, the head of the government, and all the ministers of the Vichy regime. The framers had the experience of this court in mind when they drew up the Constitution of 1946. This explains some of the features of the present High Court.

The High Court of Justice is made up of a president, a vice-president, thirty judges, and thirty deputy judges. The president and vice-president are elected by the National Assembly on a two-thirds majority by secret ballot. Two-thirds of the judges and their deputies are elected by the Assembly from its own members proportionally to the size of the parliamentary groups. Each group puts forward a list containing twice as many names as it has vacancies to fill. The remaining judges and deputies are elected by the Assembly from outside its ranks by a two-thirds majority by secret ballot. Extraparliamentary judges have thus been introduced into the High Court.

Under the Third Republic, the Senate as High Court held jurisdiction in two cases: in the case of prosecution of the President of the Republic and ministers; in the case of a private individual accused of an attempt against the security of the state. Today High Court can judge only the President of the Republic and ministers. It holds complete jurisdiction in regard to ministers and it applies to all acts committed by them in the exercise of their office. The High Court can decide only in accordance with the penal code, however; its judgments are concerned with crimes and penalties legally established. This point was made clear because the Senate under the Third Republic had sometimes departed from this principle. In dealing with the President of the Republic, the High Court's jurisdiction is restricted and exclusive; it can try him only on a charge of high treason. In practice these arrangements are as yet untested and unclear, since this crime was not envisaged in the penal code and there exists no legal definition of high treason.

The High Court established by the Constitution of 1946 has never functioned. The Senate of the Third Republic was very rarely called on to act as a High Court. Apart from the case of a man accused of treason in the 1880's, its judgments were concerned with ministers and other persons accused of communicating with the enemy in World War I. No President of the Republic has ever been brought before the High Court. The institution therefore has no importance in normal times.

PART II

POLITICAL FORCES

INTRODUCTION

After describing in general outline the French political system, we must now consider who works it and to what end. The rules of the game have been explained; let us see who are the players and how they play their roles.

The game of politics in France has the reputation of being very complicated. To all appearances, the parties are numerous and difficult to distinguish from one another, especially on the Right; the political vocabulary is abstract, teems with historical allusions, and proves very difficult for an uninitiated foreigner to understand; the pressure groups conceal their activity and flee the observer. However, beneath all the conventions and formulas, the basic cleavages of opinion are fairly easy to discern. The over-all pattern of French political life is not really very different from that in other western European countries.

The contrast between appearance and reality is still more striking when we consider the instability that is often held to be the chief characteristic of French politics. Nothing, at first sight, could be truer: French governments last on an average eight months, the lowest average in western Europe. Yet a closer examination reveals that changes in government rarely involve changes of policy and changes of personnel. "Ministries go but the ministers remain" is the remark often made. In reality the dominant feature of French political life is not instability but stability, *immobility* as it has come to be described in the last few years. Behind this political immobility, however, lies much greater economic mobility than is usually thought.

CHAPTER 6

PARTIES

France is known for its many political parties. At the present moment there are thirteen political groups officially registered in the National Assembly; there were twelve in the 1936 Chamber of Deputies. But there are fewer really organized parties, half a dozen perhaps. The truth is that the French party system is not in essence different from that elsewhere on the Continent. On the Right there is no major, organized Conservative party, and so there arises the impression of a multitude of small groups. If, however, we except the native parties of the French Union, the number of fundamental political tendencies in France is scarcely any higher than that in Scandinavia or anywhere else on the Continent. The history of the formation of the French party system best reveals its similarity to other European systems.

FORMATION OF THE PARTY SYSTEM

Conservatives and Liberals

The Revolution of 1789 is the starting point for all present-day French parties, for it brought about in France and throughout Europe an enduring pattern of conflict between conservatives and liberals. This conflict was social as well as political. The conservatives represented the aristocracy of landed wealth, and their chief electoral supporters were the peasants who remained faithful to the local gentry. In national politics conservatives supported the monarchical *ancien régime,* that is, a society founded on "natural" differences, in which the nobility had a right to special powers and privileges and political authority belonged to a hereditary monarch. Conservatives saw political power, in short, from a paternalist angle: a king's authority over his people was no different in essence from a father's authority over his children.

Religion was an important factor in this view. Authority, whether monarchical or paternal, was in accordance with the divine law, and the king was considered to be chosen by God. In prerevolutionary France, moreover, the king was consecrated in the Cathedral of Rheims in the course of a religious ceremony sometimes called the "eighth sacrament." In 1824, Charles X resuscitated this rite for the last time. Conservatives were generally opposed to political liberties: particularly dangerous in their view were freedom of thought and freedom of expression, for these were believed to spread error and lead the people astray.

In opposition, the liberals defended the ideas of the American and French revolutions. Their political philosophy was based upon eighteenth-century ideas. They thought the social order ought to be founded on reason: the traditional order could be altered and replaced by a rational order. All men were born equal and should enjoy equal rights; none had a natural prerogative to rule over others. In consequence the only valid political power must be set up by mandate of the entire community in an election. Further, the liberals were defenders of individual liberty and in particular of liberty of thought. They were, on the whole, suspicious of religion and of the Catholic Church, though there were occasional alliances between liberals and Catholics in some countries during the nineteenth century. The alliance between French Catholics and conservatives, very close in 1815 at the Restoration, in 1850, and in 1871 on the establishment of the Third Republic, naturally encouraged the liberals to show themselves somewhat anticlerical. The liberals found their chief supporters in the towns and among the urban middle class, among the merchants, shopkeepers, industrialists, and members of the liberal and learned professions. To some extent, therefore, the conflict between conservatives and liberals took on the appearance of a class struggle as well as of a struggle between country and town.

Obviously, party divisions did not exactly coincide with the cleavages between social classes; there were middle-class conservatives and liberal aristocrats. During the French Revolution the younger members of the nobility—Lafayette, for example—were often attracted to the new ideas. From the Revolution of 1848 onward, the middle classes became uneasy about the dangers of socialism and tended to draw closer to conservatism.

During the nineteenth century, neither conservatives nor liberals formed a clearly separate party in France, and this is one of the reasons for the present-day multiplicity of parties. The explanation is to be found in history. The great Revolution of 1789 continued for a decade through several different phases, and the revolutionaries of 1789 appeared as moderates by 1793, when the extreme Jacobins were ruling. Thus two traditions were established in the liberal camp, a moderate wing and a radical wing. In 1830 the former subdivided on the question of Orleanism, that is, of a view that accepted a monarchical government so long as it was liberal and parliamentary. At that period there were, therefore, three tendencies among liberals: Orleanists (or moderate monarchists), moderate Republicans, and the descendants of the Jacobins.

As for the conservatives, they experienced similar difficulties. The restoration of the monarchy in 1814 produced a cleavage between moderate monarchists, who supported the reforming policy of Louis XVIII, and the absolute monarchists, or ultraroyalists, who were said to be more royalist than the king himself. Conservative differences were increased by the Revolution of 1830 and the establishment of a liberal monarchy. After 1871 and the restoration of the republic, some conservatives officially declared themselves republicans with traditional conservative views. Bonapartism became another complicating factor in the situation.

Bonapartists and Orleanists

Two nineteenth-century French political phenomena deserve attention for their novelty—Bonarpartism and Orleanism. Both correspond to the same fundamental idea: an attempt to reconcile conservatives and liberals on the basis of a compromise policy.

It is difficult nowadays to realize just how deep was the gulf separating what were then sometimes known as the "two Frances," that of the *ancien régime* and that of the Revolution. Those who chose sides disagreed in their very conceptions of political society, in their whole philosophy of life. The struggles of the Revolution and the "white terror" of the Restoration had been so violent that the two parties were also separated by their desire for revenge. The cleavage was so profound that it inspired historians like Thierry to propound the fanciful theory of "two races" already referred to. The monarchists were identified with the aristocracy descended from the Germanic conqueror, and the liberals were identified with the Gallo-Romans.

No political system could endure in the nineteenth century unless it succeeded in satisfying the two opposing factions. Bonapartists and Orleanists attempted in different ways to do this. The First and Second Empires both witnessed an effort to conciliate liberal doctrines and the idea of the sovereignty of the nation with an authoritarian monarchical system designed to please conservatives. Considerable effort was made to fuse the two conceptions of legitimacy: legitimacy founded upon election by the nation and hereditary legitimacy founded upon appointment by God. Napoleon I was proclaimed emperor after a national plebiscite based on universal suffrage, but he had himself consecrated by the pope in order to win the advantages of royal investiture. Furthermore, he took as his second wife the heiress to the oldest royal family in Europe, the Habsburgs, to give his monarchy a more authentic air. In short, an attempt was made to establish a monarchy to the taste of the revolutionaries of 1789. It must be remembered that Bonaparte was promoted to general by Robespierre, that he was of Jacobin persuasion, and that the Convention used him to save the republic from a royalist insurrection.

The Napoleonic episode represented an effort to save the idea of civil equality by sacrificing political liberties, since at the time it was impossible to establish a republic. The effort succeeded in part. In particular, the conceptions of Napoleon spread the ideas of the Revolution far and wide in Europe and prepared the way for the great liberal movement of the nineteenth century.

The attempt made by the Orleanists from 1830 to 1848 was diametrically opposed. They sought to preserve the traditional monarchy by making it adopt liberal policies, that is, in brief, by imitating the development of the British political system. Because the elder branch of the dynasty, the Bourbons, were opposed to this attempt—the Revolution had already sought such a compromise with Louis XVI and the Constitution of 1791 was its fruit—it became necessary to remove them from the throne and replace them by the younger branch, the Orleans family, whence the term Orleanists. This experiment had the merit of acclimatizing the parliamentary regime in France. The intelligent King Louis XVIII had already attempted to introduce it between 1814 and 1824. But Louis Philippe's monarchy was always out of step. The royalists did not consider a king who had been placed on the throne by a revolution as a legitimate monarch, hence the opposition of the so-called "legitimist" party. The republicans would not allow political power in the hands of a king. The experiment could have succeeded if Louis Philippe had accepted a gradual liberalization of the system. But after 1840 he refused to agree to any reform, and this brought about the Revolution of 1848. It is worth noting that in 1871, after the proclamation of the Republic, an attempt was made to re-establish a parliamentary monarchy on the Orleanist pattern.

New Parties in the Twentieth Century

Already during the first half of the nineteenth century the conflict between conservatives and liberals was being overshadowed by
a social conflict produced by the development of large-scale industry and the appearance of a proletariat. Before this, the working
class was relatively small. The large factories were situated in the
country rather than in the town, and the workers led the life of
countrymen. Workers in the towns were predominantly craftsmen,
and social conflicts were less marked than they are in large-scale
industry.

In the nineteenth century the Industrial Revolution totally altered
the situation in France and in the rest of Europe. It led to the formation of a proletariat whose material conditions were frightful.
The investigation carried out by Dr. Villemain in 1847, at the request of the Academy of Moral and Political Sciences, gave definite
and damning evidence of the horrible working conditions in the
textile industry. It was this situation which inspired the development of socialist thought.

There were practically no Socialists at the time of the Revolution
of 1789. Some Jacobins, Robespierre and Saint-Just especially, formulated a social policy, but they remained attached to the private-
property and private-enterprise system. It was left to Gracchus
Babeuf under the Directorate to create one of the earliest Socialist
parties; he died on the scaffold for conspiring against the regime.
The real birth of socialist movements, however, followed the coming of large-scale industry and the proletariat. The Revolution of
1848 revealed their strength but also their lack of organization. Socialist movements were very strong in Paris, strong enough to
frighten the other social classes. The liberal middle classes drew
nearer to the conservative aristocracy in common hatred of the
"Reds." At the elections of 1848 they together formed the party of
"Order" which united Legitimists, Bonapartists, Orleanists, and
moderate Republicans. In the eyes of the Order party, the blood-
letting of June, 1848, did not seem adequate to prevent the subversion of society, and, to guard against subversion, they finally established the dictatorship of the second Bonaparte, who became
emperor under the name of Napoleon III.

In 1871 the moderate Republicans similarly clashed with the socialist working class, who, for patriotic reasons, revolted against a
humiliating armistice and occupied Paris for several weeks. This
was the bloody revolution of *La Commune;* its repression, after the

strife of civil war had ended, claimed ten times as many victims as the Jacobin Terror of 1793. Once again moderate Republicans, Bonapartists, and conservatives united against the Socialists. The suppression of the Commune wrecked the organization of the Socialist party for several decades. It slowly re-emerged toward the end of the century, split into different factions which did not fuse until 1905.

After the Russian Revolution of 1917, one wing of the Socialists came out in favor of the Bolsheviks, while the other maintained more reserve. This produced the 1920 split in the party, which gave birth to the Communist party. Similar trends were to be seen at the time in the rest of Europe; but in most countries the Socialist parties were strong enough so that the Communist breakaway did not greatly weaken them, and the Communist parties remained small, exercising little influence in elections and in political life. Things were different in France and Germany. In both countries, Communists rapidly formed a major party, larger in Germany than in France until 1933 when Hitler's regime put an end to the party system. World War II increased the power of the Communist party in France.

At that period of the nineteenth century when the first Socialist parties were emerging, some Catholics turned their attention to social problems and so gave birth to the Christian-Democratic or Christian-Socialist movement. The two terms initially had quite different connotations, but they have come to mean the same thing. Until 1914 this attitude remained the province of small groups which did not succeed in organizing themselves into major parties. Although Pope Leo XIII advised the French to rally to the support of the republic, the Catholic majority remained conservative. Not until the eve of World War I did a popular Christian-Democratic movement of any size, *Le Sillon,* make its appearance. Condemned by the pope, however, it disappeared. Between the wars another Christian-Democratic movement appeared in 1925, under the name of "People's Democratic party"; it was chiefly successful in Parliament, where it had a small number of deputies. Not until 1944, with the Liberation, was a major Christian-Democratic party born—the MRP.

THE RIGHT

In France there has never been an organized and coherent Conservative party of major importance. Today the Right is made up of small groups important chiefly in Parliament. There is no corre-

sponding powerful organization in the country, and only in exceptional times do the factions unite temporarily in movements that
tend toward dictatorial views.

Origins

In discussing the French Left or Right or Center, it is important
to define the period concerned. In 1871 the Orleanists were on the
Right, but in 1830 they were in the Center; the moderate Republicans were a Center party in 1871, while today they are on the Right.
At the beginning of the Third Republic, the Right was made up of
opponents of the republican regime. By 1877 the division was quite
clear: Republicans on one side, on the other the Right which included Bonapartists and Monarchists, both Legitimist and Orleanist. The position has greatly changed since then as a result of the
development of new parties to the left of the 1877 Republicans, who
have been driven toward the Center.

There were two wings inside the Republican party in 1877: the
Radical Left and the Moderate Left, dubbed "Opportunist" by its
enemies and later self-styled "Progressive." Until 1885 the Opportunists governed alone against both the Right and the Radicals.
After 1895 the Opportunists lost their majority in the Chamber of
Deputies, and they had therefore to choose between alliance with
the Left or with the Right. For some time they hesitated, though a
section went into coalition with the conservatives to form the Rou-
vier government of 1896–98. These moderate Republicans finally
split, however, over the Dreyfus affair: those who took his part
went over to the Radical Left, and the rest went over to the Right.
This affair greatly inflamed French public opinion at the end of the
nineteenth century. Briefly, it concerned an injustice suffered by a
Jewish army officer who was found guilty of treason and sentenced
in dubious circumstances by a military tribunal to life deportation.
Invoking the Rights of Man and the liberty of the individual, the
Left campaigned violently in favor of Dreyfus, who was innocent.
Invoking national security and the dangers of national division in
face of Germany, the Right opposed any revision of the case. Finally the case was retried, and Dreyfus was declared innocent and
reinstated. The Dreyfus affair marked a regrouping of political parties; the positions adopted on that issue are highly indicative of the
fundamental cleavage between Left and Right in France.

Thus at the beginning of the twentieth century the Right included, alongside the former Monarchists and Bonapartists, the
moderate wing of the Progressives. The other wing, which in 1901

assumed the title of Democratic Alliance, gradually drew nearer to the Right as the development of the Socialist and Communist parties made the Radicals lean toward the Center and hence the Center toward the Right. Men like Paul Reynaud and Antoine Pinay, who today are definitely on the Right, would at the end of the last century have been Progressives. The union of the Democratic Alliance and the Right was finally consummated just before the outbreak of the war in 1914 on a nationalist and military issue, the three-year military service law, and on a fiscal question, their opposition to income tax. After World War I and even more after World War II, one wing of the Radical party similarly moved to the Right, and this explains the difficulties now being experienced by Radicalism, as we shall see later.

History explains the marked division of the Right into two wings. First we have those who were opposed to the republic in 1875 and who have never paid it more than lip service. Then we have the moderate Republicans who moved to the Right between 1895 and 1914. Traditionally the first wing attacks the parliamentary system whenever possible and has often launched out into authoritarian and dictatorial adventures. It took part in the Boulanger episode in 1885, in the Nationalist movement of 1900, and in the Fascist escapades of the 1930's. It had a share in the Vichy regime set up by Marshal Pétain, and subsequently it has been active in both the Gaullist and Poujadist movements. In contrast, the other wing, the parliamentary Right, traditionally believes in the republic and in liberal ideas. It follows in the footsteps of the nineteenth-century liberals, the Orleanists and moderate Republicans. Paul Reynaud and Louis Marin, who are both men of the Right, took part in the Resistance movement against the Vichy government and were opposed to the Fascist movements of the thirties.

In normal times this division within the Right does not show because the great majority of Frenchmen accept the republican regime. Only in periods of crisis or at some threat of danger, whether Socialist or Communist, does the authoritarian Right recover its virulence and venture on activities that may imperil the regime.

Links with the Catholic Church

The religious question is extremely important in contemporary French politics, although it is somewhat less important than it was during the Third Republic. The heart of the matter is that the Catholic Church was linked with the Right throughout the nine-

teenth century and the early years of the twentieth. Religion was
the only bond that in practice linked Legitimists, Orleanists, and
Bonapartists, the three parties of Order in 1848. At the time, the
middle classes, who were not very devout, saw in the spread of
religion a means of combating the Socialists. That is why they encouraged the development of religious instruction in schools.

It must be added that some Catholics entered the political arena,
especially at the outset of the Third Republic. The attitude adopted
by several religious orders, especially the Assumptionists, over the
Dreyfus case was very revealing. There is no doubt that most Catholics looked askance at the republican regime. There was therefore
a bond *de facto* between the Right and the Church. The efforts
of Pope Leo XIII to break this bond failed as a result of the opposition of the majority of French Catholics. The policy of *Ralliement*
he preached in 1891, calling on the French to support the republic,
did not succeed.

The collusion between religion and politics was most manifest on
the private-school question. Most private schools are run by the
Church, and the private-school question is therefore a "religious"
question. This explains its political importance. The Right had from
the middle of the nineteenth century supported the development
of Catholic schools, both because they provided religious teaching
corresponding to its convictions and because they produced future
conservative voters. On the other hand, the Left had developed
public secular schools in order to give the younger generation an
education that was republican and liberal. The conflict became very
acute at the turn of the century. The Republicans fought against
clericalism, that is, the interference of the clergy in politics and
particularly on the question of schools. The establishment of a general system of public education had been the chief task performed
by the Third Republic before 1914. Freedom to open private schools
had been maintained, but such schools were run at the expense of
those who wanted them, whereas public education was free at all
levels. In addition to the schools question, relations between the
Vatican and France had in 1905 brought about a breach in the Con-
cordat of 1801 and led to the separation of church and state. Some
religious orders, considered as particular enemies of the republic,
were banned.

After World War I anticlericalism declined. It had never been
very serious. No Catholic, for example, had ever been prosecuted
or imprisoned for being a Catholic. The religious orders had returned to France during the war and had taken part in the fighting.

Furthermore, the clergy was tending to rally to the support of the republic, as were many lay Catholics. After 1945 the formation of a Christian-Democratic party, the MRP, put the question in a different light, since this party was trying to detach Catholics from the parties of the Right. Its success was only partial. In 1951 the debate on church schools, which ended in the passing of the famous Barangé Law to subsidize them, demonstrated the continued importance in French politics of the religious question and showed that there are still close links between the majority of Catholics and the Right. Since 1945 the MRP has itself moved toward the Right. Opposition to colonial policy in Indo-China and North Africa, however, have strengthened left-wing Catholic movements.

Economic Ties

The Right has always been qute closely linked with business circles and economic interests. In the nineteenth century the Legitimist extreme Right, largely supported by the traditional wealth of the landed aristocracy, viewed with disfavor any financial liaison with business, but the Orleanists and Bonapartists soon established such alliances, which they therefore viewed more indulgently. The reigns of Louis Philippe and Napoleon III witnessed a marked development in the relations between politics and business. On the establishment of the Republic in 1871, the moderate Republicans continued the Orleanist and Bonapartist tradition. Sometimes they acted as links with the new fields of business interest, e.g., railways, public works, and colonial trade. There seems to have been some conflict between the new Republican fortunes and the older fortunes and businesses of the Orleanists and Bonapartists, just as under the July monarchy there had been conflict between the rich Legitimist property owners and the financial and industrial Orleanist midle classes. The move of the moderate Republicans to the Right between 1900 and 1914 represents the fusion of the two interests in common fear of socialism.

The Right has thus always been linked with economic pressure groups. There is no doubt about the liaison, though it is often difficult to define. By contrast with what happens in the United States, no one in France dares to admit any open association between politics and business. In particular, the financing of political parties by economic groups, which certainly happens, is shrouded in mystery. Furthermore, the Right is not alone in being linked with economic interests; many other parties, especially the Radicals and even the Socialists, have now linked up with economic circles. These relationships are more recent, but for the Right they are traditional. It has even been suggested that the absence of organization on the Right results from the fact that the parties are really based on pressure groups.

Attempts To Organize since 1946

It has stated that the Right is traditionally split up into small rival groups. We must, however, note that in recent years an interesting attempt has been made to impose some discipline upon right-wing members of Parliament, especially when there are government crises. A real co-ordinating office for groups on the Right has been established under the name of the National Center of Independents. Its backing is much sought after in elections. In the Assembly elected on January 2, 1956, the Right is much less split than it was in previous chambers. However, it is far from having the discipline of left-wing parties, especially the Socialists and Communists.

In addition, interesting attempts have been made to develop contacts between right-wing deputies and agricultural trade unions. This could give rise to a true people's party on the Right. However, the efforts are still in the initial stage. So far the Right is made up almost entirely of parliamentary groups and local politicians. It is therefore not a mass party but a cadre party and weakly organized at that.

THE EXTREME RIGHT

Part of the Right, as we have explained, is not really in favor of the republican system of government. Originally this part was royalist with the exception of the small group of Bonapartists, but the monarchical principle has almost entirely lost its appeal for the general public. In France today the royalists are only a tiny group without real political influence. Even the claimant to the throne, the Count of Paris, who favors the Orleanist type of monarchy, has in practice accepted the republic and entertains few illusions about his chances of becoming king. The antirepublican Right has therefore abandoned the monarchical principle but this has led it to dream of dictatorship of one kind or another.

Under the Third Republic

These dreams of dictatorship first took concrete shape during the Third Republic in the Boulanger adventure of 1895, which threatened to establish military rule. It was a strange episode, for there was a kind of alliance between the antirepublican extreme

Right and the extreme Radical Left. The Radicals very soon withdrew from this curious combination and fought against Boulangism. General Boulanger had great success in the elections and could have seized power, especially as he enjoyed the support of the army, which was at that time hostile to the republic in that most of its officers were the sons of the aristocracy. But the General lacked both character and energy.

Between the wars there were a number of Fascist movements. The first wave between 1924 and 1926 was unimportant, but the success of the extreme Right between 1933 and 1940 was far more serious. Though flurries of agitation by students and intellectuals had no real influence on the public, some groups were more important. The most notable were the French People's party led by Jacques Doriot, a former secretary of the Communist party, and the Croix de Feu movement led by Lieutenant Colonel de la Rocque, which was later called the French Social party. These movements were active less at the electoral level than at the level of street-corner agitation. However, if the 1940 elections had been held, it is probable that the French Social party in particular would have won many seats.

The French People's Rally

Although it is in many ways different, the party led by General de Gaulle between 1948 and 1953 may be classed with these movements of the extreme Right. The General was very dissatisfied with the Constitution of 1946 and the political system it had established; furthermore, he considered that party strife was harmful to France in the exceptional postwar conditions. Hence he organized a body which officially opposed political parties but which was really itself a political party, the RPF, or French People's Rally. The General cannot honestly be accused of aspiring to dictatorship, however, for, if he had wished, he could have exercised absolute power after 1944, whereas he used all his influence for the re-establishment of republican liberties. Nonetheless, the danger of communism led a large section of the authoritarian Right to support the RPF. This support was neither enthusiastic nor unreserved, for the extreme Right had rather favored the Vichy experiment and the government of Marshal Pétain.

The RPF won a great success in the 1948 senatorial elections and in the 1951 elections to the Assembly; but its parliamentary group, which was the largest in the chamber, was unable to follow the orders of General de Gaulle, who refused to allow any participation in the government. A first split in 1952 led to the creation of a dissident group under the name of Social and Republican Action, which lost no time in securing ministerial posts for some of its members. Then in 1953 the General himself took the step of breaking off all contact with the RPF parliamentary group, and this led to the disappearance of the party. The former RPF deputies went to the 1956 elections under the new name of the Social Republican party, only to experience a serious defeat.

Poujadism

The Poujadist movement is very different from the RPF, and we must beware of any facile comparison which might suggest that Poujadism in 1956 is the heir to the RPF of 1951. It is true that one French politician has called Poujade "the poor man's de Gaulle," but this was merely a witticism with no real foundation.

Initially the Poujade movement was a pressure group defending the interests of small shopkeepers and artisans, as its official title indicates: Union for the Defense of Shopkeepers and Artisans (UDCA). Its main aim was to fight against taxation, which these groups of society consider excessive. Actually, the small shopkeeper pays on the whole a smaller tax in proportion than the large firm. Tax inspection, however, is irritating, and the keeping of exact accounts exasperates the artisan and the small shopkeeper. The Poujadists first protested with violence against the inspection of accounts. They organized street meetings (at which crowds of artisans and shopkeepers gathered to prevent inspection on the premises of their fellows) and punitive assaults on tax offices. After some hesitation, Pierre Poujade decided to put forward candidates at the January 2, 1956, elections. His electoral propaganda was quite simple. There were no ideals, no concrete proposals for reform. There was simply a meaningless cry for a meeting of the long defunct States-General, and there was the resounding slogan "Get rid of them!" directed against the deputies running for re-election. It was predicted that the Poujadists would win 5 to 10 seats; instead, they won 52 and polled 2,500,000 votes—almost 10 per cent of the electorate.

The Poujade movement differs radically in organization from other parties by its corporatist character. It is made up of a series of parallel occupational defense unions—Union of Shopkeepers and Artisans, Union of Agriculturalists, Union of the Working Class, etc.—while those without a trade are grouped in the Union and Brotherhood of France. In practice, there is no autonomy in the groups. Everything is closely centered on the leader, who exercises absolute authority over the unions. Moreover, the UDCA continues to provide the principal strength of the movement. Initially the supporters were shopkeepers and artisans defending their corporate interests, particularly small provincial shopkeepers economically on the decline who were in revolt against modern trends that threatened them with extinction. The weakness shown by the government in face of Poujadist agitation and the considerable tax concessions that it made to medium-sized businesses had given prestige to the UDCA. Around this small-business nucleus there gathered at the 1956 elections supporters of authoritarianism and enemies of Parliament, that is, part of the authoritarian extreme Right. In composition, in methods of agitation, and in general tendencies, Poujadism is akin to fascism, but it is a very elementary, primitive kind of fascism. Pierre Poujade more nearly resembles a huckster than a Hitler or a Mussolini.

There is also a popular side to the movement. It unites the "little men against the big men." But there are no intellectuals and no representatives of the upper middle class or of the world of big business, who on other occasions have supported authoritarian right-wing movements. It is typical too that Poujade's electoral victories were won in the areas of France that are most backward economically. In the few economically progressive departments in which Poujadism gained some success (e.g., Isère), careful study has revealed that this success came principally in the backward cantons within the department.

The star of Poujadism has waned considerably since the triumph in 1956. The mediocrity of its parliamentary representatives, who have certainly not shone in debate, does it harm. No complete bill on any subject has been introduced by the Poujade group. Furthermore, the personal failure of Pierre Poujade at the by-elections in Paris in January, 1957, showed that the electoral tide had turned against him. Poujadism is certainly on the decline. It is probable that the movement will last no longer than the other authoritarian movements whose activities under the Third Republic have been described.

THE RADICALS

The Radical party played a vital part during the Third Republic, and it has sometimes been evaluated as the party which best represented the spirit of the Third Republic, which is often called the Radical Republic. The party's first steps under the Fourth Republic were uncertain. It was very weak when Liberation came, but it has since made a fine recovery so that it now again occupies an important place. Since 1955, however, it has been rent by internal schisms which bear witness to the complexity of its composition.

Origins

The Radical party was the extreme left-wing party of the early republic. It was the embodiment of intransigence and called for a program then considered bold: revision of the Constitution, a single chamber, nationalization of the Bank of France, the mines, and the railways, separation of church and state, a graduated income tax, election of judges. At that time its chief supporters were town workers and almost the same social groups who today support Poujade, that is, small shopkeepers and artisans. Poujadism, however, spread particularly in small towns, whereas left-wing Radicalism was a large-town product. In foreign policy, it was nationalist, longing for revenge against Germany, and it quite faithfully embodied the Jacobin tradition.

Between 1900 and 1914 the social basis of the party changed; it enlisted supporters throughout rural areas—in the Paris basin, Burgundy, central France, and then in the southwest—so that it gradually won the backing of the peasantry. Its class character decreased, and it put secularism in the forefront of its program at the same time that it began to keep quiet about nationalization of the Bank of France, the mines, and the railways. Graduated taxation stayed as a plank in the platform, however, because in peasant eyes this represented some hope of decreasing land taxes, which were then quite heavy. It was at this period too that the party made contact with business circles.

The rise of a powerful Socialist party between 1900 and 1914 compelled it to choose between alliance with moderate republicanism or alliance with socialism. Generally, it preferred the latter and joined the left-wing coalitions: the 1906 Bloc des Gauches, the Cartel des Gauches in 1924, 1928, and 1932, and the Popular Front in 1936. In economic and social matters, however, the Radical program tended to approximate closer to moderate republicanism. Furthermore, one section of the party declined to ally with the Left, and the whole party broke with the Left several times, especially in financial crises. Under the Fourth Republic the right wing was initially the stronger, and this led the party to support a policy very like that of the Moderates and to fight for a liberal economy against planning (1944–54). After 1954, however, the experience of the Mendès-France government increased the power of the left wing within the party. When Mendès-France took over the leadership of the party in 1955, the struggle between the two wings became so intense as to lead to the splitting of the party.

The Mendès-France Experiment in Neo-Radicalism

As we have seen, the Radical party has almost always been divided, one wing leaning toward the Right and the Moderates, the other toward the Left and the Socialists. It is the coexistence within one party of these two wings that constitutes the special characteristic of the Radical party. There have been Radical ministers in almost every government, whatever its political complexion. Often, moreover, they were the same individuals, and they applied the brakes on conservative policies in right-wing governments or on reformist policies in left-wing governments. In every important ballot the Radical party divided into three sections: For, Against, Abstention.

In 1955 when he accepted the vice-presidency, and the virtual leadership of the party—Édouard Herriot being too old and tired to exercise effectively the presidency that he clung to so obstinately—Mendès-France wanted to make a complete change in the style of the party. His basic idea was to replace the old Radical party with its long-standing divisions by a disciplined and homogeneous party. This really would have entailed the victory of one wing over the others. The Mendès-France faction is situated on the left wing of Radicalism, with some leaning to the Jacobin tradition, and shows a certain understanding of social problems. This is the wing that Edgar Quinet and Louis Blanc represented in the National Assembly of 1871, the same trend that at different times the younger generations of Radicalism, e.g., the "Young Turks" of 1934–36, have represented. From 1945 to 1955 the right wing, represented by such men as Martineau-Deplat and Bourgès-Maunoury, dominated the party. The 1955 party congress, at which Mendès-France triumphed, reversed the position. What was new about the situation, however, was that once at the head of the party, Mendès-France wanted to reorganize it from top to bottom.

So far the results have been disappointing. Two successive splits have divided the party into three sections. In December, 1955, after dissolving the National Assembly in defiance of the party's opinion, Premier Edgar Faure was excluded from the party. He then formed a new party of Radical views with the title of Union of Left-Wing Republicans (RGR).

45818

To begin with, this was a grouping around the Radicals of a number of small parties, some to the Right, e.g., Democratic Alliance, and some to its Left, e.g., Democratic Socialists, Union of Democratic and Socialist Resistance (UDSR). Faure's cleverness lay in using the name of the RGR, which in the 1946 and 1951 elections had been merged in practice with the Radical party, to found a new party. The UDSR and the Radicals soon quit the RGR, however, and it is now no longer an alliance between several parties but simply a small party reduced in effect to the parliamentary group centered on Faure.

At the Radical congress of 1956, another group from the right wing left the party under the somewhat mediocre leadership of André Morice. To create confusion they chose the name Radical Socialist party, which is part of the official title of the Radical party. A lawsuit has been brought to decide the question of usurpation of title. These two splits did not settle the principal question. Within the main party itself, the majority of deputies were opposed to Mendès-France, and their leader was Bourgès-Maunoury, one of the engineers of the Suez expedition. Finally, in June, 1957, Mendès-France resigned the leadership, and the Radical party will now probably return to its old ways.

The Mendès-France attempt at reform was directed toward the organization of the party rather than its ideology. In fact, the changes in doctrine were minor; Mendès-France and his supporters limited themselves to insisting upon a strategic policy aimed at alliance with the Left and especially with the Socialists. From the point of view of organization, however, the reforms suggested were new and important.

The traditional Radical party furnished the outstanding example of a well-organized cadre party. It consisted of a network of small committees covering the whole of France. Essentially, the committee was a grouping of the important people in each *canton* or *arrondissement*. In national party meetings, representation was not based upon membership figures, the concept of membership not being at all precise. In practice, anyone could purchase an admission card to a Radical congress and influence discussion and voting, a fact which favored all kinds of intrigue. The directing body of the party was the Executive Committee, consisting of all parliamentary representatives, all the municipal councillors from the large towns, and delegates from the federations. This made some 1,200 members, but decisions were considered valid so long as 150 members were present.

The whole organization of the party was arranged so as to insure effective control not to the militant members but to small groups clustering round particular individuals, to what might be called "clans." Rivalries and alliances between "clans" finally determined the direction of party policy. It was this that Mendès-France wanted to change. He wanted to transform the old cadre party into a mass party organized more or less after the pattern of the Socialists. The party congress would become a meeting of delegates from the federations with voting strength proportional to the number of members they actually represented; control of the party would be in the hands of a small executive committee elected by the congress. A recruiting campaign carried out in 1955 increased by 50,000 members the strength of the party, so that by the beginning of 1956 it numbered approximately 100,000 members, about the same as the Socialist party.

Finally, Mendès-France wanted to introduce voting discipline into the traditional anarchy of the parliamentary group. In March, 1957, the principle was accepted that Radical deputies should vote in accordance with the decision adopted by their parliamentary group, although abstention was allowed. This marked a considerable improvement over the previous system, in which it was possible not only to abstain but even to vote against the decisions taken by the majority of the group. However, the principle of voting as a group was not put into practice, and it was because of the refusal of the parliamentary representatives to conform to the decisions of the 1957 congress on this issue, although they had formally accepted them, that Mendès-France resigned the leadership of the Radical party. The majority of party members supported him, but the majority of the parliamentary group, even after the 1955–56 splits, remained hostile to him. This hostility arose because the *de facto* leadership of the party was traditionally in the hands of the parliamentary group. The attempts of Mendès-France to give supreme authority to an executive committee emanating from the general membership ultimately failed. Such conflicts in political parties between parliamentary representatives and executive committees are not infrequent. Socialist parties, in particular, have at different times had the same experience.

UDSR

Similar to the Radical party in political views is the UDSR, which was one of the few parties to emerge in 1944 from the clandestine resistance movements against the Occupation authorities. Originally it was composed of former *résistants,* who were on the whole Socialist in tendency but had not found any place in the hierarchy of the Socialist party. A very small party, it is now little more than a parliamentary group, split into two rival wings, each of which is headed by an outstanding figure. The right wing is led by former Premier René Pleven, the left by François Mitterand, who aspires to become Premier. The former is pro-European and anti-Mendès-France, the latter anti-European and pro-Mendès-France. One of the distinguishing characteristics of the UDSR is that it has always maintained close contact with political associations in the French Union. This enabled it after the 1956 elections to form a common group in Parliament with the largest of the African parties, the African Democratic Rally (RDA). At present the UDSR and the RDA are united in a group which is close to Radicalism in its general policy.

THE SOCIALISTS

In its present form, the Socialist party dates from 1905, when there was a fusion of several Socialist groups that had been created at the end of the nineteenth century. It then took the name of the French Section of the Workers' International (SFIO), and it remains today linked with other Socialist parties of the world through the Socialist International. In France, as in other countries, the Socialist party introduced a new technique in political organization. It substituted for the former cadre parties, based on support of individual politicians, as developed by the Right and the Radicals, the conception of a mass party based upon a large number of members properly recruited and organized.

General Organization

In structure the Socialist party is much more complex and rigid than parties of the Right or the Radicals of tradition. Supreme power lies in the party congress, which meets annually and elects an executive committee responsible for managing the party. Branches send delegates to the congress in proportion to their membership, and delegates have one vote for every twenty-five members. Care is taken to enrol members every year; they take out an annual card and pay a monthly subscription by buying a stamp to put on the card. Theoretically, the leaders at all levels are elected; in practice, nomination by retiring officers or from headquarters plays a considerable part. The organization of the party nevertheless is democratic: motions for the national congress are proposed by the branches, discussed at federal congresses, and presented by the delegates, who often have strict instructions from their local group. Motions adopted by the national congress constitute in a sense the party's law.

On the executive committee elected by the congress to manage the party, Socialist deputies have only one-third of the seats. By contrast with the Radicals and the Right, the Socialist party is dominated not by its parliamentary representatives but by the representatives of its militant members. Conflicts frequently break out between executive committees and parliamentary representatives. One of the most serious disputes to occur during the last few years arose over EDC; the majority of Socialists in Parliament voted against it despite a contrary decision by the executive committee. In fact, this crisis enabled the executive committee to reassert its control over the parliamentary group. Thanks to the untiring activity of present General Secretary, Guy Mollet, who keeps a firm grip on the party machine, the SFIO is more united and more centralized than ever.

One of the defects of this organization lies in the difficulty of renewing membership and making it possible for newcomers to secure rapid promotion. The mass of militants and the branch and federation secretaries are indeed an obstacle to any rapid promotion. The branches do not like new faces and new appointments. The result is that it takes a long time in the Socialist party to get to the top. Many young men entering politics are put off by this and so lost to the Socialists. It is especially noteworthy that the party failed in this way to renew itself after the Liberation. At that moment many outstanding young men from the Resistance wanted to make their careers in the Socialist party. Instead of offering them candidatures at the next election, the party preferred to put forward its venerable federal secretaries. In the legislatures of 1946 and 1951 it was the party with the fewest young representatives in Parliament.

Doctrine

Officially the party remains attached to Marxism, and on this point it has never revised its original program. Theoretically it even remains a revolutionary party. Before World War II many of its speakers would still talk in public meetings about the "great revolutionary upheaval." Today, there is no reference to it, although a certain amount of revolutionary phraseology still occurs. In practice the party puts forward a reformist policy, insisting on an improvement in the standard of living of the worker. It also proposes, rather more vaguely, a number of reforms in economic organization. It tends to favor increased state control of the economy, and in this respect it supports planning. This however is not exclusively Socialist or Marxist.

From the beginning there has been an antithesis between the revolutionary phraseology of the program and the moderate reformism of the party's activity. This is in part explained by the fact that French trade unionism, by refusing to ally with the Socialist party and by remaining aloof from politics, has driven the party toward the doctrinaires who have been more intent on theory than on immediate reforms. After 1920 the emergence of the Communist party, produced when the Socialist left wing broke away, severed the main revolutionary elements from the party and accentuated its reformist leanings. Its participation in government in 1936 and since 1954 has finally reconciled it to the workings of the present system. Consequently the party makes increasingly fewer allusions to its revolutionary doctrine, though it has not replaced the doctrine by a systematic program. Today the Socialist party, by and large, lacks a doctrine.

Strategy

Three periods in the development of the Socialist party can be discerned. From 1905 to 1936 the party strictly applied the decisions of the Amsterdam International Congress, which prohibited any Socialist participation in bourgeois governments. This prevented its deputies from entering any Cabinet, although the parliamentary group supported left-wing Cabinets, mostly made up of Radicals. Their support was moreover limited; in particular, they never voted for military appropriations. These tactics were maintained until 1936 except for an interruption during World War I when the Socialists took part in the *Union sacrée* Cabinet. On several occasions Socialist splinter groups broke away from the SFIO to enter governments.

The system of support without office encouraged an increasing divorce between doctrine and fact. Since they did not share ministerial responsibilities, the Socialists were able to maintain intact their doctrinaire revolutionary attitude. On the other hand, when participating in electoral alliances and parliamentary voting, they were led into supporting a very moderate, scarcely even reformist, economic and social policy. Their moderation gave satisfaction to the minor state officials and middle-class citizens whom the party began to recruit after 1920, thus taking over from the Radicals; but these developments allowed for the spread of communism among the working class after 1920.

From 1936 on, the Socialists participated in government, first of all in the Popular Front government that was headed by their leader Léon Blum. Important social and economic reforms were carried out in 1936. The opposition of the Moderates, however, led to the fall of the government in 1938.

At the Liberation the party returned to power in governments that relied on left-wing, MRP, and Communist support. This was the Tripartist experiment, a kind of Popular Front in which the Christian-Democrats had taken the place of the Radicals. From 1947 onward, after the Communists had been eliminated from the government and became a permanent opposition, the Socialists formed the left wing of a majority known as the "Third Force." This was primarily a coalition between SFIO, MRP, and Radicals. At the 1951 elections the Third Force lost its majority and the Socialist party went into opposition. There it stayed until 1954, when it emerged to support the Mendès-France government, but without accepting ministerial office. The passing of the Barangé Law to subsidize private schools had alienated it from the MRP.

A fourth period opened in 1956 when the party returned to power after the elections. Its support came from a majority similar to that composing the Third Force (Radicals and MRP), but its policy was definitely farther to the Right as a result of the pressure of events in Algeria and the wave of nationalism that they provoked in France.

THE COMMUNISTS

The French Communist party was founded in 1920. When the Socialist party split at its congress in Tours, the majority decided to join the Third International created in Moscow after the Revolution of 1917, while the minority remained faithful to the Second (Socialist) International.

Organization

The Communists have built a new type of political party in which organization and structure are essential elements. Like the SFIO they depend on mass and not on cadre, but several important features distinguish the Communist party from the older Socialist organization. In the first place, the basic unit of the party is differently constituted. The Socialists group members from the same district in a branch, whereas the Communists group members in "cells" according to their place of employment, whether factory or shop, university or office. The militant members of the Communist party are thus organized in the very place where they work, which makes contact easier and more intimate. There are district cells in the country, but they are of less importance.

Second, the different cells are connected by a well-defined system of vertical links. This means that in theory the cells do not communicate directly with one another but only through the medium of a higher level. This insures the party when it is being persecuted or when it has to go underground. It also enables the party to quell any attempt to provoke trouble or to break away. Discipline within the party is, furthermore, very strict. The instructions of headquarters must be applied without fail at all levels. This centralization is, however, considered "democratic" because considerable discussion takes place in the cells and federations before any policy is adopted, so that headquarters is well informed before coming to its decision.

The party relies upon an inner circle of devoted and well-tried militants whom it endeavors to employ full time whenever possible in accordance with Lenin's theories about the "professional revolutionary." With all due reserve, the role of these militants might be compared with that of the clergy in the churches.

Membership is more all-embracing in the Communist party than in other parties. In other parties membership does not involve the private life and does not command attitudes other than the political. Admission to the Communist party, however, influences the member's attitude to religion, science, art, morality, the family, and so on. This is a result of the totalitarian character of the Communist doctrine.

Doctrine

We cannot here hope to study Marxism itself but must content ourselves with showing its influence on the party. This influence is very considerable, for the Communist party pays more attention than others to instructing its members in doctrine. Furthermore, Marxism lends itself readily to vulgarization and can be reduced to a kind of catechism easily mastered by the militant. It is also a doctrine primarily directed toward action and therefore easy to apply in concrete terms to political life.

The French Communist party adheres to Marxism in the most orthodox terms and defends it against all deviationist activity. In this respect the difference between Communists and Socialists arises not so much from the philosophical bases of the doctrine as from its consequences in practice. The Communists claim to be "Leninist"

Marxists and hold that the transition from capitalism to communism can only be effected by a violent revolution. Like most Communists elsewhere, the French Communist party faithfully follows the leadership given by the Soviet Union, and it has, in fact, since its reorganization in 1942 never shown any signs of independence. Every attempt at independence has led to the expulsion of those who began it. At the moment the French party is very far from the positions adopted by the Yugoslav and Polish Communist parties, for example. It is considered to be one of the most Stalinist of Western Communist parties. Some hidden disquiet is suspected among militant members, especially in intellectual circles since the Hungarian revolution of 1956. So far, however, there has been no sign of change at party leadership level.

Strategy

The party was initially slow to develop. After a good start in 1920, its growth was checked by its electoral tactics and by the difficulties of establishing stern discipline. In 1936, at the time of the Popular Front, membership increased a great deal, but it reached its ceiling in 1945–46 after the Liberation. Since then there has been a slow decline: in ten years the party has lost almost two-thirds of its members.

Communist political strategy has passed through four phases. From 1920 until 1935 was a period of deliberate isolation in which the party practiced "class-war" tactics. It refused to make electoral alliances, to support any government, to enter any ministry, and it proclaimed itself the enemy of all other parties, including the Socialists, whom it stigmatized as "social traitors." This considerably restricted its representation in Parliament but gave it a reputation for intransigence.

In 1935 the danger of fascism in France and in other countries led to the introduction of Popular Front tactics which were simultaneously applied in most Communist parties throughout the world. In France this brought alliance with the Radicals and Socialists. It was a very close alliance, for the three parties agreed on a common program that they presented jointly to the electorate. After the Popular Front had won the 1936 elections, the Communists refused to enter a government led by Socialists but gave it their votes. They thus followed the same tactics of support without participation that the Socialists had practiced from 1905 to 1936. Within the Popular Front, the party asked many favors as the price of its participation, and it considerably hampered the activity of the Socialists, who still have bitter memories of their alliance with the Communists, a fact which continues to influence their political attitude today.

During the Occupation, the Communists behaved very courageously in the Resistance—once the Soviet Union had entered the war in June, 1941. At the Liberation they joined General de Gaulle's government. Throughout Europe they were applying the same tactics by joining National Fronts. In 1947 the French Communists returned to opposition, and at the same time a similar tendency on the part of other European Communists was observable. This was a consequence of the breach between the Allied powers and the opening of the Cold War. Communist opposition was violent, including strikes and obstructionist tactics in Parliament. On the death of Stalin, however, the party attempted to emerge from its isolation. In 1954 it offered its votes in support of Mendès-France, who refused them, however. In November, 1955, it saved Edgar Faure's government on a vote of confidence. It proposed electoral alliances to the Socialists, who refused. After the 1956 elections it openly prepared for the setting up of a Popular Front. Events in Hungary, however, put an end to all these efforts by rekindling a very strong anti-Communist feeling.

Auxiliary Organizations

Almost all parties try to foster auxiliary organizations that have the twin merits of attracting sympathizers who would not formally join the party and of tightening the bonds linking the members proper. Many associations are thus to some extent under party control. Trade unions, women's clubs, youth movements, pacifist movements, art clubs, tourist associations, and sports leagues are the principal kinds of such ancillary organizations. In this domain the Communist party has made special efforts, and its network of auxiliary organizations is the most extensive and the most highly articulated. The Confédération Générale du Travail (CGT), the most powerful of French trade-union bodies, is such an auxiliary organization, having come under Communist control at the time of the Liberation.

THE MRP

The MRP is connected with certain intellectual traditions of Christian democracy, though more directly it is the descendant of the small People's Democratic party founded in 1924. The phenomenon is not of course peculiar to France. The growth of the MRP cannot be dissociated from that of other large Christian-Democratic movements in Germany, Italy, and Belgium.

Doctrine

The party's doctrine is a result of the emergence of a Christian-Democratic trend of opinion. In Europe during the nineteenth century the Church was on the whole a conservative force. In France particularly, Catholicism served as a bond of union among right-wing groups. A similar situation existed in most other countries, though in Germany at the end of the nineteenth century there arose a Catholic party which refused to be classified as right-wing and proclaimed itself a Center party in opposition to Bismarck. In practice it was somewhat conservative but, by comparison with the German Right, it stood out as a truly Center party. In Italy after 1919 Don Sturzo's People's party adopted the same attitude. It is with these political movements that the MRP must be associated.

Its prime aim is to be a party of the Center; firmly supporting the republican and democratic regime, it here parts company with the traditional Right and with the attitude of hostility to the regime adopted by French Catholics at the outset of the Third Republic. The party is a product of the Resistance, and the Resistance was as much the enemy of Vichy dictatorship as of German occupation. The MRP helped to found the Fourth Republic, whereas in 1875 the Catholics opposed the establishment of the Third.

In its place at the Center, the MRP has adopted certain attitudes of modern liberalism. It voted for the various measures of nationalization and for social security, and it continues to defend these policies. It recognizes the existence of the class struggle and of capitalist exploitation. It is concerned with the problems of the working class, and it finds some support among them. Obviously its program is less revolutionary in phraseology than the Socialist program, but when it comes to action, the two are not very far apart. Thus the MRP is in this important respect separated from the Right; it is even farther to the Left than the majority of Radicals.

It is not a religious party, but it claims to be a party "inspired by Christian ideals." Hence moral and spiritual questions play an important part, in their own right, in its doctrine. It holds that the class struggle can be ended, not by the suppression of capitalism, but as the result of an effort to reconcile the interests of employer and employee according to the dictates of justice. The MRP expects a transformation of society to come not solely from a change in institutions but also from an improvement in individual morality. In this respect, its attitude is akin to that of the Right, for the idea that social problems are moral problems is a right-wing idea, the Left tending on the contrary to the view that moral problems are social problems. Its Christian inspiration makes the MRP very sensitive on all issues affecting religion, e.g., the parochial-schools question. This tends to bring the party into line with the Right, as, for example, in the case of the Barangé Law for subsidizing parochial schools.

Strategy

The ambivalence of its doctrine leads the MRP to fluctuate from Left to Right and from Right to Left. Its leaders have a preference for alliance with the Socialist party, but pressure from its supporters, who are mostly Moderates, tends to push the MRP toward the Right.

At the time of the Liberation the MRP took the place of the Radicals in a coalition that united Socialists, Communists, and Christian-Democrats in a tripartite government that effected important social and economic reforms. After the eviction of the Communists from the government in 1947, the MRP became the leading spirit in the Third Force, that is, in the alliance with the Socialists and the Radicals which excluded both the extreme Right and the extreme Left. In this combination, the MRP saw the realization of its fondest dream, that is, the formation of a bloc or coalition of Center parties against both extremes. The 1951 elections brought the coalition to an end, since the Third Force lost its majority. The elections were fought on the parochial-schools issue; the Right, by raising the question, obliged the MRP to adopt the same position in order to avoid offending its supporters. The subsequent legislature was therefore dominated by the "Barangé majority," based on an alliance between the MRP, part of the Radicals, and the Right. The Socialists went into opposition and declared themselves the bitter enemies of the MRP. However, the MRP tried to reach common ground with them again on the European Union issue. The defeat in Parliament on August 30, 1954, of EDC marked the temporary defeat of the "European majority" that might have renewed the Third Force. After the 1956 elections and the formation of the Mollet Cabinet the MRP gave indispensable support to the government. The European treaties for free trade and pooling of atomic resources have aided the development of a new Third Force. On North African questions the MRP has adopted a liberal attitude, more liberal even than the Socialist attitude. The party is therefore moving away from its conservative allies.

FRENCH UNION PARTIES

The overseas territories send deputies direct to Parliament in Paris. Some of these deputies belong to French political parties, but most of them form autochthonous parties. Today there are no longer any Algerian parties, because elections did not take place in Algeria in 1956, but other African parties play quite an important part. It is difficult to describe them exactly, for they are still in course of development. Three major bodies can be distinguished, however.

The first political party to develop in French Africa was the Socialist party, which was strong in Dakar and Senegal under the guidance of an important leader, Lamine Gueye. The African Socialists separated from the French Socialist party in 1956 to form the African Socialist Movement (MSA), still under the leadership of Gueye. This party is losing ground but still remains strong in Senegal and the Niger area.

In opposition there has grown up since 1946 a truly African party based in the Cameroons and the Ivory Coast. Led by an outstanding personality, Hophouet Boigny, it has assumed the name of the African Democratic Rally (RDA). To begin with, the RDA was associated with the Communist party and was violently opposed to France, but since 1951 it has changed and has become more reformist. Because of the influence of Mitterand, of the Radical splinter group, it allied itself in Parliament with the UDSR. Very well organized, the RDA has won adherents throughout the greater part of French Africa, and at the March 31, 1957, elections it became the largest African party. It seems to have a great future before it.

The MRP had something to do with the development of a party known as the Overseas Independents party (IO), which has produced an outstanding personality in Leopold Senghor. He is Lamine Gueye's rival in Senegal, where he succeeded in ousting him as mayor of Dakar. In 1956 Senghor organized a Senegalese People's Bloc which forms the nucleus of a party that is trying to develop an "African Convention." More localized than the RDA but strong in Dakar, the largest town in French Africa, Senghor's bloc supports a policy of African unification, or at the very least of Unification of French West Africa, which would give Dakar greatly increased importance.

These overseas parties play a not inconsiderable part in French political life. Because the margin between the government majority and the opposition is often slender, they can exert a decisive influence. Cabinets never fail to seek the support of the African parties, which have often seized the opportunity to secure worthwhile concessions for the territories they represent.

CHAPTER 7

PRESSURE GROUPS

In the widest sense of the term as it is used at the present time in France, "pressure groups" include not only economic interests and trade unions but also ideological groups, such as the churches and the universities, and technical and administrative groups as well as the press. In brief, pressure groups represent all the forces at work in political life other than political parties proper.

TRADE UNIONS

Characteristics

Trade unions are less well developed in France than in Great Britain and the Scandinavian countries. They differ too in political tradition and modes of activity from American unions. Historically speaking, the fundamental characteristics of the French labor movement are its class animosity and its non-political attitude.

The class basis of the French labor movement rests on the idea of a permanent conflict of interests between employer and employed. Exploitation of the employed by the employer was thought to result inevitably from the capitalist system. Thus from the outset the workingmen's unions evolved as organizations for class war. Unions for a long time refused even to make collective agreements with employers. The first important collective bargaining did not take place until 1927, and not until the Popular Front of 1936 did the practice really spread. Even such moderate union organizations as the Force Ouvrière and the Confédération Française des Travailleurs Chrétiens (CFTC) still show in their activities and policies a traditional spirit of class conflict.

French unionism is non-political insofar as it is heir to the doctrine that at the beginning of the twentieth century was called anarcho-syndicalism. Unions, according to this doctrine, ought to fight independently and self-sufficiently for material advantages and for social revolution. They ought not to rely upon political parties and parliamentary action. They naturally looked upon Socialist parties as parallel and fraternal bodies, but they considered that action at the electoral and parliamentary levels was ineffective and even dangerous, for it plunged the militant members of the working class into middle-class circles in which they lost their aggressiveness. (The transformation of some Socialist deputies shows that this suspicion was not always ill-founded.) Consequently, from the beginning, the unions always treated the Socialist party with considerable reserve. They always refused to collaborate with it in any organized and institutional way, as contrasted to the practice of British and Swedish unions. The French Socialist party has thus been deprived of powerful backing, which has left it weak.

These early views have lost their sway but traces still remain. The French trade unions of 1956, for example, were quite closely linked with political parties, but they did not admit it officially. It is true that the Force Ouvrière and some Christian trade unions agreed to sponsor productivity campaigns, and this implies some recognition that employer and employed have a few interests in common. They did it with some reticence, however, and their propaganda was never very extensive. It is true that the Confédération Générale du Travail (CGT) itself agreed to take part in the Renault experiment in which employees are given a direct share in the profits of the firm. It did so under constraint, however; the mass pressure of its members forced it to agree. Furthermore, the Renault factory is a nationalized concern. French trade unionists conceive of the strike in a manner very different from that of American trade unionists. It is also very difficult to make them admit that they have a common interest with the employer in increased productivity. They are therefore less susceptible to economic arguments, such as the need for stability of currency or for industrial expansion.

History

One of the most deep-seated myths in French trade unionism is that of unity. At the beginning of the twentieth century there was only one central trade-union body, the CGT. There were also a few Christian trade unions, but they were very weak and were not taken very seriously in working-class circles. The accusation was often leveled at them that they were "blackleg" unions, that is, strike-breaking bodies organized by the employers.

After 1919 the monopoly of the CGT was broken in two ways.

The first and most important was that the Communists created their own central trade-union body, the Confédération Générale du Travail Unitaire (CGTU). This was not very strong in numbers and was closely dependent on the Communist party, which controlled it. It was violently revolutionary in attitude. Second, the Christian unions of the CFTC increased their strength, especially among white-collar workers. Nevertheless, the CGTU and the CFTC were much weaker in numbers than the CGT, which remained far and away the most powerful central trade-union body.

In 1936 the Popular Front achieved the merger of the CGTU with the CGT, but the CFTC remained independent. In the re-unified CGT the Communists were in the minority, but they made life very difficult for the ruling majority, which has retained unpleasant memories of the period. During the Resistance, the Communists, who were better organized, progressively conquered the posts of command in the CGT with the result that at the time of the Liberation they were masters in the house. By comparison with 1936, the balance of power had been reversed.

The non-Communist minority found it hard to get a hearing. Finally, therefore, after the exclusion of the Communists in Parliament from the majority supporting the government, the minority in the CGT decided in 1949 to break away. Pressure from American unions was certainly not without influence on this decision. Subsequently, a new movement of opposition to the Communist leadership has developed within the CGT, and events in Hungary have powerfully reinforced it. The third central body, created thus in 1949, retained in its full title the name Confédération Générale du Travail, which has enormous prestige among the working class, and by adding Force Ouvrière, the name of the newspaper in which until then the minority had expressed its views, became the CGT-Force Ouvrière. Many people now think the the split was a mistake and that if the Force Ouvrière group had remained in the CGT, it would now have the opportunity of recovering majority control, which would be a very important event in French political life.

Policies

Because of the non-political tradition in French unionism, each of the central bodies affirms its independence of political parties, but independence is no longer the reality. The three bodies are all associated in some degree with a party. The CGT is very closely bound up with the Communist party: Benoit Frachon, its General Secretary, is a member of the Political Bureau of the party; and at almost every level the CGT officials are Communists. There is, however, an active non-Communist minority led by Pierre Le Brun. The association with the Communist party is very one-sided; it is the party which dictates policy to the unions. This is different from the situation in Britain or Scandinavia, where the reverse often occurs.

The Force Ouvrière is quite closely linked with the Socialist party. However, all its leaders are not Socialists. In this case it is difficult to say whether the unions are more influenced by the party than is the party by the unions. On the whole, it seems that the former proposition is the more accurate. It is not, however, always true where purely labor problems are concerned; the pressure of the Force Ouvrière generally compels the Socialists when in power to carry out some measures of social reform. The increase in workmen's old age pensions effected in 1956 by the Mollet government is a case in point. It is to be noted that within the Force Ouvrière there has been growing for some time a "Labor Party" tendency, the supporters of which are demanding an official institutional linking of the party with the unions. Such a link would strengthen them both.

The relations between the CFTC and the MRP are much less extensive. Primarily they are personal contacts. It seems that the CFTC exercises some influence on the left wing of the MRP, which it tends to reinforce. The CFTC has continued to grow since 1945 and is now no longer viewed with suspicion by the working class, which accepts it as an authentic trade-union organizing body. In elections to public works councils and social security committees it has won votes, often at the expense of the Force Ouvrière and sometimes at the expense of the CGT. Within the CFTC, one section, composed of young militants, is eager to abolish the reference to Christianity in the title of the organization and in particular to withdraw from membership of the International Federation of Christian Trade Unions, which is not very powerful. In a number of strikes the CFTC joined forces with the CGT when the Force Ouvrière refused to take part in joint action.

The French trade-union movement is weakened by its present divisions, but even more so by the CGT link with the Communist party. The situation is paradoxical: the majority of French workers are connected with the CGT, but because the CGT is connected with the Communist party, ministries often refuse to negotiate with it. On many joint committees it has no representation. This situation to some extent paralyzes its activity. At the same time, the Communist party has involved it, especially between 1947 and 1952, in a series of political strikes that have gravely weakened the working-class movement.

ECONOMIC INTERESTS

In this section we shall briefly examine the main employers' groups and the artisan and farmer groups. It may seem strange to deal with them under the same heading, but, generally speaking, they themselves determine this classification by their opposition to the workmen's trade unions, although there are some exceptions.

Employers' federations and organizations of artisans and farmers were slow in developing in France, where the spirit of individualism is extremely strong in the upper and middle classes and even more intense among the peasantry. The strikes and Popular Front of 1936 frightened French employers by revealing the power of collective working-class action. This led them to collective action of their own. The wartime economy of the Vichy regime added to the co-operative experience of employers. In order to distribute products in a period of scarcity, the Vichy regime built up a system of co-operative bodies—an employers' committee, interprofessional committees, a farmers' association, and so on. The greater part of this corporative system has since been destroyed, but it left a legacy: employers and farmers have acquired the habit of collective organization. The postwar development of employers' and farmers' syndicates has little in common with the prewar situation.

Employer Groups

French employers are not grouped in a single body. The Confédération Nationale du Patronat Français (CNPF) does not, in spite of its name, include all employers but is in fact an association of industrial and big-business operators. Small-business operators and artisans are, in general, not members. They tend to unite in an organization of small and middle-sized firms known as the Confédération des Petites et Moyennes Entreprises (PME). It must be noted, however, that the power of the PME has greatly diminished since the Poujade movement began. The shopkeepers in the country and the small towns were always hesitant about joining the PME. They have readily become members of Poujade's Union de Défense des Artisans et Commerçants (UDCA). It is quite characteristic of French society, though too much should not be made of the point, that there exists this threefold stratification of employers' organizations into large, medium, and small businesses.

The CNPF has no great cohesion. In fact, the different industrial

federations are very independent of one another, their power varying according to their economic strength. Some distinction might
perhaps be made among the old industries, e.g., textiles, the new,
e.g., plastics, and the recently modernized, e.g., metals. On many
issues their points of view are not the same. A particular example
may be seen in the important question of tariff protection; the new
or modernized industries, being far more competitive, favor a return
to free trade. The differences may be far-reaching, extending even
to questions of the overseas territories. For example, the less modern
industries remain attached to classical colonialism in order to con-
serve their African markets, while the others often favor a withdrawal from the colonies, which would allow a concentration within
France proper of all productive investment. On the whole, the PME
comes closer in attitude to the older industries. On the question
of protection, in particular, it is quite intransigent.

There is a deep-rooted tendency among French businessmen to
seek state protection even when their firms are not economically
sound. As a result, in some fields grave breaches have been made
in the freedom of commerce and industry. It is very difficult for
the government to defend itself against such pressure, because the
shopkeepers and artisans are not only very numerous but also exert
considerable influence on elections. In daily contact with the public
in their shops, they play a very important part in the formation of
public opinion.

Employers' groups operate in different ways. The CNPF and its
member federations very much resemble the American "old lob-
bies"; that is, they make direct contact with ministers, members of
Parliament, and senior civil servants. The PME does not neglect
such means but tends also to make use of mass action; in the last
few years, for example, there have been strikes of shopkeepers.
Such mass action is a transposition of the means habitually used
by employees in their conflicts with employers. Originally, Poujade's
UDCA was a direct competitor of the PME, and it has taken over
a good many followers by organizing a new form of mass action—
fighting the tax collector. The typical Poujade procedure consists
in mobilizing all the shopkeepers in a district to prevent tax inspection of a neighbor's business. This has occasioned some riots, though
these have not generally been very serious. As we shall see, the
farmers too have adopted mass-action tactics in setting up road-
blocks.

It is difficult to say which of the employers' organizations has
most influence. This depends primarily on the circumstances but
also on which parties are in power. Particular note should be taken

of the influence commanded by the oil and automobile pressure groups. They are less often under attack than the beetroot growers but have exercised a decisive influence on some aspects of French economic policy. In particular, they were responsible for insuring that automobile production was given priority over housing, whereas the national interest would have been better served by the reverse. This is a result of the power and variety of the groups with an interest in the question: oil companies, motor manufacturers (including the powerful nationalized Renault Company, which the government had an interest in favoring in order to demonstrate the success of nationalization), trucking agents (a group composed of dynamic young people in close contact with the electorate), and clubs and associations of automobile users managed by men who are generally hand in glove with the oil companies and motor manufacturers. It is probable, however, that the group would not have achieved such considerable results if middle-class opinion had not supported it. The highly individualistic Frenchman, in fact, tends to consider the automobile as a means of increasing his personal liberty. Investigations have shown that many people would rather have a car than make their home more comfortable. There are many more cars than bathrooms in France!

Trucking agents have considerable influence in another sphere. By exerting pressure on members of Parliament they have insured that tariffs on the nationalized railways (SNCF) are so arranged as to give them an advantage. Thus they have done away with the competition on main-line routes—the only ones which are profitable to the truckers—and have left the railways with the burden of the unprofitable secondary routes. This is the principal cause of the deficit shown by the SNCF which has to be made up by the state, that is, out of the taxpayer's pocket.

Farm Groups

French farmers are rather unwilling to submit to collective organization. This is connected with the fact that there are large numbers of individual family concerns. Nevertheless, peasant syndicates were formed and have been the subject of party strife. Such syndicates were created at the beginning of the Third Republic by the landowning nobility of western France, who used them to maintain conservative influence in the countryside and thus insure the victory of the Right throughout the nineteenth century. At the end of the century, the Radicals, who were then a party of the Left, set out to win over the peasants. To this end they organized co-

operatives and a system of agricultural loans; the Ministry of Agriculture set up at this time was mainly intended to win the support
of the peasants for the republic by giving them concessions, especially as regards credit. This policy attracted farm votes, but it
accustomed the peasants to count upon the backing of the state.
The tendency was accentuated, especially after the Méline ministry
of 1898, by the establishment of a high protective tariff that safeguarded a large section of agriculture from foreign competition.

The struggle between two rival peasant groups, extreme Right
and moderate Left, continued until the end of the Third Republic.
The Vichy government, in creating the Peasant Corporation, sought
to assure the preponderance of conservative tendencies by placing
rightists at the head of the organization. At the time of the Liberation, however, the Corporation was dissolved and replaced by the
Confédération Générale de l'Agriculture (CGA), which was headed
by the other group. Under the influence of a Socialist Minister of
Agriculture, the CGA first tended to be left wing. Soon, however,
the old conservative forces, more numerous on the whole, regained
the ascendancy, and this led in 1953 to the breaking up of the CGA.
Although it still exists officially, the CGA is now nothing more than
a façade. The various peasant syndicates have regained their autonomy under the leadership of a new and loosely organized agricultural federation (FNSA) that tends to be conservative.

Generally speaking, the political power of agriculture is considerable. To some extent the large, modern agricultural enterprises
north of the Loire ally themselves with the small, traditional concerns elsewhere in France; for when commodity prices are fixed
uniformly at a figure high enough for small, inefficient concerns to
show a profit, large-scale farming brings an unusually high return.
This is the case with wheat raising and dairy farming, for example.

In some private sectors the strength of farm organizations is
particularly marked. At the moment, owing to press campaigns, one
such sector is much in the public view: the alcohol industry. A
curious piece of legislation compels the state to buy alcohol from
the distilleries at a price four times that of the world price. This
is primarily to the advantage of the beetroot producers as well as
the cider-apple growers and some winegrowers. The alcohol, moreover, is treated to make it unfit to drink. Under the Third Republic
the beetroot producers of the north and the winegrowers of the
south were often at loggerheads, and this enabled the state to
escape to some extent the clutches of both sides. However, in 1930
the two groups united. Recently some signs of renewed discord

have been evident, and it is possible therefore that some remedy for this absurd system may be found.

Another curious aspect of the alcohol question is the *bouilleurs de cru* (private distillers). There are very heavy taxes on all spirits intended for consumption, but any Frenchman producing wine grapes, cider apples, or any other product from which spirits may be made is entitled to distil ten liters of pure alcohol (about two and a half gallons) tax-free. This encourages widespread fraud, for the ten-liter limit cannot be checked. It also contributes to alcoholism and sickness brought on by adulterated liquor. However, it is not practical politics to abolish the privilege, so fierce is the opposition of the farmers, who in some districts are ready to riot in defense of their right to distil. This is a curious feature of French life that may well disappear as the general standard of living rises.

The agricultural groups exert their pressure on ministers, members of Parliament, and on public opinion. The Minister of Agriculture generally tends to see himself as the defender of the farmers against the state rather than as the representative of the state in farm questions. Both ministers and deputies set high store by the support of the farmers in view of their electoral strength and the general mentality already described. The farmers do not hesitate to use mass action, and the methods used by trade unions have proved contagious. Recently the farmers have taken to blocking roads and thus causing gigantic traffic jams as a way of showing hostility to government policy.

IDEOLOGICAL GROUPS

The Catholic Church

Of the ideological forces which play an important part in French political life, the Church must be mentioned first. Clericalism is not easy to define exactly, but we can say that the principal issue involved is the intervention in politics of Church authorities as such.

The explanation lies, as for so many things in France, in the history of the nineteenth century, when Catholicism was frequently the bond between different conservative forces. When the Revolution began in 1789, the clergy, and especially the lower clergy, welcomed the new ideas. The Civil Constitution of the Clergy passed by the Constituent Assembly was inspired not by anticlericalism but by the traditional Gallicanism of French Catholics, that is, their traditional independence of Rome. Nevertheless, the implementation of the Civil Constitution led to religious persecution. This was the first example of an association between Catholicism and conservatism. The refractory priests who opposed the Civil Constitution of the Clergy were more often than not royalist agents.

A second association between Catholicism and conservatism occurred after the Restoration during the period 1814–30. At the time there was talk of an "alliance between altar and throne" and of the activities of a secret society called the Congrégation, composed of militant Catholics. It was thought to exercise a decisive influence over the promotion of state officials, the choice of ministers, and the general trend of policy. Allowing for some exaggeration, the links between Catholics and ultraconservative Royalists were obvious at the time. Reaction to this explains the anticlericalism characteristic of the July Monarchy (1830–48).

In 1848 the clergy initially favored the republic. Certain young priests had in the preceding years become aware of social problems and had spread this awareness among the public. In every corner of France, *curés* were called upon to bless the tree of liberty. However, fear of socialism was to lead a large section of the bourgeoisie, though they were generally not believers and were somewhat anticlerical, to turn to religion as one of the most effective means of preserving the social order. This was the principal motive behind the Falloux Law of 1850, which provided for freedom to establish schools and in practice gave the clergy considerable influence in education.

During the early years of the Third Republic the majority of the clergy were hostile to the regime. Some publicly announced their desire for the return of the monarchy. Christian texts were used in antirepublican argument. A natural reaction led the republicans to fight the clergy, and there followed the banning of extrareligious congregations, the separation of church and state in 1905, and the development of public, non-religious education.

World War I diminished the hostility between clericals and anticlericals without completely removing it. The problem of the secularization of education was an important issue in the 1924 general election. World War II tended further to diminish the importance of the old clerical problems. The large part played by Christians in the Resistance movement was decisive in this respect. Whereas at the turn of the century a Catholic was almost inevitably a conservative, the MRP offered the spectacle, on the morrow of Liberation, of a Christian party that was definitely leftist in views.

The clerical problem was, nonetheless, resurrected at the 1951 elections. The parties of the Right, in order to separate the MRP from the Socialists, revived the issue of subsidizing private schools,

which in practice meant Church schools. The MRP was compelled
to support this policy. After the elections a government majority
including the MRP and the Right passed the Barangé Law to give
financial aid to denominational schools. This, as we have seen, separated the MRP from the Socialists and gave the whole legislature
a right-wing slant.

The private-school issue is no doubt difficult for foreigners to
understand. There exists in France a system of free and public
education that is completely detached from any religion. However,
each Thursday is set aside for pupils to receive the religious education of their choice, and there are chaplains in the state-supported
lower schools. Outside the public system, anyone may set up a
private school at his own expense. In practice, more than 90 per
cent of private schools are Catholic. The whole of France is now
agreed on the maintenance of this system. The sole point of discussion is whether the state should give financial assistance to these
schools so that the opportunity of attending them is available to
all children, however poor. The parties of the Right are strongly
in favor, the Left strongly opposed. It is said that secret negotiations were undertaken with the Vatican in 1956–57 to solve this
irritating problem. In any case it is losing its virulence. In spite of
the efforts made by the Right, the private-school issue was of only
minor importance during the 1956 elections, and the clergy wisely
did their best to insure that the attention of the electorate was not
focused upon it.

If, in the majority of cases, Catholic forces in France are still
conservative forces, a liberal and social Catholicism is growing and
spreading. The worker-priest movement, in which a number of
priests went with workers to the factories, made a very great impression on the mind of the nation and showed that the rejuvenation
is affecting the clergy itself. Although the MRP is today more conservative than it was in 1946, there are important Catholic groups
which are definitely left wing in their views. Few Catholics, however, come anywhere near communism or deserve all the connotations of the name "Christian Progressives" that their opponents
apply without distinction to any liberal Christians. In ecclesiastical
circles some groups adhere to an ultraconservative doctrine: this is
referred to as the "Integrist" movement.

The Universities

The universities constitute another ideological force that must
be considered, though it is difficult to measure it exactly. Officially,

the French university system is centralized to the extent that all teachers are state employees and all syllabi are uniform in every university. In fact, however, the teachers have considerable independence in status; they can be dismissed only by a decision of a national committee composed of their own elected representatives. Moreover, French universities are passionately attached to the principle of the intellectual independence of their members and consequently to the idea of a variety of opinions among them.

The universities have by their intellectual influence played an important part in some periods of French history, as, for example, during the July Monarchy and at the beginning of the Third Republic. Today that influence is still considerable. University teachers are frequently asked to sign political manifestoes which both press and parties are happy to quote, so that public opinion clearly considers this important. Furthermore, French university teachers are imbued with a sense of mission transcending their academic duties— that of being to some extent the guardians of the Rights of Man and of personal liberty. This may well be a survival from the period when the universities were in the hands of the clergy, and it is true that French intellectuals willingly accept the title of *clercs*.

In a sense the university is the focal point of what has been called the "Republic of Letters," gathering round itself writers, philosophers, artists, journalists, and so on. The "Republic of Letters" certainly enjoys considerable political influence, which is generally exercised in favor of parties on the Left. There are, however, some exceptions to this generalization: successful writers, who have "arrived," and members of the French Academy, which is their voice, are generally very conservative.

Philosophical Societies and Protestantism

Other ideological groups should be mentioned, including, for example, the contemporary successors of what the eighteenth century called "philosophical societies." Freemasonry was very powerful at the beginning of the twentieth century and was closely associated at that time with the Radical party. Since then its political importance has declined. The League for the Rights of Man, established at the time of the Dreyfus affair, retains some moral influence, protesting against every violation of personal liberty. The Teachers' League, which is mainly composed of elementary and secondary schoolteachers, is liberal in politics and remains traditionally anticlerical in attitude. Initially, it was associated with Freemasonry.

Some attention should also be paid to the political role played by Protestant groups. On the establishment of the Third Republic, when the Catholics were hostile to the regime, the Protestant bourgeoisie helped to provide the rulers of the nation. Studies in electoral sociology have demonstrated that the few regions with a Protestant majority vote rather differently from the Catholic regions. French Protestants today, however, are as divided as the French Catholics.

THE PRESS

At the time of the Liberation, the French press was subjected to a unique experience. All newspaper enterprises were taken away from their proprietors, who were guilty of publishing their papers during the Occupation. The various papers were handed over to teams of independent journalists with sufficient initial capital. In this way was established a press that was free from interference both by the state and by monied interests. Unfortunately, financial difficulties led to the gradual disappearance of this independent press, and today the newspaper *Le Monde* claims to be the only one retaining its original status as a free agent.

Parisian and Provincial Press

One of the results of centralization in France is that no provincial newspaper has any political influence. Before the war there were some exceptions to this rule, e.g., *La Dépêche de Toulouse, L'Ouest-Éclair, Le Progrès de Lyon*. Today the political influence of local newspapers has almost entirely gone. Even before 1939 local journals of opinion could by no means sustain comparison with the Parisian press.

Paris newspapers are in fact read everywhere in France. Frenchmen who want to "keep up to date" read two newspapers: the local paper for town gossip and a Parisian paper to keep in touch with political affairs and the main news of national importance. The vast majority of provincials, however, read only their local newspaper. From the point of view of national and international news such papers are rather inadequate, but they are much less "localized" or "provincial" than local newspapers in other countries, the United States especially. International events in particular always occupy considerable space in the French press, even in local papers.

Another aspect of the situation is that the local newspaper generally balances its budget with ease. Consequently it could take an independent line in political matters, but in fact it does not dare to do so for fear of losing readers. Parisian newspapers, in contrast, generally experience more financial difficulties but are less timid. Some distinction should here be made between journals of opinion and journals of information. The latter, represented by such large-circulation papers as *France-Soir* and *Le Parisien Libéré,* do not in general take sides on political questions and they publish few editorials. They restrict themselves to giving the news with headlines and photographs after the style of the American press, though with fewer pages and far fewer advertisements. This kind of newspaper experiences no great financial difficulty. Journals of opinion, in contrast, have a smaller circulation and so find it more difficult to subsist. In fact, apart from the Communist party, no major party today controls a Parisian newspaper, whereas in 1944 each had its own. *L'Aube,* the daily associated with the MRP, has disappeared, while *Le Populaire,* the Socialist party's daily, only survives in the form of a confidential newssheet.

The Press Industry and the Press of Industry

Some newspapers can be considered purely and simply as commercial undertakings. Their proprietors try to sell the maximum number of copies and to make the maximum profit. This kind of press considers itself to be a capitalist undertaking subject to the laws of competition and the newspaper to be a commodity like any other with the main aim of pleasing the consumer. This view, which is widespread in some countries, particularly in the United States, is not the dominant view in France. Even the directors of journals of information do not willingly admit that they are the heads of a press "industry."

Public opinion remains attached for the most part to the idea that the press has a mission to educate the public, to mold it, to enlighten it, and therefore to defend certain ideas and principles. In a different form, this is another example of the concept of the intellectuals' mission which we mentioned when discussing the universities, for in France journalists are considered in a sense to be intellectuals. The difficulty in putting this idea into practice arises from the fact that the vast mass of the public is more or less inclined to take the path of least resistance, and so journals of opinion have a comparatively limited circulation. Thus most of the journals of opinion, so-called, survive only because they are backed by large concerns which are willing to lose considerable sums of money in this way. The aim of these backers is to get the papers they finance to defend particular political policies. The newspapers in question are run not as businesses with a view to making as much money as possible but somewhat like organs of political publicity. The immediate loss of money is supposed to be compensated for by the effect of propaganda against revolutionary socialism, against high taxes, against government intervention, and so on.

Thus alongside the press industry there is also a press run by industry. It would be a matter of some interest, though difficult because of the many subterfuges that are practiced, to discover with what industrial or commercial interests certain of the chief journals of opinion are associated. It is known, for example, that *L'Aurore,* a right-wing paper widely read by small tradesmen, is the property of Marcel Boussac, the biggest French textile manufacturer. Perhaps an examination would reveal some antithesis between the traditional industries clinging to protectionist and conservative policies and the more modern and more dynamic industries willing to accept new ideas.

The press of opinion proper, which succeeds in living on its own resources, independent of economic and financial interests, is very limited in extent. There are some weeklies, e.g., *L'Express, France-Observateur,* and only one national daily, *Le Monde.* The last-named merits particular attention. Founded in 1945, under the same conditions as the rest of the Liberation Press, to take the place of *Le Temps,* the great conservative organ of the Third Republic which since 1930 had been under the control of the iron and steel trust, Le Comité des Forges, it has succeeded in creating for itself an extensive public and in balancing its budget by practicing severe economy. Its circulation is now over 200,000 copies, three and a half times greater than that of *Le Temps.* The reliability of its news is such that a fair proportion of its readers, at least one-third, continue to read it although they do not agree with its political views, which, however, are not purely partisan. Since 1950 *Le Monde* has been in favor of a decrease in international tension and also of a "neutralist" policy, though it is definitely opposed to the dictatorship of communism. Its complete independence from all French Cabinets has done little to win their sympathy. On several occasions it has been the target of unsuccessful attempts by financial groups to seize control. Its position is something of a paradox.

TECHNICIANS AND ADMINISTRATORS

The senior civil servants and the technical officers of the large industrial firms, although not usually organized in pressure groups proper, are influential forces and are playing an increasing part in the affairs of State.

Senior Civil Servants

The influence exerted in the government by senior civil servants is of prime importance, for they form an elite. The most brilliant university students seek high office in the civil service, not because it pays well—salaries are often less than half what they would be in private business—but because of the prestige and power attached to these posts. Another explanation is to be found in the fact that recruitment to managerial posts in industry and commerce still has a family bias: access to the highest posts in private concerns is by birth or family connections. Recruitment to the senior ranks of the civil service, however, is impartially based on competitive examination. No favoritism can be shown by the government. Once the examination hurdle has been passed, very young men are sometimes given senior posts.

Senior civil servants do not form a united group but belong to one or another of the administrative "corps," each with its own traditions. The most important corps are: the Council of State, the Inspectorate-General of Finance, the Court of Accounts, the Department of Mines, and the Department of Civil Engineering. Entry to all these important bodies is by competition. Once admitted, a civil servant receives automatic promotion, and there are few grades in the hierarchy. Members of these corps carry out the appropriate administrative duties corresponding to the function of their organization: Councillors of State advise the government and serve as administrative judges; Treasury Inspectors supervise the implementation of the budget by the different departments; the Court of Accounts inspects and judges the records presented by state accountants, and so on. In addition, the members of each of the corps may if they wish spend several years in other duties, where they master a secondary specialty. Thus these great corps act as a kind of reservoir for the filling of senior posts throughout the public services. Furthermore, ministers draw heavily on the corps for the staffing of their personal offices. In these ways the members of the corps hold in their hands the most important posts in the administration of the state.

Civil servants, properly speaking, have no common doctrine which they apply in the exercise of their functions. They are of different political opinions and employ varying methods. Liberalism and the independence of the individual are fundamental traditions of the senior civil service, however, and some general tendencies are quite evident. Seeing the effectiveness of economic intervention by the state, these officials tend to be "planners" and followers of Keynes. Their duties also give them the opportunity of observing the mediocrity of some heads of private undertakings. They can also see the harm caused by the privileges that certain pressure groups obtain. They were the first to denounce the alcohol scandal and to unmask the procedure involved. They also see the present impossibility of solving problems at government level. They wish not to substitute themselves for the government but to receive clear orders, which more often than not never come. Some civil servants attempt to remedy the deficiencies of political authority, but most look upon it with unalloyed skepticism.

Technicians

The technical officers in the national public utilities and in private firms generally come from a few schools to which admission is as competitive as for the civil service. The most important of these institutions are the Polytechnic, founded by Napoleon to produce military engineers and now sending its best pupils into civilian occupations, the School of Mining, the School of Art, and the Central School of Industry. The technicians often retain a sense of belonging to the same school, and sometimes a particular kind of undertaking is put entirely in the hands of people who have had the same education. The state railways, for example, are almost entirely run by former Polytechnicians. School loyalty, however, generally has more influence in private careers than in the public service. The sense of belonging to the same state corps is stronger, for the jobs done by former Polytechnicians or old students of the Central School or of the School of Mining are too varied and too dispersed.

We must also note that private enterprise seeks recruits from the great administrative corps. In particular, banks, financial corporations, and even industrial and commercial firms welcome with open arms Inspectors of Finance, to whom they offer much higher salaries than the state pays. Such transfers from public to private administration are called "taking it easy" (*pantouflage*). The practice of transferring has important consequences, for it establishes close and friendly relations between the two sectors. The former Inspector of Finance who is "taking it easy" remains in close contact with his former colleagues in the civil service. In some respects these contacts are useful, but they are harmful where they allow collusion between private economic interests and political authority.

CHAPTER 8

THE DISTRIBUTION AND DEVELOPMENT OF POLITICAL FORCES

The two preceding chapters enumerated the various political forces at work in France. Now in studying the development and distribution of these forces we shall still be dealing primarily with the political parties. It is far more difficult to evaluate pressure groups, and they in any case depend upon the parties. An election that shows the strength or weakness of a party will likewise reveal the strength or weakness of the pressure group associated with the party. By the same token, the strength or weakness of a party at the polls will influence the strategy of a pressure group.

DEVELOPMENT OF ELECTORAL FORCES

As is true in all countries of long-established democracy, voters in France are relatively stable in their attitudes. There is little variation in voting from one election to the next, other things being equal, and such variations as occur are more often apparent than real. The man who voted Radical before 1914, Socialist before 1939, and Communist after the war will think he has always voted for an extreme left-wing party. Studies in electoral psychology have revealed an astonishing permanence in political attitudes. Such features should not be overemphasized, however. Most electoral studies in France have dealt with the rural areas rather than the towns, that is, with the parts of the country that are most stable by nature.

The Distribution of Votes

The election held on January 2, 1956, gave the following distribution of votes over the country as a whole: Communists 25 per cent, Radicals and associated parties (RGR and UDSR) 14.7 per cent,

Socialists 14.7 per cent, traditional Right 14.7 per cent, MRP 10.7 per cent, Poujadists 12.4 per cent, Social Republicans (ex-RPF) 3.8 per cent. These rough figures are based upon votes cast and take no account of abstentions. Compared with previous elections under the Fourth Republic, there are considerable differences.

Only one party has remained stable, the Communist party. It polled 26 per cent in 1945, rose to 28 per cent in 1946, and declined to 25.6 per cent in 1951. This is an impressive record of stability. The MRP on the contrary has greatly declined: 25 per cent of the poll in 1945, 28 per cent in 1946, 12 per cent in 1951, and then a further fall to 10 per cent in 1956. It has lost almost two-thirds of its votes. The Socialists have lost almost half of theirs: 23 per cent in 1945 as against 14.7 per cent in 1956. The traditional Right has had a slight increase: 11–12 per cent in 1945–46, 10 per cent in 1951, and 14 per cent in 1956. In contrast, the Radicals have remained very stable: 14.2 per cent in 1945, 13 per cent in 1946, 12.4 per cent in 1951, and 14.7 in 1956. Compared with these parties, which figure in five elections, two are both new and ephemeral: the RPF, which in 1951 received 21.5 per cent of the poll but in 1956 received only 3.8 per cent, and the Poujadists, who did not exist in 1951 but proved more powerful than the MRP in 1956, and who are now already on the decline.

It will be observed that apart from the stable forces of the Radicals, the traditional Right, and the Communists, there is a section of French opinion which is floating. There is no doubt that the success of the RPF resulted from the fact that many conservatives voted for it. Right-wing voters abandoned their usual candidates in 1951 to vote for the RPF, only to abandon it in 1956 for the Poujadists. However, the general pattern that emerges from a first glance at these statistics requires some modification. All the votes cast for the RPF in 1951 did not come from the Right, and many of the 1956 Poujadist votes did not come from former RPF supporters. We must remember that the success of the RPF lay particularly to the north of the Loire while the Poujade movement was chiefly successful south of the Loire. Many electors who voted Socialist at the time of the Liberation voted Radical in 1956. Many electors who voted Radical at the Liberation must therefore have voted differently in 1956, probably for moderate candidates.

On the whole, voting during these first ten years of the Fourth Republic has been less stable than voting under the Third Republic. Before 1940 the percentage variations from one election to another were much slighter. Since the turn of the century there have been no successes so rapid and so fleeting as those of the RPF and the Poujade movement, to say nothing of the upsurge of the MRP in 1945–46. There is no doubt that public opinion fluctuates more than before World War II, and this probably means that many voters have not yet found the party which expresses their opinions and desires. This is an important fact to be borne in mind.

Significance of the Communist Vote

The Communist vote raises a special problem. All public opinion polls and all political science investigations made on this question show that the majority of those who vote Communist are not Communists but voters who simply want to express their opposition to government. Indeed a vote for any party other than the Communist party is not really a vote for the opposition, since all the other parties have taken some share in government. It remains for us to define the exact nature of this opposition vote.

The opposition is generally thought to be primarily the result of discontent with the economic system. The majority of those who vote Communist are people discontented with their material lot. This is strikingly evident in the case of the workers in the large towns, whose wages are sometimes satisfactory but whose housing conditions are generally deplorable. It is equally obvious for the rural Communist voter: many owners of very small farms vote Communist because their holding is so tiny that they cannot live by their work and can have no hope for the future. In a sense their position is the same as that of the proletariat.

Furthermore, there is no doubt that the attitude of the Communists during the Occupation (and the propaganda they made of it at the time of the Liberation) greatly contributed to swelling the party vote. In 1945–46 the territorial distribution of Communist votes in the countryside coincided very closely with the map of the *maquis* areas under the Occupation. Later, Communist propaganda directed against the United States reinforced a certain amount of chauvinism that had been fostered by American military aid and French dependence on the United States. Furthermore, Communist peace campaigns created a certain stir in public opinion, especially at the time during the Cold War when the Eisenhower administration was producing propaganda in favor of a "Crusade" and "rolling back" the Russians.

These various explanations do not seem adequate, however. In particular, the Communist vote is very high among sections of the working class whose wages are not inadequate and whose material

conditions are certainly better than those enjoyed by salaried workers in commerce and by clerks. Here it is probable that class feeling
is the dominant factor. As a result of the struggles of the working
class in the nineteenth century, the savage repressions of 1848 and
1871, the lack of understanding shown by the employing classes in
the same period, and the spread of Marxist propaganda, class feeling is very deeply rooted in the mind of the French workman. Many
members of the working class vote Communist because they feel
they cannot vote otherwise without betraying their fellows. It will
be very difficult to dispel this feeling unless some other party can
create the impression of defending the interests of the working class
or until social and economic changes gradually efface the class feeling. In some areas the Communist vote also corresponds to a tradition of revolution. For example, in some departments of southern
France many people always vote for the party "farthest to the Left."
They voted Radical in 1890, Socialist from 1910 to 1930, and today
they vote Communist. They feel that in this way they are remaining
true to themselves.

We must also take account of discontent with the political system. The Third Republic was an adequate regime until 1914. Between 1920 and 1940 it proved obviously incapable of facing the
problems that France had to solve. Since 1945 the Fourth Republic
has shown itself similarly incapable of settling vital issues. Consequently, opposition to it has developed from two sides: on the extreme Left from the Communists, on the extreme Right from the
Gaullists and the Poujadists. These extremist votes may well be a
sign of fundamental dissatisfaction with the political system itself. It
is by no means sure, however, that many Communist or Gaullist
voters would not energetically defend the parliamentary regime if
it were really under attack. Republicanism is very deep-rooted in
the French mind, and so far republicanism has always been identified with the parliamentary system.

The Division between Left and Right

To understand French politics, one must understand the meaning
of the terms Right and Left; and this is by no means easy, since
their content has changed a good deal. The Right at the present
time will not admit to its name. It is not the politically expedient
thing to be rightist; one must always claim to be leftist. This is no
doubt due to the fact that in the nineteenth century the Left represented the ideas of the French Revolution, and they in the end triumphed. No one today willingly appears hostile to these ideas.

At the turn of the century the fundamental division between Left and Right centered on the form of the political system. On the Left were those loyal to the republic; on the Right were its enemies—Bonapartists, Orleanists, Legitimists, and supporters of dictatorship. The cleavages coincided fairly accurately with the division already discussed between anticlericalism and clericalism. Catholicism being at that time the bond uniting the forces of the Right, clericalism was the touchstone of the Right and anticlericalism the touchstone of the Left. In many small French villages there was a cleavage between the "Whites" who supported the *curé* and the "Reds" who were his enemies—in politics, that is, for often perfect amity reigned in private life within the village.

Toward the end of the nineteenth century the traditional cleavages between liberal and conservative, republican and antirepublican, clerical and anticlerical, were disrupted by the question of socialism. Many liberals, republicans, and anticlericals were still attached to private ownership of the means of production and to economic competition; hence they were anti-Socialist. On this issue they joined forces with the traditional conservatives in an anti-Socialist coalition. Consequently, from this point of view the Right could be defined as upholding liberal capitalism and private enterprise, while the Left would be composed of those who desired the coming of a Socialist system or at least state control of the production of wealth and egalitarian distribution of the national income. Obviously, there exist intermediate positions. To support the extension of social security, state control of investments, the intervention of public authority in the distribution of the national income, and a certain amount of Keynesian "planning" is a long way from socialism proper, but it is equally far from laissez faire capitalism. Thus there emerges a cleavage between a Right that favors private enterprise and a Left that favors planning and controls.

This division is tending to become the fundamental cleavage in the Fourth Republic, which was founded by the three major parties, Communist, Socialist, and MRP, then considered to be "planners," while the Right fought them energetically in the name of free enterprise. Since then the pressure of international events has somewhat blurred the division. Fundamentally, however, it still exists. Since attitudes are long-lived in political life and since new attitudes are superimposed upon them, some contemporary political parties, such as the Radicals, are able to label themselves Left according to the ideas of Third Republic, though they are on the Right according to the Fourth Republic. On the other hand, the MRP in 1946 appeared to be Left according to Fourth Republic terms, though it was clerical and Right in the terminology of the Third Republic.

In view of these difficulties in distinguishing between Left and Right in French politics, it is not easy to estimate the distribution of strength between the two sides. They would appear to be equally matched, as under the Third Republic, though the Left is perhaps slightly the larger. Voting strength does not correspond in this case to strength in Parliament, because the Left is deeply split by the isolation of the Communist party.

COALITIONS AND MANEUVERS IN PARLIAMENT

As we have seen, the presence and seesawing of so many parties force all French governments to be coalition governments. If a single party does form a Cabinet, it is at the very least obliged to rely on the backing of others in Parliament. The question of alliances thus dominates the whole of political life. There have been considerable changes of alliance since the Third Republic.

Third Republic Coalitions

The classic works of André Siegfried and François Goguel have described the political history of the Third Republic as an alternation of right-wing majorities (parties of "Order") and left-wing majorities (parties of "Change"). The interchanging of right-wing coalitions in 1919, 1926, 1928, 1934, and 1938 with left-wing coalitions in 1906, 1924, 1932, and 1936 seems to bear out the description. Slight modifications are necessary, however; for it must be remembered that the great party of the Third Republic, the Radical party, always allied with the other parties of the Left at elections, but in forming the Cabinet it sometimes made alliance with Center or even Right parties. The so-called Left governments were really governments of the Left-Center; until 1936 the Socialists never entered a Cabinet. As for the so-called Right governments, they were really governments of the Right-Center. The alternation between Left and Right is thus really an alternation between Left-Center and Right-Center. Political life under the Third Republic does not create the impression so much of a series of swings from one extreme to the other as it does of a gentle wobbling from one margin of the center to the other. Moreover, one of the ambitions cherished by the Radicals and by some members of the Right-Center was to achieve a lasting alliance between the parties of the Center, excluding both extreme Left and extreme Right. Before 1914 this desired alliance was spoken of as the "union of the Center," and after 1914 it was spoken of as "consolidation" of the Center. It never resulted in a lasting majority.

In the last years of the Third Republic the swinging of the Radical party between Right and Left often led to curious changes of majority during the life of a single legislature. The same general pattern emerged in 1924–28, 1932–36, and 1936–40. The elections gave a majority to the alliance between parties of the Left, that is, Radicals and Socialists in 1924 and 1932; Radicals, Socialists, and Communists in 1936. During the first two years of the legislature the victors exercised power in unison. But then the misgivings of the Radical party led it to change horses in midstream and make alliance with Right-Center and even Right parties. This produced National Union Cabinets based on an alliance of all parties except those of the extreme Left. It was in this way that Poincaré came into power in 1926, Doumergue and Laval in 1934–35, Daladier in 1938. On the eve of each of the elections, the Cabinet was defeated in order to prepare the way for a new electoral alliance between parties of the Left.

Fourth Republic Coalitions

Parliamentary maneuvers have been quite different under the Fourth Republic, since 1947 at least. Before then the government was an all-party coalition reminiscent of the united front of World War I. However, the breakup of the alliance of the great powers in the international field and the division of the world into two blocs led to the breaking up of the united front in the domestic field and to the isolation of the Communist party. On May 6, 1947, the Communists were expelled from the Cabinet and from the parliamentary majority; they have never returned. Since then the swing from Left to Right practiced under the Third Republic has become impossible. The Left is divided into two sections of almost equal strength, Communist and non-Communist. No government of the Left is conceivable. The choice, therefore, lies between majorities of the Right or majorities of the Center in the image of the consolidated Center that had been dreamed of in vain under the Third Republic. Right-wing government obtained throughout the 1951–56 legislature except during the short life of the Mendès-France ministry. The Radicals and the MRP allied with the traditional Right, with which was associated part of the RPF, the new Right; only a few intransigent conservatives refused to join the majority. The Socialists and Communists were in opposition. Between 1947 and 1951 a Center majority governed under the name of the Third Force. The nucleus was formed by an alliance between the Socialists and the MRP, and they were joined by the Radicals and some of the moderate conservatives. At the time the Radicals were considered to be more to the Right than the MRP and much closer to the moderates.

The Republican Front, constituted for the 1956 elections, was nothing more than a close alliance between Socialists and Radicals which drove the MRP toward the Right. This was important, since the French political mentality does not look kindly on the Right. The maneuver was made possible, as we have seen, by the passing of the Barangé Law for subsidizing private schools. Since then the MRP has fought back. It has played on the European question and on the personal enmity of Guy Mollet, secretary of the Socialist party, for Pierre Mendès-France. The European treaties concerning atomic resources and the establishment of a Common Market facilitated a rapprochement between the MRP and the Socialists. Moreover, the final failure of Mendès-France to reorganize the Radical party drove the Radicals toward the Right.

In the middle of 1956 it seemed possible that the isolation of the Communist party might end and that a new Popular Front majority might again be established one day. However, the repression of the revolution in Hungary and the subsequent hardening of the Russian attitude made this solution impossible. At the moment, then, the situation is unchanged: the Left, divided into two sections, has no hope of governing.

INSTABILITY OF MINISTRIES

The preceding analysis makes it possible to understand the real causes of the instability of governments in France. Contrary to what is often believed, even by Frenchmen, instability is caused not by the structure of the political system but by deep cleavages in public opinion as they find expression in the parties and at elections. It is also caused by the structure of the parties themselves.

Lack of Cohesion in Parties

The situation in France as regards the number of parties is little different from that in most countries on the Continent. In all or almost all, there are more than two parties; in all or almost all, government has to be by coalition, but elsewhere than in France coalitions are easier to maintain, because of the internal discipline of the parties. Coalitions are sometimes difficult to organize. Indeed, long and arduous negotiation by the party leaders is required to achieve an agreed basis of alliance. In Holland, for example, ministerial crises are interminable partly for this reason. However, once the majority has been established, the cohesion of the parties renders it relatively firm. Party discipline makes the deputies conform generally to the directives issued by the party leaders.

In France party discipline is much weaker. It exists in a strict form only in the Communist and Socialist parties. The former has been totally excluded from government since 1947, while the latter has often been in opposition and, in any case, constitutes only a minority in Parliament. In the MRP there is a form of discipline, but it does not extend to all important questions. In other parties there is no discipline at all. We arrive at the paradoxical situation in which a head of government (Mendès-France in 1955, for example) is defeated by his own party, which splits and turns upon itself. The result is that a Premier is never sure of his majority, and so he spends a great deal of his time trying to persuade deputies to support him. His task does not end with convincing party leaders; he has to scrape together individual votes. For this reason, the attempted reform of the Radical party by Mendès-France and of the moderate right-wing groups by Roger Duchet might have profoundly altered the conditions of parliamentary activity and have increased the stability of government. They failed, however, in the face of a long tradition.

Varied Composition of Majorities

Though it is sometimes said that in France no majority can be found on any issue, this is not true. There are majorities on every issue, but they frequently differ from one issue to the next. One majority combination of deputies passes social reforms, another favors some particular foreign policy, a third moves to balance the budget, a fourth favors European co-operation, and so on. This compels ministries to indulge in feats of tightrope walking that often lead to a fall.

From 1952 to 1954 successive ministries were obliged to put off the ratification by Parliament of the treaty setting up the European Defense Community, because the issue of ratification would have split their majorities. But the anti-EDC majority in Parliament could not agree on a single other issue; once Mendès-France had got EDC rejected, he was defeated on other questions. Obviously, one can imagine a Cabinet that relies on a core of support from single party or from a small group of men while seeking differently composed majorities in Parliament according to the question at issue; that is known as the "alternative support" procedure. During the initial period of the Mollet government something of this kind was practiced, the ministry relying on the extreme Left for support in some questions, on right-wing support in others. But this is difficult because deputies do not like to lend their support time and time again to a Cabinet in which their party has no share. Furthermore, the isolation of the Communist party, not only in Parliament but also its moral isolation throughout the country, makes it difficult to form alternative majorities in which it is to be a frequent participant.

Consequences and Cures

Instability of governments is caused by many factors other than those already indicated. We must also take account of customs and traditions. Parliament is used to overthrowing Cabinets. Of the six hundred or so deputies, about half have some prospect of attaining ministerial rank, and they are anxious to do so. When a Cabinet has lasted six months, deputies begin to think the time has come for a change.

Nor are the consequences of ministerial instability all bad. It is certain that a government needs to enjoy a comparatively secure period of existence if it is to perform its duties. No important project can be undertaken in the knowledge that in six or eight months' time one will very likely have been driven from power. Ministerial instability is a deep-seated evil; that cannot be denied. Nonetheless, this evil has some compensating advantages. Ministerial crises are often a means of solving problems that otherwise would not be solved. When a new government has been set up, it enjoys a honeymoon period lasting several weeks. Parliament cannot in all conscience overturn it so soon; moreover, deputies are pleased with the change and curious to see what the new ministry will do. The Cabinet is allowed to take energetic action during this period. It is often the case that Cabinets are defeated because Parliament refuses to agree to reforms that it is obliged to pass for the new Cabinet.

Instability is less pronounced than one might think. The remark that "ministries change but ministers remain" expresses a profound truth. Ministers in the defeated Cabinet often find a seat in the new one. In this way teams are formed to alternate in power. The majorities on which Cabinets rely vary little; in fact, over the last ten years there have been only three changes in majority, in 1947, 1951, and 1956. Some ministers retain their posts over a long period in successive governments; in the ten years from 1944 to 1954 there were only two Ministers of Foreign Affairs, and they belonged to the same party.

The remedies usually envisaged for the instability of ministries do not seem to have much bearing on the situation we have just described. Generally, thoughts turn first to reforming the Constitution, especially the power of dissolution. As we have seen, such reforms would be difficult to handle. Furthermore, it is difficult to see how dissolution could work the miracle of creating artificially a majority that did not exist in fact. The majority is no more clearly visible after an election than it is before. However, it is true that dissolution used as a means of bringing pressure on Parliament to keep a government in power would insure a certain longevity for ministries; this occurs in Denmark, where ministries last approximately two years, at the end of which they are defeated, Parliament is dissolved, and new elections take place.

Another cure put forward is electoral reform. This is an excellent way of changing the composition of an assembly in a country where political stability is fairly high. But the Third Republic single-member majority system with second ballot (*scrutin d'arrondissement*) did not produce Assemblies of any greater stability than the Fourth Republic system of proportional representation. In many respects a change in balloting procedure would prove interesting. But it is not certain that it would promote party discipline sufficient to prevent the defeat of governments. In this connection it is significant that the longest Fourth Republic Cabinet was led by Guy Mollet, and the real explanation is to be found in the arithmetic of Parliament and the discipline of the Socialist party. In the Assembly elected on January 2, 1956, it was impossible to form any majority without the Socialist party, and under Mollet's leadership that party had been subjected to even stricter discipline than in previous legislatures. Since the Socialists were likely to oppose any government set up by parties which had defeated Mollet, Parliament was constrained to maintain him in power for an unprecedented length of time.

The outlook for ministerial stability is poor. Although during the last few years internal party discipline has tended to increase, especially among right-wing moderates, there is little likelihood of forming stable majorities in France on the model of those in northern Europe. There is equally little prospect of any modification of the power of dissolution to insure its regular use after the defeat of a Cabinet.

This explains why of late the solution to the problem has been sought in other directions. Although, since the unfortunate episode of 1848, the presidential system of government has been viewed with disfavor in France as tending to dictatorship, a campaign in favor of it was opened in the spring of 1956. It was observed that the French multiparty system was more like the pseudo-party system of the United States, since American parties are notably lacking in internal cohesion and discipline. If a parliamentary system operated in the United States, it was claimed, it would be just as difficult to form a coherent majority as it is in France. Consequently the idea was put forward that the American presidential system, which provides executive stability, should be transposed to France. Others have proposed a mixed system retaining the President of the Republic to represent the nation at ceremonies but providing for the Premier to be elected directly by the voters at the time they elect deputies to the National Assembly. According to this system the Assembly could defeat the Premier but would then have to face the voters at the same time as they were electing a new Premier. These proposals have been discussed in great detail, and quite eminent men have been converted to them, even on the Left, though it is the Right which traditionally favors this kind of system. In practice, however, these proposals have no chance of being adopted by Parliament by means of any regular constitutional revision.

PART III

INDIVIDUAL LIBERTY AND LOCAL AUTONOMY

INTRODUCTION

The subjects to be treated in the last part of this book, civil rights, administrative centralization, and the evolution of the French Union toward federalism, seem to be very different one from the other. In reality they are various aspects of the same problem, that of the relations between those who are governed and those who govern, between ordinary citizens and those who hold the reins of power.

France, like the other Western democracies, has a liberal regime. The French state does not claim to have a right to interfere in every aspect of life. It allows individuals a sphere of personal action. It is not totalitarian. This liberal aspect of the French system is highly developed, more so in some respects than in other countries of the West, and especially more so than in the United States. France is a plural democracy and even permits the existence of revolutionary parties that are opposed to the very basis of the established political regime. However, unlike other Western democracies, especially the Anglo-Saxon countries, France shows a very definite tendency to centralization and an obvious distrust of decentralization. This characteristic is constant throughout the history of France. The *ancien régime,* the Jacobins in 1793, the Napoleonic Empire, and the democratic republic all show the same tendencies in this respect. If the democratic republic is more decentralized than the preceding regimes, it is only in details. The main lines of the system remain identical. The very phrase "one indivisible Republic," repeated by those who drafted the Constitution of 1946 in imitation of their great ancestors of the Revolution, is typical. France conceives political relations as a dialogue between citizens and the state. Intermediary bodies are viewed with suspicion. There is great tolerance for individual liberty, but local autonomy is frowned upon.

The development of the French Union is opening up new perspectives in this connection. Individual liberalism combined with administrative centralization led France to develop her colonies in the direction of assimilation. The practical impossibility of applying this system today and the obligation to recognize the autonomy of federated states are opening an ever-widening breach in French centralization. With the *loi-cadre* of 1957, which introduced a great degree of autonomy in the overseas territories, France is turning her back on a considerable part of her tradition. Individual liberty is being complemented by self-governing communities. The "one indivisible Republic" is turning into a federal republic.

CHAPTER 9

CIVIL RIGHTS

"Here begins the land of liberty." The foreigner visiting revolutionary France in 1792 met this inscription at the border. During the same period some paper money bore the words "Liberty or death." These heroic times are gone, but the tourist can still read over the entrance to the municipal hall of the smallest French village the old republican motto which figures on all public monuments and all official documents, "Liberty, Equality, Fraternity." The attacks on government, ministers, and Parliament in the press and in conversation, the habit of perpetually evading official rules and regulations, a certain attitude of opposition and constant criticism—all these are signs which point to the fact that the feeling for liberty is still very much alive in France. They also show that liberty is quite often conceived as opposition to those in power. Nevertheless, an important change has taken place in this respect since the middle of the nineteenth century. One of the aspects of political strife in contemporary France is that several concepts of liberty, founded on very different bases, now confront each other.

THE FRENCH CONCEPT OF LIBERTY

The French concept of liberty has no great originality. To a certain extent it is the reflection of general ideas. At the present moment there is a certain equilibrium between these ideas and some effort to co-ordinate them. France no longer accepts in its entirety the idea of liberty characteristic of the nineteenth century, which is still dominant in some countries, as, for instance, in the United States. It rejects as a whole the Marxist idea of liberty as currently formulated in the Soviet Union. It is trying, however, to define a kind of intermediary position that has more in common with the first concept but that nevertheless borrows some of its elements from the second.

Liberty as Resistance

Throughout the course of the nineteenth century, civil rights were conceived in France and in the rest of the Western world as a means of resistance to governments. Libertarians began with the idea that in social life there was a domain closed to government activity, a zone of private action reserved for individuals. In this sense, freedom was a protective device. It determined the frontiers of this zone of action reserved for individuals, of this private domain forbidden to governments.

Moreover, even within the domain allowed to government action, the government could not do everything. Citizens had to have means of restricting it and opposing it. Political freedom was a weapon for opposition. Anyone studying the development of the freedom of the press, the freedom of assembly, the freedom to demonstrate, and the freedom of association in France throughout the nineteenth century will see that these rights have always been conceived as a means of making it possible for citizens to oppose those in power. It is true that each of these rights does, in fact, extend beyond the realm of politics and political opposition to the government. There is a sporting press, a feminine press, and a technical press. Most meetings and associations are not concerned with political life or the government. Nevertheless, historically, it was because of their role in the political field that the government refused to recognize them and that their supporters demanded freedom for them to develop. Once recognized, moreover, they were very widely employed as a means of political opposition.

Liberty as Particpation

Benjamin Constant, who lived at the height of the nineteenth-century struggle for freedom, and who was ardently in favor of liberty conceived as a means of opposition, made a definite distinction between the modern idea of liberty, which he defined as the "peaceful enjoyment of individual independence," and the classical idea of liberty, which consisted in active participation in collective power. He was violently opposed to the latter idea, which he considered a sophistry, and which is the concept to which we are giving the name liberty as participation. According to this idea, the freedom of citizens consists in their having the power to participate in collective decisions. They must, however, accept these decisions without opposition.

The works of Jean-Jacques Rousseau are one source of this idea.

He defined liberty as the participation by each individual in the formation of the general will. Rousseau's disciple Mably developed his ideas and added details, and they were adopted by the Jacobins. In the society dreamed of by Robespierre and Saint-Just, in that virtuous and rational Sparta, the general will was to exercise a strict dictatorship. Liberty was not the ability of the citizen to resist power but the fact that he shared it. Marx, Lenin, and the present Soviet regime are the heirs of this concept of democracy and liberty. To those who describe the Soviet regime as lacking freedom, the apologists of the system reply that under it everyone is free, since the people are in power. Liberty can be conceived as resistance only if the government is bad. If it is good, if it expresses the will of the people, the very basis of the theory of liberty as resistance no longer exists.

Formal and Real Liberty

The French doctrine of liberty has been influenced to some degree by Marxism. Marx distinguished between formal liberty, which is purely legal and depends on laws, and real liberty. What does freedom of the press signify if economic conditions are such that all newspapers are in the hands of powerful financiers? What does freedom of domicile mean to a man with no home or to one who lives in a slum? What does freedom of thought mean to those who have to work when they are children and never have the time to receive the instruction and education which should lead them to exercise their thought? In fact, freedom as conceived in the nineteenth century was the freedom of a few. Marxism develops this analysis and shows that for the great mass of the workers the legal rights recognized by "bourgeois" democratic constitutions are only formal rights without real substance. They also constitute a means employed by "capitalists" to maintain oppression. The rich pretend to grant freedom of the press, freedom of association, political rights, and the possibility of opposition to everybody, but they arrange matters so that in practice these prerogatives can be exercised only by those who have the money, that is to say, the capital. These rights serve, therefore, to conceal from the eyes of the proletariat the oppression of which they are the victims. For Marx the conclusion is that there is no liberty possible so long as the capitalist system and the class struggle continue. It is only by ending this system that man will achieve freedom. Contemporary French thinkers do not accept these conclusions or all the arguments in the analysis that leads up to them. However they retain the idea that it is necessary to concern one's self with material conditions for the exercise of these rights and that a simple legal definition is not sufficient.

The Present French Concept

It is difficult to define precisely the present concept of civil rights in France. To conciliate the different points of view already enumerated leads to theoretical contradictions. These contradictions, however, are often not so acute in practice.

First of all, it must be noted that the traditional concept, entertained by nineteenth-century liberals who considered liberty as a means of opposition to power, has definitely not been abandoned. On the contrary, it remains very much alive and rooted very deeply in the mind of the public. In this respect the French idea of liberty is quite different from Marxist concepts and the doctrines of the Soviet Union. The state is considered as representing a danger to the freedom of citizens. Distrust of power remains extremely widespread, and the laws provide the citizens with effective means of resisting power.

French public opinion is, however, just as alive to the dangers of the influence of private economic powers. In this respect it clearly breaks with nineteenth-century ideas, which were founded on an integral economic liberalism, optimistic by nature, and which held that financial and economic combines cannot act otherwise than in the general interest. Though the preoccupation with the protection of the individual from the state continues, there is also today in France a preoccupation with the protection of the individual from private powers, which are essentially the powers of money. In certain cases this can lead to a demand in favor of state intervention against the action of these private interests.

Finally, the idea that some material means are essential for the exercise of rights has led to the development of what the Preamble to the Constitution of 1946 calls "economic and social principles" considered "particularly necessary in our time." These principles apply to the right to work, a guaranteed minimum wage, the right to leisure, and social security schemes as a protection against every risk (sickness, accident, old age, maternity). These are elements of the welfare state.

There is some difficulty in harmonizing the different viewpoints. Certain branches of production are nationalized in order to protect the individual from the action of private economic powers. The Preamble to the Constitution makes it obligatory to nationalize "any property, and undertaking, which possesses or acquires the character of a public service or of a monopoly." This, however, increases the power of the state, and so a simultaneous attempt is made to increase the influence of private forces capable of opposing it. The present French concept of freedom necessitates a series of continual compromises. It cannot be strictly defined in the abstract. It can only materialize in concrete action of a very flexible nature.

CIVIL RIGHTS

Freedom of the Person

Personal liberty means freedom from hindrance to the individual's free movement from place to place, freedom from encroachment on the privacy of his home, and freedom from arbitrary arrest and detention. These are the traditional liberal ideas of the nineteenth century.

It should be noted that these rights are perhaps less well protected in France than in Anglo-Saxon countries. The French tendency has been to put the accent on freedom of thought and expression (for example, religious freedom, freedom to teach, freedom of the press, freedom to publish, and freedom of the theater) and on freedom of political action (demonstrations, meetings, associations) rather than on personal rights. The French term *libertés publiques*, which corresponds approximately to the Anglo-Saxon term civil rights, expresses a fundamental difference in trend. This can no doubt be explained by history. In France the struggle for civil rights was one of the forms taken by the struggle for a democratic regime. The demand for rights was made by men as citizens rather than as private individuals. Nevertheless, this trend must not be exaggerated. France has never lost interest in the habeas corpus. *La sûreté*, which is approximately the same thing, has been listed since 1789 as one of the rights of man.

La sûreté, however, is equivalent to several Anglo-Saxon terms besides habeas corpus. In addition to protecting against arbitrary arrest and detention, it insures an equitable arraignment system. No arrest can take place without a warrant from a magistrate, the *juge d'instruction*. There are exceptions in the case of those caught in the act and in the famous case of Article 10 of the Code of Criminal Procedure, which dates from the time of Napoleon I and which authorizes the prefect to have recourse to police arrests, searches of premises, and seizure of goods in the case of crimes and offenses against the security of the state. The prefect has to inform the Public Prosecutor's Office within twenty-four hours and send him the relevant files. The essential safeguard is the independence of the examining magistrate, the *juge d'instruction,* who is responsible to the Minister of Justice. Here we come once more to the problem of the impartiality of the judiciary, which will be examined later. In exceptional cases of serious troubles, foreign or domestic, the proclamation of a state of siege or of a state of urgency, such as exists at present in Algeria, has the effect of limiting this safeguard by transferring the powers of indictment to military courts.

Once the arrest has been made, the essential problem is that of preventive detention, to which habeas corpus is one solution. In France the decision rests with the magistrates. The examining magistrate may order the prisoner to be set at liberty provisionally, but he is not obliged to do so except for trivial charges. If he rejects the request, the prisoner may seek relief from the Court of Appeal. There have been certain abuses in this matter in the last few years, and reform of the procedure is under consideration.

As for due process of law, the guaranties of procedure are similar to those of other Western nations. Penalties must be statutory rather than improvised, and laws may not be retroactive. The trial takes the form of a public debate, the opportunity of legal counsel is obligatory, and judgment is pronounced by a citizen jury. In practice, the police try to circumvent some of these fundamental rules. For example, when they summon and question as a "witness" a suspect, they may make him speak without his lawyer being present. On the whole, it is true to say that there are abuses but that they are rare. Obviously, exception must be made of the measures taken in Algeria in the struggle against the nationalist rebellion, in which certain abuses seem to have taken place.

The freedom to choose one's place of abode is the second of the personal rights of the individual. With certain exceptions, the citizen is free to live where he chooses and to move his domicile without any duties or formalities. The married woman's domicile is fixed by her husband, but she may request the court to fix a separate domicile. The domicile of minors is the same as that of their parents. Army reservists are obliged to report any change of domicile, so that they may be reached in case of mobilization. The individual's domicile is inviolable; that is to say, officials have no right to enter except in specified cases. Judicial authorities may search homes in order to look for accused persons or proof of crimes.

The search must be made by the examining magistrate, however, or by a person designated by him with a formal warrant. The collectors of indirect taxes, of customs duties, and of certain other taxes also have the right to enter private residences in certain specified cases. Similarly, government inspectors may visit factories, workshops, and other premises in connection with the social welfare laws. Finally, force may be used to enter a home in order to seize goods if a legal judgment has been made to this effect. As a general rule, no visit or search may take place at night except in the case of a state of siege, a fire, a flood, or a call for help from within.

Freedom of movement is another of the personal rights of the individual. Any person may move freely within French territory. There are a few exceptions to this fundamental principle. Naturally there is stricter legislation about foreign travel, but it is very liberal compared with that of many democratic countries, and in particular of the United States. French citizens may not leave their own country unless they have a passport delivered by the authorities, who for reasons of national interest may refuse to grant one. If it is refused, the person concerned has the right to appeal to the Council of State, and this is a very precious safeguard. In practice, it is only in extremely rare cases that a passport is refused. A passport is not required for visiting certain neighboring countries—Belgium, Switzerland, Germany, and Italy, for example. It is therefore very easy for any Frenchman to leave his own country.

Foreigners wishing to enter France must have a passport from their country unless they are inhabitants of certain neighboring countries with which an agreement has been made. A visa as well as a passport is required of the citizens of certain countries. This especially concerns those from countries which themselves insist on a similar visa from French citizens seeking admission. Nevertheless, citizens of the United States enter France without a visa, whereas the French must comply with the general requirements of the American visa in order to enter the United States. In any case, the issuing of a French visa is accompanied by no special formality; in this respect there is no comparison with the very severe restrictions governing the issue of visas for admission to the United States.

Finally, the Preamble to the Constitution solemnly proclaims the right of asylum in these terms: "Any man persecuted by reason of his action in favor of freedom has right of asylum in the territories of the Republic." In practice, there is a certain difficulty over the right of asylum, and a government decision is needed before it can be granted. Public opinion, however, is very alive to the problem.

Freedom of Thought

We are here concerned in practice with the freedom of expression, of education, and of religion. Thought itself remains the secret of the individual, the most inviolable domicile of all.

Religious freedom is the first of the freedoms of thought. Any religion may be freely practiced on French territory. The state does not subsidize or give special recognition or favor to any one religion. Such is the situation since the law of December 9, 1905, which established the separation of church and state. The state safeguards the free exercise of all religions. Those who try, by compulsion or threats, to force a person to practice a certain religion or to prevent him from practicing one are liable to imprisonment or a fine. Churches of all denominations usually belong to the state and the communes, which make them available to the various ministers without cost and assume financial responsibility for their upkeep. Anticlericalism never attacked this freedom of religion, but only the influence of the clergy in political life.

The French concept of freedom of education is very different from the Anglo-Saxon concept. The point of departure is the organization by the state of free public education without religious or political bias, at all stages, primary, secondary, higher, and technical. Private individuals, however, are at liberty to set up educational establishments at any level. Private institutions for higher education, however, are not allowed to call themselves universities or faculties.

It is the state that grants university diplomas. Pupils from both public and private schools receive these diplomas, which are awarded on the passing of an examination judged by teachers from the public educational system. There is nothing to prevent the private schools from awarding their own diplomas. Some of them are very highly prized, but, with a few exceptions, it is only state diplomas that enable one to qualify for civil service examinations. These diplomas are awarded impartially from whatever institution the candidates come.

The freedom of the universities is very great despite the fact that all the teachers are nominated by the state and are virtually civil servants. They are recruited by completely free competition, the jury being formed of practicing teachers. The appointing minister is obliged to nominate those whom the jury designates. There are very strong guaranties against dismissal. The university is very jealous of its prerogatives and its independence. In fact the French university system is one of the freest in the world, although it is one of the most centralized. A teacher may pass from one to the other university on request. Naturally, they all dream of ending up at the University of Paris, which has the greatest prestige.

Since the nineteenth century, freedom of the press has been considered the most important of all freedoms of thought, and throughout this period it has played a most important part in political struggles. The only consideration at the time, however, was the freedom of the press vis-à-vis the state. A press was considered free to the extent that the government had no means of interfering with it. This matter was settled in 1881, when complete freedom to set up a newspaper and to publish any news that one wished was granted. Currently the problem of the press is to acquire financial independence.

Freedom of the theater is one of the freedoms of thought, but it is also very akin to the right to hold meetings. Censorship of plays did not disappear until 1906, and municipalities still have the right to forbid a performance if it endangers public order. The exercise of this right is, however, very strictly controlled by the administrative courts.

There is still censorship of the cinema by the Minister of Information, who is advised by a board consisting of representatives of some ministries—National Defense, National Education, Foreign Affairs, and Public Health—together with representatives of the cinema—writers, directors, distributors, cinema owners, and critics. All films pass before it, whether they are made in France or imported. A visa must be obtained before the film can be shown. Usually the censorship is tolerantly applied.

For radio and television the situation is quite different. Since 1939 there has been no private radio or television station in French territory. It is forbidden to set up such stations. Radio and television are therefore entirely in the hands of the state. Quite strict rules oblige the government to respect political freedom at election time. Radio and television time are shared equally between the candidates. Otherwise, the government has complete discretion. Abuses are frequent. News bulletins, whether on radio or television, often put the case for the ministers in power. This was especially so for the Mollet ministry. A radio and television bill is still in process of preparation. The public hopes that there will soon be some reform. The present system is being criticized more and more violently.

Freedom of Association

In all countries and under all political systems the problem of the freedom of association is different from that of individual freedom, for groups may become powerful and well armed and then oppose the government, so that the latter naturally views them with distrust. This was particularly so in France for a long time. The revolutionaries of 1789 did not trust "intermediary bodies" which came between the state and the individual. They considered them as dangerous to individual liberty. For this reason freedom of association has developed at a slower pace than the other freedoms.

Public demonstrations have always played some part in French life. The great demonstrations of the Revolution of 1789, those of the July Monarchy, and the riots of February 6, 1934, are but examples. Many processions and marches are traditional, as, for example, the procession of left-wing parties and trade unions on July 14 from the Place de la République to the Place de la Bastille, that of the right-wing parties on the feast of St. Joan of Arc, the march of the extreme leftists past the wall in the Père-Lachaise cemetery against which, in 1871, the last supporters of the Commune were shot, and working-class demonstrations on May 1. All demonstrations are not of a political nature, as, for example, religious processions on the streets.

Public demonstrations must be authorized by the government. This authorization can be refused only if there is a risk of disturbing the peace. Appeal to the Council of State is always possible. In practice, the government shows itself more or less strict according to circumstances. In times of trouble it tends to forbid demonstrations. In normal times it generally allows them to take place without interfering otherwise than by taking precautionary measures lest the demonstrators should go too far or there should be a counterdemonstration. Private meetings to which individuals go only by invitation do not require authorization.

Freedom of assembly was introduced by the Revolution of 1789 and great advantage was taken of it. The clubs of the time, where people met daily, were of great political importance. During the nineteenth century, however, meetings were generally forbidden, except immediately after the Revolution of 1848. Government permission was necessary before a meeting could be held even if its purpose were scientific, economic, religious, or literary. The principle of freedom of assembly was established in 1881 under the Third Republic. Thenceforth, the participating group needed only to make a declaration to the authorities.

Freedom of association proper (that is, of more or less permanent groups as distinguished from temporary assemblies) was established by law in 1901. There is complete freedom to form any kind of association, but if it is desired to have legal status (the right to take legal action and own property), a declaration must be made at the prefecture, and the by-laws must be deposited there. Existing associations cannot be forcibly dissolved unless they cause a disturbance of the peace or offend morality. This dissolution can be pronounced only by the legal authority.

Such is the general rule. There are special rules. Some associations are subjected to stricter controls; private leagues and militia, for example, can be dissolved by the government and not by the courts, according to the law of 1936, which was aimed at the political agitation conducted at that time by groups with Fascist tendencies. Religious orders must have an authorization from the government in order to have the right to function on French territory. This regulation is a result of the anticlerical movement at the beginning of this century. To begin with, authorizations were rarely granted. Today they are given freely. Moreover, the law is no longer applied. In practice, most orders function on French territory, and most of them without any authorization.

The state has recently changed its attitude toward associations. For the last ten years the tendency has been to intrust private associations with matters of public interest and to establish co-operation between them and the state. This is the exact opposite of the spirit of 1789, which did not tolerate "intermediary bodies." At present they are looked upon with favor. They were encouraged by the Vichy government, which granted legal privileges in return for a strengthening of government supervision. The tendency is less marked since the Liberation, but associations of radio listeners, interprofessional committees of commerce and industry, and family associations, for example, are now intrusted with semipublic functions.

Economic Freedom

In economics more than anywhere else we can see the duality of the present French concept of civil rights. The ideas of laissez faire liberalism, according to which economic freedom can be defined as a policy of no interference and no obstruction, clearly persist. But there is also a tendency to extend the control of the state over certain economic interests in order to prevent the latter from bringing pressure to bear on citizens and attacking their personal liberty. There is also a tendency to limit the unfettered operation of the

market in order to guarantee to every individual a minimum standard of living and a certain security which are deemed indispensable
for the normal enjoyment of civil rights.

Freedom to work in the traditional sense meant nothing but the
free choice of employment where a worker could find it. This idea
was made use of throughout the nineteenth century in order to fight
strikes, which were considered to be attacks on the free determina-
tion of conditions of work. Today freedom to work is understood
quite differently. One aspect of it is to make possible, or less impossible, the real choice of a profession or career, and great improve-
ments were effected in this respect by the educational reforms of
the Third Republic, which made primary and secondary education
obligatory and free and provided maintenance grants for education. A second aspect is the recognition of the fundamental inequality between employer and employed, and the establishment for the
latter of guaranties of work which afford him a certain freedom.

First of all, the principle of the right to work has been admitted,
and thus it is taken for granted that the unemployed worker has a
right to relief. In the second place, the idea of stability of employment has gradually developed. In state enterprises employees cannot be dismissed except when this is recommended by a disciplinary
committee on which their own representatives sit, and after they
have been informed of the complaints made against them and have
been given an opportunity to defend themselves. There is nothing
similar in private enterprises except that employees' delegates can
be dismissed only with the consent of a committee or of the government inspector. The only general measure which can limit the employers' abuse of dismissal is the obligation to pay an indemnity. In
the third place, the disciplinary power of employers and their representatives, the foremen, has been limited by the stipulations of
workshop rules. These rules must conform to clauses inserted in collective agreements, which can be extended and made to apply to the
whole industry by the state. Finally, and most important, the state
fixes a minimum wage that must be paid by all employers. No real
freedom is thought to exist without a tolerable minimum standard
of living.

Freedom to form trade unions was recognized for the first time in
1864 under the Second Empire, but in a limited form. Complete
freedom was established under the Third Republic by the law of
1884. There is now no restriction on the formation of labor unions.
They enjoy considerable legal rights. They cannot be dissolved unless by court order they are found to be inimical to public order or

morality. Every worker is free to belong to the labor union of his choice. Unions are not permitted to insert closed-shop clauses in collective agreements, for such clauses are considered to be a negation of union freedom. Conversely, an employer may not bring pressure to bear upon his workmen to prevent them from joining a union: it is a case of wrongful dismissal if a wage earner is fired because of his union membership and activity.

The part played in public life by labor unions is changing. To begin with, they were considered exclusively as organizations for furthering the working class against employers, but they are now becoming organizations for co-operation. Many factors have contributed to this change in the nature of the trade unions, among them the development of collective agreements which may by government decree be made obligatory for a whole profession or branch of a profession, a procedure for arbitration of labor disputes, the appointment of employees' advisers, the nomination of judges in the courts dealing with disagreements between employers and employees, and union representation on the Economic Council.

French unions differ a great deal in their attitude from American unions. They consider that the union's first duty is to gain advantages for its workers, but they are very reticent with regard to active collaboration in the running of the business. On the whole, they do not approve of the capitalist system, and they continue to believe in class warfare.

The French economic system is still based on free enterprise, but this is limited in two ways. First, there is a very important public sector of the national economy. Mines, electricity, gas, railways, most of municipal transport, atomic energy, arms factories, and the Renault car factories are run by the state or by certain local communities. This nationalized sector exerts a very important influence on the economy through its very extent and also because of the basic character of most of the industries it includes. Nationalized industries have come into being in order to protect the freedom of individuals from the possible stranglehold of monopolistic private enterprises. It was considered that in certain industries the growth of enormous organizations would dominate the state and the elected representatives of the nation.

The state also has important means of control of private enterprise as a whole. It can regulate economic activity in general. It can aid any category of business it chooses through subsidies or investment. It can favor exports or imports. These economic powers were very great in the years immediately following the war, because the scarcity of goods made free competition impossible. Today these powers are much more restricted. The most important are concerned with welfare regulations, as, for example, minimum wage, regulation of hours of work, and obligatory paid holidays. This is all meant to insure every citizen of at least a minimum standard of living that will permit him to take a real share in the life of the nation. With the same end in view, a comprehensive system of social security has been developed.

PROTECTION OF CIVIL RIGHTS

It is not sufficient to give legal recognition to rights. Respect for the law must be insured. In France this problem has been considered of the highest importance. Article 16 of the Declaration of the Rights of Man states that "any society in which the citizen's rights are not guaranteed has no constitution." This was meant to proclaim clearly that the most solemn declarations of rights and the most liberal constitutions are worthless if they are not enforceable. It is not easy, however, to implement civil rights. Legal procedure is not enough. Public opinion and the general attitude of citizens toward these rights are an essential complement.

Legal Safeguards

The first legal safeguards organized in France were related to the right of resistance to oppression and to the right of petition. They were both in keeping with the spirit of the French Revolution, but they were of no practical use. The Constitution of 1793 contained the following declaration (which is reminiscent of Lincoln's Second Inaugural Address): "When the government violates the rights of the people, insurrection is for the people and for each section of the population the most sacred of rights and the most indispensable of duties." But this declaration was of necessity void of any practical results. The French system of civil rights safeguards developed slowly; it is less the result of legislation than of the formation of legal custom bit by bit. The fundamental legal protection of civil rights lies in the existence of a high administrative court, the Council of State, which has the power to annul all government acts, whether of ministers or of local authorities, which it finds to be contrary to the law. The Council of State enjoys very great independence and is accessible to ordinary citizens. Any individual may apply directly to the Council or may appeal to it from the lower administrative courts. There is no special form of procedure. A letter addressed to the General Secretary of the Council of State will bring about an investigation of the matter without any other formalities. There is no need of a lawyer, and the only expense is a registration fee (equaling about ten dollars) if the case is lost.

Any act of the government or the administration which violates a civil right recognized by law, by the Constitution, or simply by the "general principles of French law" may be annulled by a decision of the Council of State as a result of an appeal by an individual. Municipal rulings, departmental regulations, orders issued by the Premier or the President of the Republic, and even certain decrees of Parliament are voidable by the court. Acts of Parliament, however, are unassailable, for the Council of State is not the judge of the constitutionality of laws. Theoretically, this is a serious loophole. In practice, it is not so important, at least insofar as civil rights are concerned. In a parliamentary country like France, where there is a very lively reaction of public opinion to all that concerns civil rights, an unconstitutional law would arouse violent opposition, which Parliament would be obliged to take into account. If it were a temporary violation, resulting from a wave of emotion, it would be quite soon put right. The chief danger comes not from laws against freedom but from the action of the government or administration, which is precisely the domain of the Council of State.

The French use of the Council of State is a very original one and has given the Council a great deal of prestige. It has been imitated abroad. Belgium, in particular, has adopted the system almost intact. Legally the members of the Council enjoy no special protection. They are not even granted the tenure of office guaranteed to the judiciary. Theoretically, the government can dismiss them. In practice, it does not do so. The power and unity of the Council are so great that for practical purposes its members are irremovable. It is recruited by impartial competitive examination. Its general character allows the Council to judge without bias the acts of even the highest governmental and administrative authorities.

The Council of State, however, is competent to deal only with the acts of administrative and executive authorities and not with those of magistrates. The police power, for example, comes under the authority of the public prosecutor's office and thus arrests, searches, and so on are not considered to be administrative. Preventive detention is ordered by a magistrate, the *juge d'instruction*. This explains why abuses are more numerous in this province and why liberty of the person is less well safeguarded than other freedoms. Appeals against this kind of abuse go to ordinary courts, whose judges are less independent than the members of the Council of

State. Foreign observers find it difficult to understand this, because they are naturally inclined to view professional magistrates and the judiciary as guardians of liberty and the administration as its enemy. In France, however, the judiciary is afraid to face up to abuses and does too little to stop them, whereas a high administrative body, the Council of State, gives proof of great independence and exercises strict control over attacks on liberty.

The only thing to be regretted is the slowness of the Council of State's decisions. Swamped with work, it is "defeated by its own success" and is the victim of the excessive confidence placed in it by the ordinary man. There is considerable delay in passing judgment. On an average, two or three years pass between the lodging of the appeal and the decision. This diminishes the effectiveness of control, especially because an appeal does not suspend the application of the contested administrative action. An important reform was therefore introduced in 1953. The jurisdiction of the lower administrative courts was expanded in order to free the Council of State from almost everything that did not concern control of the essential acts of the administration. This reform has not yet taken full effect because of the immense backlog in the Council's docket. Nevertheless, the delays are beginning to be shorter.

Gaps in the System

The absence in France of safeguards that are widespread in other countries naturally strikes the foreign observer. There is no mechanism for controlling the constitutionality of laws as there is in the United States. Such control has been attempted on several occasions in a different form. It was exercised by a political body instead of by a court, and it did not work in practice. At the present time, as has been seen, the Constitutional Committee is not authorized to examine legislation in terms of the Preamble to the Constitution, and it is in the Preamble that civil rights are enumerated.

The limited independence of the judiciary is another defect in the French system, of which those who know the independent, respected position of judges in Great Britain are particularly conscious. French judges are honest and independent as regards litigants, but they are far less independent as regards the government, for their advancement depends partly on the latter. There are a great many grades in the hierarchy of the French judiciary, and salaries are quite low at the bottom of the scale. There are few posts at the top compared with the total numbers in the profession, so that the main preoccupation of a judge is to insure his own advancement, which can be done only through loyalty to those in power. Nevertheless, the creation of the Supreme Council of the Judiciary in 1946 is a first step toward reform. It has given judges a measure of independence that was lacking in the past.

Individual Responsibility

No procedure can ever by itself insure absolute protection of rights. If English judges, members of the American Supreme Court, or French Councillors of State were themselves lacking in the spirit of freedom, these supreme guarantors of liberty could destroy it instead of protecting it. Besides legal institutions and the men who compose them, however, there is the great mass of public opinion, the whole country, in fact. The general structure of the nation and the spirit that prevails in it are the ultimate guardians of civil rights. No legal control, no machinery for appeal, no body of magistrates, no institution, can guarantee the freedom of a people which does not value freedom, and a people which does value it will always finally achieve respect for it, whatever the defects in the legal system.

The history of the development of civil rights in France shows a link between the existence of a liberal regime and that of a democratic regime with free elections. This same link is to be found in most of the countries in the world, so that the following general statement may be formulated: civil rights in a country exist in direct proportion to the degree of democracy to be found there. This is not a logical connection but one based on actual fact. Democratic procedure (election of parliamentary representatives and separation of powers) weakens governments and decreases their efficiency to a certain degree. Precisely this loss of efficiency is a guaranty of freedom. Democratic procedure is a means of strengthening citizens at the expense of those in power and of making it possible for them to resist power.

The pluralist structure of society has the same effect. If liberty is the possibility of opposing authority, this opposition must find support in the social system. There must, therefore, be a certain amount of division in society. There can be no freedom in a unanimous society, for opposition there can be the work of only isolated individuals, who would be considered social deviants. If French society seems relatively egalitarian as regards standard of living, it is extremely diversified in its other aspects. Social forces are numerous, opinions and beliefs are different, and each point of view is represented to a certain extent either in the government or in the opposition. This provides an extremely solid support for liberty. In the nineteenth century, the only forces that counted in practice were economic ones. The masses were unorganized. Senior posts in the civil service and throughout the state as a whole went to the industrial and commercial middle class, the members of which defended the regime because they accepted its doctrines and ideology. The press, the parties, the leading posts in politics and administration—nearly all the instruments of power were in the hands of the privileged economic groups. The opposition had no real power. Today the situation is different. The organization of trade unions and working-class parties has given the mass of the people a very powerful instrument for action, and high officials in the administration are detaching themselves more and more from the monied middle class in order to pursue disinterested aims and to formulate doctrines of their own. The opposition has now become real and powerful, so powerful that in some exceptional circumstances it has managed to seize power. This social pluralism gives reality and authenticity to freedom.

The very nature of public feeling seems to be one of the essential guaranties of this exercise of rights. There is something constant in the national character. However vague this idea may be, it is incontestably a fact. It has been said that a Frenchman has only to see the notice "Keep Out" to experience an irresistible desire to enter, which he would not have felt if there had been no notice! This natural tendency to defy authority can be traced far back through history. Traces of it can already be found in the description Caesar gives of the Gauls. A peasant tradition that is still very much alive has fed this fundamental spirit of opposition to the state, this natural resistance to the government. Instinctively, when any action is proposed by the state, the Frenchman is immediately opposed to it. It is difficult to persuade him to agree to it. At bottom he considers disobedience and insubordination as virtues. This feeling is strengthened by his education. The part given to the French Revolution in the teaching of children is important. It is dealt with not in the form of a description of the dead past but as a source of lessons that have some bearing on present-day life. The language, style, ideas, and doctrines of the revolutionary period powerfully reinforce this feeling for freedom, for opposition, and for resistance to oppression. The history of the Revolution is the basis of civic education in France, and it teaches less to obey the state than to resist it. In secondary education, literature and philosophy only reinforce this general tendency.

It should be added that the whole history of the nineteenth century, during which French opinion was divided, has accustomed people to the idea that a plurality of doctrines is a natural phenomenon and that liberty consists in respecting this plurality. There are democratic countries, like the United States, where opinion is almost unanimous concerning the form of the state, the structure of the government, and the fundamentals of public life, but the situation in France is quite different. For the last 150 years there has been, as we have seen, a struggle between two or three irreconcilable concepts concerning the form of the government, its philosophical basis, and its methods of wielding power. The present opposition between Communists and the rest of the French is in many respects no greater than that between conservatives and liberals immediately after the Revolution of 1789 and during the whole of the nineteenth century. Thus the French have learned to live surrounded by radically contradictory political philosophies, with the result that they now believe that the coexistence of such philosophies is one of the essential conditions of freedom.

One special characteristic, which the foreign observer finds difficult to understand, adds strength to all these ways of safeguarding freedom. This is the respect that the public shows for thought, mind, and intelligence. French intellectuals enjoy considerable influence and prestige. Within the Republic exists a "Republic of Letters," which often sets itself up as a guardian. Its members make a noteworthy effort to rise above class prejudice, to achieve a calm, impartial view of things, and to be a kind of incarnation of justice among men. French intellectuals are thus continuing the tradition of the clerks of the Middle Ages. They are trying to set themselves up as guardians of civil rights, and to a certain extent they are succeeding.

CHAPTER 10

ADMINISTRATION

The word "centralization" is not in favor in France today. Every political party and every newspaper claims to support decentralization. Nevertheless, centralization has been the rule, and the republic has followed the example of Napoleon, who himself continued the work of centralization begun by the monarchy. Centralization can be studied with reference to local government, civil service, and the judicial system.

LOCAL ADMINISTRATION

During the French Revolution, the Girondins and Jacobins came into conflict over the problem of local administration. The former wanted a kind of federal republic on the American pattern, while the latter entirely disagreed. It was the Jacobins who were responsible for the formula, "The Republic is one and indivisible," demonstrating the importance they attached to unification and centralization. In general, theirs was the victory, thanks to Napoleon, who in 1800 as a former Jacobin laid the foundations of the present system of administration in France.

Centralization varies in degree according to the unit of local government in question—commune or department.

Communes: Limited Decentralization

In theory the organization of the commune is decentralized, for it is self-governing by way of elected authorities. The commune is the modern equivalent of the oldest of French territorial units, corresponding in general to the parishes of the *ancien régime,* which were largely a continuation of the divisions made by the Gauls. Consequently, the organization of the commune can be traced back a thousand years.

There is a large number of communes (38,000), and they are very different in size: 35,000 have less than 2,000 inhabitants, and only 22 have more than 100,000. In spite of this disparity their administrative system is uniform, apart from the special case of Paris, and thus gives evidence of the spirit of unification. Before the Revolution, on the contrary, the system of administration in the communes varied a great deal according to the region.

There are in every commune two organs of administration: the municipal council and the mayor. The council is an assembly elected by universal suffrage every six years, and its membership varies from 11 in the case of communes with less than 500 inhabitants to 37 for those with a population of 60,000 or more. Before 1947 the electoral system was the same for all communes. In 1947, as we have seen, proportional representation was introduced for communes of more than 9,000 inhabitants, while simple-majority list-voting with a second ballot was applied in smaller communes. The distinction was made in recognition of the fact that the size of the commune has considerable bearing on the significance of the vote. In small communes, voting is in the main determined by the personality of the candidates, and political issues, though not ignored, do not weigh heavily. But in large towns the vote is dominated by the conflict between the parties, and the personal qualities and administrative capacity of the candidates take second place in the considerations of the voter, who makes his decision primarily on political grounds.

The municipal council is the deciding body in all communal matters. It meets four times a year for sessions lasting two weeks, with the exception of the May session, which is devoted to passing the budget and may last six weeks. Certain duties are mandatory for the council: in particular, it must provide such public services as fire protection and sanitation, and it must allow for the necessary funds in its budget. On the other hand, it is forbidden to undertake certain activities, notably competing with private enterprise unless the services of private enterprise are inadequate and inefficient.

The municipal council is subject to the authority of the central administration. It may be dissolved by decree of the Council of Ministers in case of a disagreement between the mayor and a majority of the council or if it neglects communal interests. A councillor may be removed from his post by the prefect in the case (a) of ineligibility for office, (b) of refusal to perform a duty prescribed by law, and (c) of absence without good cause from three consecutive council meetings. The prefect also has power, in the name of the government, to annul decisions of municipal councils which are contrary to law or which exceed its competence. He also has power of annulment, within two weeks, when a decision has been taken after discussions in which a councillor with a personal interest in the question has taken part.

The mayor is, in a sense, the executive authority in the commune. He is elected by the council from among its members and is assisted by deputies, varying in number according to the size of the commune. The mayor may delegate some of his powers to his deputies. Broadly speaking, the mayor carries into effect the decisions of the municipal council. He also presides over its discussions and has the initiative in drawing up the agenda. He has personal power in that he and not the council decides certain questions in regard to the employees of the commune and to matters of public safety, order, and hygiene within the commune. The mayor is also an agent of the state and in this capacity performs a number of duties for which he is placed directly under the control of the government. He acts as registrar, registering marriages, births, and deaths for the Registrar General's office, and he is an officer of the police insofar as he is concerned with the investigation of breaches of law and the pursuit of lawbreakers. These activities of the mayor as agent of the state are not very important, however.

Technically, the commune is self-administered, but actually the controlling powers of the higher authorities are quite extensive. The limit to decentralization is primarily imposed by the financial position of the commune, not by the provisions of the law. The main taxes in France are state taxes, and to meet their expenses the communes have only comparatively minor resources. Nor have they the right to levy duties as they wish; they can fix the rate of only certain taxes laid down by law. The result is that many communes have insufficient funds to meet their needs. Therefore they seek state help, which makes them dependent upon the central government. Nonetheless, an ingenious system has been set up to limit their dependence: state aid is compulsory for a whole series of communal services, provided that the commune raises a certain proportion of the needed revenue. School buildings are a good example. The communes, however, are obliged in this case to submit their plans to intermediary authorities, and this allows the central government to postpone decision for a long time.

Departments: Open Centralization

The division of France into departments dates from the Constituent Assembly in 1791. The aim was to replace the former provinces, which varied greatly both in size and in method of government, by a uniform system of administration. The Assembly gave departmental authorities considerable power, but this was replaced under the Jacobin dictatorship by a centralized regime. Present-day organization in the departments dates, generally speaking, from Napoleon. In particular, he established prefects, who are in a sense the modern equivalent of the intendant of the *ancien régime*.

In appearance, the department is organized like the commune. There is an assembly, the general or departmental council, elected by universal suffrage on a single-member ballot with one councillor for each *arrondissement*. Executive power is in the hands of the prefect, who roughly corresponds to the mayor in the commune. There are, however, two important differences to be noted. Whereas the mayor is elected by the municipal council from its own members, the prefect is a civil servant appointed by the government. And whereas the commune is responsible for many public services, the department is concerned with very few. Moreover, its financial resources are very slight. In fact, the department is not so much a geographical community as a framework within which state services function. The prefect is not so much a departmental authority as the representative of the government in the departmental area.

The general council meets twice a year and decides on departmental matters, but, as we have just seen, there are very few departmental services and very few departmental questions. The council may also express hopes and give opinions, but political matters are excluded. It elects a president and a departmental committee which sits in the period intervening between council sessions. The Constitution of 1946 clearly sought to make the president of the general council a kind of departmental mayor who would rival the prefect; but the necessary laws to implement this step have never been passed, and it is unlikely that they ever will be. The president of the general council has a certain influence in the department because he is an outstanding figure and is in contact with political circles, but he has no great authority.

The prefect is an officer peculiar to the French administrative system. He is a senior civil servant appointed and dismissed by the government. There is a prefectoral corps that offers a professional career, but the appointment and promotion of prefects are, nonetheless, much affected by politics and depend on the individual's relations with one of the parties. The prefect is closely supervised by the government, and absolute loyalty is considered necessary. He may be dismissed by the government without any reason being given, which is not the case for other civil servants.

Legally, the prefect's powers are not great. Essentially, he is an agent of the state and executes the decisions of the government within the framework of the department. Article 10 of the Criminal Investigation Codes gives him the right in emergency to investigate crimes and offenses against the security of the state; particulars must be forwarded to the Public Prosecutor within twenty-four hours. He is also the government's representative in dealing with state public services operating in the department, though most of these are run by regional chiefs who come under the direct control of the appropriate minister. Although the prefect represents the entire government, he is under the control of the Minister of the Interior, to whom he is more directly responsible.

If the powers of the prefect are not very extensive legally, politically they are very important. It is he who keeps the government informed on the state of mind prevailing in the department, on the functioning of public services, and so on. It is he who supervises the activities of the local authorities, and he remains in close contact with all the mayors. Furthermore, he has under his orders from two to five subprefects according to the importance of the department, and each subprefect supervises a particular area. He has quite a large staff directed by the general secretary of the prefecture and by his own personal secretariat.

The Problem of the Region

The department has long been the subject of a controversy, although the issue has somewhat died down since World War II. The parties of the Right leveled at it the traditional criticism that it was an artificial division, for they considered that the *ancien régime* provinces were the only natural division. But memories of the former provinces have faded away, and it would not be possible to resuscitate them.

It has been argued that the departments are too small from the economic point of view. It has also been said that the Minister of the Interior cannot possibly supervise ninety prefects and that it would be better to regroup the departments into some twenty regions. As can be seen, the regional question is raised in several forms: historical and traditional regionalism, now obsolete; economic regionalism, based on a division of the country into natural regions; political regionalism, motivated by a desire for closer government control. The Vichy government thought it had solved the problem by putting a regional prefect in charge of several departmental prefects. At the time of the Liberation the regional prefect was temporarily replaced by a civil servant, the state commissioner. Today these posts have been abolished. In each region, however, the prefect of the most important department is given the title and duties of chief administrative inspector on special duty (known by the initials I.G.A.M.E.). He has his offices in a town, which thus becomes a sort of regional capital. He summons meetings of his prefectoral colleagues in the department, supervises their work, and co-ordinates the activity of the heads of public services in the region.

It must further be noted that the creation, in some regions, of committees for economic development has given a new impulse during the last few years to regional co-ordination. The regional concept is beginning to emerge from the world of imagination into the realm of fact. It began purely for the sake of administrative supervision of a number of prefects; it is now part of the economic and social life of the region.

THE CIVIL SERVICE

The organization of the civil service is a powerful factor contributing to centralization. The number of communal and departmental officials is quite low in comparison with the number of civil servants working in the same area. The total number of state civil servants comes to 1,550,000, with an additional 860,000 employed in public economic undertakings (nationalized enterprises). This makes a grand total of 2,410,000 state officials, compared with some 400,000 departmental and communal officials—an indication of the preponderance of central administration.

Unification

There is a definite trend toward unification of the different branches of the service. Before World War II each ministry had its own branch with its own personal policies. Recruitment was by separate competition for each branch and each grade. Since 1945 two main reforms have been carried out. First, a law was passed in 1946 establishing general conditions of service applicable to all state officials except magistrates and the military. Common regulations were laid down for promotion, discipline, and so on.

Second, reforms made in 1945 unified the system of recruitment. For the higher grades a single system of competitive entry to the National School of Administration now replaces all the individual forms of selection for the different branches. The aim of the reform was to make recruitment more democratic. There had, in fact, been criticism that the individual selection panels composed of members of the recruiting service had been influenced by considerations of social prestige. In practice, the only candidates who had any chance of success were those who had prepared by following courses at the École libre des Sciences Politiques, a private institution of somewhat conservative tendency. Moreover, these courses were taught by civil servants from the different branches. The 1945 reform created a common selection panel for all higher grades. Furthermore, the École libre des Sciences Politiques has been taken over by the state and turned into the Institute of Political Studies of the University of Paris, while similar institutes have been created in different universities in the provinces. A special system of scholarships for young people of modest means was set up to allow them to study in the institutes for entry to the National School of Administration. Competitive admission to the National School of Administration is divided into two parts, one restricted to candidates with certain examination qualifications, the other to candidates who have completed five years in the civil service. This has made it possible to admit to the higher grades civil servants from the lower ranks, generally of working-class origin.

Recruitment to the lower and medium grades has itself been unified by the institution of a national system of competitive appointment for administrative clerks. This has led to a decrease in political influence on recruitment, since it is more difficult to bring influence to bear on a national competitive examination than on the individual examinations of individual ministries.

Many public servants, however, remain outside the civil service code laid down in 1946. This is the case with the magistrature, which has its own separate competitive entry, and with the various technical branches, mining, forestry, civil engineering, and so on. The same is true of nationalized enterprises, each of which recruits in accordance with procedure it has itself determined. In this respect, true decentralization exists. Local officials are also recruited by separate competition for each commune and department. Here, too, however, some measure of unification has been achieved, particularly by the creation of a special branch of service for the prefectures.

Independence

A special feature of the French civil service is the existence of measures designed to safeguard the official's independence from the government. This can no doubt be explained by the vicissitudes of French political history in the nineteenth century, which produced many changes of political system. Another reason is the frequency of changes in the Cabinet and in the parliamentary majority. An effort was made to prevent the civil service from suffering from the same instability.

Civil servants benefit from a series of privileges which safeguard them against political pressure exerted by the government. Naturally this does not free them from the obligation to obey their superiors, but it allows them to dissent from the political doctrines of the ministers in power. An exception must be made for certain posts of a political nature, notably the position of prefect. Prefects, however, enjoy considerable security by comparison with the insecurity of ministers.

The effort to insure independence and to provide for the security of the public official has not met with general success and is not, as yet, generally applied. Many posts are still filled by direct nomination without competition. This is the case for all minor posts, especially for auxiliaries who do not have the legal status of civil servants but whose position is somewhat similar. Here political influence plays a considerable part; it is a way in which members of Parliament can dispose of some patronage in their constituency. Nor does competitive entry apply to certain nationalized enterprises which are purely industrial in organization, especially in the case of workers in mining, electricity, gas, and so on. Finally, there is no competitive entry for some semipublic services like the social security offices.

The rules for promotion show the same desire to avoid as far as possible the effects of political arbitrariness. In consequence, promotion by seniority is an important feature of the civil service. This is not very satisfactory as regards stimulation and professional ability. The rules for promotion by seniority are, however, tempered by exceptions that make room for choice on the basis of ability. Furthermore, the highest ranks are to some extent filled by officers from the great administrative corps (Council of State, Finance, Mines, Accounts, Engineering, Forestry, and so on), which are filled by direct competition. This allows able men to reach posts of responsibility while still very young and is an effective counterbalance to the often regrettable results of widespread promotion by seniority.

The arrangements for disciplinary penalities that the government may impose upon its officials similarly bear witness to the desire to safeguard independence. No sanction of any kind may be imposed on any civil servant unless he has appeared before a disciplinary committee on which sit representatives of his branch of the service and unless he has had prior notice of the complaints alleged against him. The Council of State severely punishes the failure to observe these rules. Certain officials, like prefects, who have political functions, are excepted.

In 1946 official recognition was given to the right of civil servants to form unions to defend their professional interests and even their service interests. It is even admitted that a strike by civil servants does not in itself constitute a breach of discipline since the Preamble to the Constitution recognizes the right to strike "within the framework of the laws which govern it," and no particular law limits this right in the case of civil servants. However, jurists think that the general principles of law may permit the denial of the right to strike to civil servants belonging to services which by their nature seem incompatible with strike action, as, for example, officials concerned with the maintenance of public safety, the police, senior officials charged with the implementation of government policy, and so on. The government cannot, however, deny to all civil servants the right to strike.

It is also acknowledged that state officials enjoy freedom of conscience. The Preamble to the Constitution states that "none shall be allowed to suffer wrong in his work or employment, by reason of his origin, his opinions, or beliefs." The civil service code forbids any entry on a man's record of his political opinions. Nevertheless, there are certain limits fixed to the expression of his opinions. On duty, the civil servant must not carry on propaganda and must observe the strictest neutrality; off duty, some officials with political duties are also obliged to maintain great discretion. It will be noted that there is no legislation in France covering the case of civil servants belonging to parties like the Communist party. In practice, however, all Communists were after 1947 excluded from senior posts of a political character—in prefectures, for example, and from the direction of ministerial departments.

Finally, the 1946 code provided for two bodies that officially represent civil servants before their service chiefs: joint administrative committees and joint technical committees. On these joint committees the representatives of the civil servants are elected by secret ballot with proportional representation by all officials of the branch. Their function is to examine with the service chiefs all matters pertaining to promotion, discipline, and so on. These bodies act as disciplinary committees.

The representatives of the staff on technical committees are nominated by the most representative of the trade-union bodies. Technical committees advise service chiefs on all problems concerning the organization and functioning of the service. They may approach the minister to whom they are responsible on any matter concerning the operation of the service.

Pay and Pensions

There is considerable discussion in France at present over the material situation of civil servants. They are "declassed" in comparison with private enterprise; that is to say, employees in private undertakings are much better paid. Some reservations must be made, however. The fundamental point to be observed is that in state service the scale of pay is much narrower than in private business. For the lower and middle grades there is no great gap between the pay in the civil service and the pay in private employment. It may even happen that the civil servant is better off. This explains the very deep envy of people in private employment, especially because at this level the civil servant is virtually alone in enjoying the considerable advantage of a retirement pension. At the higher levels the position is entirely different: the differences in pay are very considerable. It is acknowledged that a senior civil servant can earn twice or three times as much in private enterprise. At the same time the advantage of a retirement pension, which was great before World War II, is no longer of any account, since very effective pension schemes have been organized for management in private enterprise.

There is also a disparity between civil servants proper and the officials of nationalized enterprises. The scale of pay is very much wider for the latter. The trade unions are particularly emphatic in denouncing this situation, since both categories of officials work for the state. One of the basic claims made by higher-grade civil servants is for equality of pay with the nationalized sector.

The situation has important consequences. In the first place, it leads to the migration of many senior officials into private employment. This is particularly common in certain technical branches (e.g., scientific research) and in the economic and financial branches. It thus happens that the best members of the state service are taken away from it by private enterprise, although the state was responsible for their training. Private enterprise can thus have a highly qualified technical staff without having to stand the expense of training it. In the second place, the inferiority of their material situation arouses in senior civil servants a certain amount of bitterness toward the state. Before World War II the senior ranks of the service were generally inclined toward conservatism in politics, and this was particularly noticeable in the great administrative corps. Today, however, without being revolutionaries, they generally tend toward moderate left-wing views. There are, of course, many other factors which have contributed to this change, particularly the economic theories of Keynes and the role of the state in the general supervision of production and in the distribution of the national income.

CHAPTER 11

THE FRENCH UNION

In 1939 the French colonial empire was second only to the British, but it was very different in composition. The British Commonwealth already included independent Dominions associating on equal terms with the mother country and forming the major part of the Commonwealth. At that time there were only white Dominions, but immediately after the war Pakistan, India, and Ceylon received similar status. The French colonial empire was entirely different in structure; it included no territory of dominantly French population and no territory that was up to date economically or politically.

THE COLONIAL PROBLEM IN 1945

Before 1939 the French colonial empire included three kinds of territories. Some were states under French protection; they were autonomous and dealt with the French Ministry of Foreign Affairs almost as independent countries. In a second category was Algeria, divided like France into departments, with prefects and mayors under the supervision of the Ministry of the Interior like those in France. A governor-general in Algeria was charged with the duty of supervising the activities of the three local prefects. Parallel with the communes proper, known as "full" communes, there were "mixed" communes where only part of the administration was in the hands of the native representatives, the rest being the responsibility of a representative of France. There was a curious mixture of assimilation to the French legal system and of local autonomy. The third category was made up of territories that were officially designated "colonies" and administered with no local autonomy. The colonial governors were advised by local councils, but the latter had little effective power. These colonies proper came under the jurisdiction of the French Minister of Colonies.

At the time of the Liberation, the independence movements that were rousing the peoples of Asia and Africa had their echo in the overseas territories of France. Consequently, some change was necessary. It could, however, mean either assimilation or autonomy, and this was a dilemma peculiar to the French colonial situation.

Assimilation

Assimilation would have consisted in progressively extending to Algeria and to the colonies proper all the features of the French governmental system. The full realization of such a development would have been the formation of a France of 100 million inhabitants, stretching along both coasts of the Mediterranean, in which all citizens were equal whatever their race or color. Another consequence would have been that more than half of the deputies in Parliament would have been colored representatives elected by the overseas territories. This was not an inconceivable dream insofar as there was real assimilation in customs, culture, standard of living, and so on, but it presupposed long-term development.

For some territories, however, immediate action might have been taken. This was in fact accomplished in Guiana, Martinique, Guadeloupe, and Réunion, which were transformed into departments of France with the same rights and privileges as other departments. Some solution of this nature would probably have been possible in Algeria, and it is significant that many present-day Nationalist leaders, in particular Ferhat Abbas, the most intelligent of them, were at that time in favor of assimilation. The pressure of conservative forces in France, backed by the French settlers, prevented the application of such measures of reform. The Algerian statute of 1947 was a complicated compromise between assimilation and self-government, and it was not even put into force.

Self-government

Another path was that being followed by Great Britain. This would have involved the progressive granting of autonomy to the different French overseas territories according to the stage reached in their development and their ability to form authentic states. These states would have been associated with France in a community modeled in some degree on the British Commonwealth. This kind of status seemed necessary for those sections of the French Empire for which assimilation appeared to be totally impossible, notably the protectorates of Indo-China, Tunisia, and Morocco. Obviously, such developments would have raised very difficult problems. Newly independent states have a natural tendency to be chauvinistic and aggressive as a result of a very understandable reaction based on an inferiority complex. However, the ease of personal relations between Frenchmen and natives and the natural absence of any racial feeling among Frenchmen would have made the task much easier.

SECTION VIII OF THE CONSTITUTION

Section VIII of the Constitution of 1946 defined the status of what it called, by a new name, the French Union. The arrangements laid down were, however, vague and inadequate.

Local Organization

Section VIII distinguishes between territories forming an "integral" part of the French Republic and "associated" states or territories. Areas forming an integral part of the republic are of two kinds: overseas departments and overseas territories. The former include both the Algerian departments and the new departments set up in 1946—Guiana, Martinique, Guadeloupe, and Réunion. The new ones are almost entirely on the same footing as metropolitan departments, with only minor political and administrative differences. The Algerian departments, however, are different from these new ones in two ways. First of all, they are not directly linked with the mother country but form a separate group of departments with their own administrative organization, having at its head a governor-general and an assembly for Algeria. In the second place, all inhabitants do not share the same legal code, the majority of natives retaining a quite distinct civil code which includes, for example, polygamy. Voters are therefore divided into two groups, French and native. The result is that, in spite of the theoretical assimilation between French legislation and laws in the overseas departments, many French laws do not apply to Algeria.

The overseas territories include all the former colonies with the exception of Algeria, Guadeloupe, Guiana, Martinique, and Réunion. Some are self-contained units; others are "territorial groups," a kind of federation such as French West Africa and French Equatorial Africa. The legislative system for the overseas territories differs from that of metropolitan France and the overseas departments. In the latter, laws passed by Parliament in the mother country are fully applicable unless they contain some clause expressly declaring otherwise. In the overseas territories, metropolitan laws are applicable only if they contain clauses expressly providing for such application. The extension of laws to overseas territories is a matter either for parliamentary decision or for government decree.

The associated states included the former protectorates of Morocco, Tunisia, Cambodia, Laos, and Vietnam. The substitution of the term "associated state" for that of "protectorate" is evidence of the will to replace domination by collaboration. Unfortunately, the status of associated state was defined by the French Constitution unilaterally without consultation of the states themselves. This seems to contradict the concept of association. The idea was that the states would have their own governments, laws, and administration but that their independence would be limited by the treaties of association with France, which would provide for some French participation in their government.

The associated territories comprise the Cameroons and Togoland, former mandated territories of the League of Nations and subsequently of the United Nations Organization, which had intrusted them to French protection. Their status was almost analogous with that of the overseas territories, but they could not be legally and formally associated with them because of the difference in their international status. Furthermore, they are under the supervision of a UN committee for mandated territories to which appeal may be made against the administration of the mandatory power.

General Organization

In addition to defining the different kinds of status for different territories, Section VIII of the Constitution sketched an embryonic over-all organization for the French Union. This was based in part on a representation of overseas territories in the metropolitan Parliament and in part on the creation of special bodies for the Union.

The representation of overseas territories in the Parliament in Paris is a traditional feature of the French Republic. Parliament in the Third Republic had overseas deputies and senators, although they were few: 9 deputies from Algeria and 10 from the colonies out of a total of 600; 3 senators from Algeria and 4 from the colonies out of a total of 300. The Constitution of 1946 established much higher proportions. Of 627 deputies in the National Assembly, 544 represented metropolitan France, and 83 (13 per cent) represented the overseas departments and territories (10 for the four departments of Guadeloupe, Martinique, Guiana, and Réunion, 30 for Algeria, 43 for the overseas territories proper). In the Council of the Republic, 246 members represented metropolitan France, 7 the departments of Guadeloupe, Martinique, Guiana, and Réunion, 14 Algeria, 44 the overseas and associated territories, 5 Tunisia, Morocco, and Indo-China. Thus 22 per cent of the members represented territories outside France. In spite of the increase, the overseas representation remained low in proportion to the population, since in contrast with the 43 million people of metropolitan France, the overseas population numbers approximately 50 million.

Representation differed widely from place to place. In the new departments of Guadeloupe, Martinique, Guiana, and Réunion there was universal suffrage with the same conditions as in France. Theoretically the same was true of Algeria, but women did not vote there. Elsewhere, although the law of May 7, 1946, known as the Lamine Gueye Law after its author, granted French citizenship to all persons born in the overseas territories, the right to vote remained restricted to certain categories of educated native citizens. In some territories natives and those of European origin voted together in a single electorate, while in others they voted separately, constituting two separate electoral colleges.

Section VIII of the Constitution provides for three institutions at the head of the French Union proper: the President of the Republic (who thus becomes the symbol of the unity of the whole French Union), the High Council of the Union, and the Assembly of the Union.

The President

The President of the Union is the President of the Republic. Following the British example, the head of state is supposed to symbolize the unity of the different parts of the French community. The Constitution does not define the powers of the President of the Union, and the spirit of the Constitution is such that these powers cannot be extensive. The very nature of the parliamentary regime prevents the head of state playing an effective part in government. Because he is not responsible to Parliament and because all his acts need the countersignature of both the Premier and a minister, who accept responsibility for them to Parliament, he cannot himself make decisions.

Despite these checks, the first President of the Fourth Republic, Vincent Auriol, took the initiative in regard to the Union. He personally intervened in the Vietnam question and especially in the Tunisian and Moroccan questions. He did not, in fact, hesitate to send his principal private secretary to get in touch directly on the spot with local leaders. With René Coty, the Presidency of the Union, like that of the Republic, has become less active.

The High Council

The High Council of the Union was intended to co-ordinate the actions of France and the semiautonomous associated states. Thus it was meant to be a body peculiar to one part of the French Union, whereas the other two institutions, the Presidency and the Assembly of the Union, were concerned with the whole. In the minds of its founders, the High Council was inspired by the example of the British Commonwealth Conference.

In practice, the High Council has scarcely functioned. Its first meeting was held in 1951, and it ceased to meet after 1954. This failure resulted from the fact that, with the exception of Vietnam, Laos, and Cambodia, the other states formerly under French protection have refused to accept the status of associated states. What is more, Vietnam and Cambodia later withdrew.

Assembly

Of the institutions set up under Section VIII for the whole of the Union, the Assembly is the most important and most interesting. It is made up half of representatives from metropolitan France, half of non-metropolitan representatives. Two-thirds of the metropolitan representatives are appointed by the metropolitan members of the National Assembly and one-third by the metropolitan members of the Council of the Republic, elected proportionally to the strength of the parliamentary groups. The system of election is that used for appointment of legislative committees. Most of the persons thus appointed are unfortunately politicians and not experts in overseas questions; generally they are individuals who have lost an election in metropolitan France. The representatives of the overseas territories are appointed in several different ways, usually by the general councils of the overseas departments or by the local assemblies in the territories. It was provided that the associated states should send representatives, but so far Morocco and Tunisia have not accepted.

The members of the French Union Assembly have a semiparliamentary status. They enjoy the same privileges, immunities, and salary as deputies and senators. The Assembly establishes its own procedure and verifies the credentials of its members in the same way as the National Assembly and the Council of the Republic. Its debates are public. But it meets only when summoned by the

President of the Union, who can call meetings, moreover, only while Parliament is sitting.

The powers of the Union Assembly are purely advisory. Its opinion must be sought, however, on the extension of French law by decree to overseas territories, on the preparation of decrees relating to the territories, on the definition of the status of each territory, and on the question of modifying statutes concerning members of the French Union. Yet there is no obligation to heed its advice. Governments of the associated states may also ask the views of the Assembly. Finally, the Union Assembly may itself pass resolutions and formulate proposals to be sent to the French government or to the High Council of the Union or else to the National Assembly.

There is a striking disparity between the powers and the recruitment of the Union Assembly. Aiming at the creation of a kind of federal body representing both France and all the other sections of French Union territory, the recruitment is quite novel; though the parity between metropolitan and non-metropolitan areas to some extent contravenes the principles of classical federalism, it corresponds to differences in political importance. The federal aspect is interesting in itself, for it may offer a possible solution to the problem of creating common institutions for the French "Commonwealth." Unfortunately, the Assembly of the French Union is almost powerless. Furthermore, great efforts have been made to undermine its prestige. For many years it was relegated to Versailles, on the pretext that there was no chamber available in Paris; not until 1956 was it established in the capital. It is fairly evident that Parliament feared it as a possible rival. Yet the Assembly of the French Union appears to be an institution with a future; it may foreshadow a kind of federal Parliament for the Union, invested with powers of decision. A Minister for Overseas France, Jacquinot, a conservative, proposed as early as 1945 that the Assembly be given the power to legislate within certain limits for overseas France.

CHANGES SINCE 1946

Section VIII of the Constitution has never been fully applied. Some of the provisions have remained stillborn; others have gradually been set aside for political reasons. There is unanimous agreement today that in this respect the Constitution should be revised. Revision will undoubtedly prove difficult, but it has already been going on in substance if not in form. The *loi-cadre* passed for overseas territories in 1956 and the decrees implementing it from 1957 onward are initiating a profound transformation of the French Union.

Obstacles to Section VIII

The application of Section VIII has encountered two kinds of difficulties: those created by French conservative circles and those created by the native peoples.

The status of associated states has proved the most difficult of all to apply. In Vietnam, after the tentative agreements of Fontaine-bleau in 1948, a civil war broke out which led finally to the Geneva agreements of 1954. Northern Vietnam, which had fallen under Communist domination, was officially detached from the French Union by the war; Southern Vietnam has subsequently drifted away of its own accord, but to a large extent under the influence of the United States. Cambodia and Laos alone accepted the status of associated states, only to reject it subsequently. In Tunisia and Morocco, local opposition was at first contained by a policy of repression. Tunisian ministers, for example, were arrested in 1952, and the Sultan of Morocco was deposed in 1953. Then, however, France entirely reversed her policy by signing agreements first with Tunisia and subsequently with Morocco. These agreements recognized the independence of the two countries but declared them attached to France by bonds of "interdependence." The conventions defining "interdependence" are still under negotiation, though particular points have been agreed upon and signed. Neither Tunisia nor Morocco has accepted the terms "associated state" and "French Union." Neither has sent representatives to the High Council of the Union or to the Union Assembly.

The second serious difficulty arose in Algeria. The 1947 statute which defined the extent of self-government in Algeria, while emphasizing the principle of gradual assimilation, has never been applied. Local conservatives are dead set against it. In 1955 armed rebellion broke out, and the fighting still continues. The problem in Algeria is more difficult to solve than the problem in Tunisia or Morocco, because Algeria has never been a state and because 1,200,000 French citizens are established there, some of whom are the third generation of settlers and consider themselves just as much Algerians as do the Moslems.

In the overseas territories the problem has not assumed so violent a form except in Madagascar, where a very violent rebellion, violently repressed, broke out in 1950. Elsewhere, after an upsurge of intense nationalism, local political leaders have preferred to use more cautious methods. They sought to obtain a large measure of self-government within the territories while formally accepting participation in the French Union or even integration into a French federal organization. The *loi-cadre* of June 23, 1956, marked a great step forward in this direction.

The Loi-cadre

In the overseas territories proper, that is, in the African territories other than Algeria, Tunisia, and Morocco, and in Madagascar, which together comprise the major part of the French Union, the law of June 23, 1956, and the decrees implementing it have accomplished a very considerable reform. It may even be called a veritable revolution. The *loi-cadre* prepares the way for a transformation of the overseas territories into autonomous states. The Cameroons have already received this status.

Before the *loi-cadre*, each territory had a governor appointed by France and a territorial assembly which passed the budget and functioned somewhat like a French departmental council. The fundamental innovation made by the law and the decrees applying it consists in creating alongside the governor a council of government which is, for all practical purposes, a real cabinet. In relation to it, the governor is intended gradually to play no more than the role of a head of state in a parliamentary system, that is, a very minor role.

Councils of government are made up of six to twelve members with the title of minister, and they are elected by the territorial assembly from among its members or outside. The council of government is not officially responsible to the assembly, but if it considers that it no longer enjoys the assembly's confidence, it may resign in its entirety, the principle of cabinet solidarity being accepted. In theory, after a vote of no confidence by the assembly, a council can remain in power. In practice, it obviously will not do so, and the system will develop toward parliamentary government.

The territorial assembly has power to decide on the establishment of public services and on budgetary and fiscal questions. It must give its opinion on the decrees proposed by the council of government for the organization of the public services, for economic and social questions, and for police regulations. It exercises a real measure of parliamentary control by means of observations and requests for information addressed to the council.

For this to become a real parliamentary system of government, the vice-president of the council of government would have to bear the title of prime minister. The governor would have to become no more than a head of state, without effective power. On these points, it is likely that there will be rapid progress. Furthermore, there is need for a revision of the line of demarcation between matters for which France is responsible and matters locally decided. Officially, the *loi-cadre* is treated as a simple measure of decentralization. Until it was passed, all services and administrative bodies functioning overseas were state organizations subject to the authority of Paris. Now only certain services, expressly enumerated, are retained within the jurisdiction of the government of France, and they are considered essential to the general interests of the republic. They are foreign affairs, defense and military affairs, courts of justice, inspection of working conditions, services concerned with safeguarding individual liberties and public security, external communications (aviation and radio), finance, credit and exchange, higher education, and semipublic companies. All other services are run by the territory, which has full power to decide on their organization and operation. The list of services still retained under the authority of Paris is long, but it may be expected to grow shorter.

The *loi-cadre* was passed under camouflage as one of the "measures of decentralization" because of the legal obstacle in the Constitution, which proclaims the republic to be "one and indivisible." Without saying as much, the law is a beginning in the establishment of federal institutions. Clearly, revision of the Constitution is now indispensable. There is still considerable opposition, but the French system seems to be evolving toward federalism.

CHAPTER 12

A BALANCE SHEET

Is the French political system, as we have described it, efficient or not? Does it allow France to solve the problems that face her? Opinion is almost unanimous in replying in the negative. Outside France, French political institutions are severely criticized. In France, judgment is often harsher still because of the critical turn of mind of the French. Running down their own institutions is one of the few points on which all Frenchmen, both Right and Left, agree.

The impartial observer must temper the harshness of these criticisms and judgments. In the first place, if we examine the efficiency of French institutions, not in the abstract and measured against some ideal system, but in comparison with other Western democratic systems, we have to admit that the latter are not very efficient either. There is a general crisis of democratic institutions, a general failure of adaptation to the problems they have to face. The crisis affecting French institutions is more serious and more acute, no doubt, but it is of the same kind.

Furthermore, certain current misconceptions concerning the defects of French institutions must be corrected. The most important relates to the instability of ministries. Contrary to opinion both inside and outside France, excessive stability rather than instability is one of the most serious defects in French politics.

Finally, though it is not yet clear what direction the necessary reform of French institutions will take, it does seem certain that reform will take place. The political system of a country always reflects in some degree its social structure. The structure of French society is at present being shaken from top to bottom by a demographic revolution, and this will inevitably have political consequences. The contemporary political system of France is a restoration of the system that operated between 1920 and 1930, which was

185

itself a reflection of an aging people. A nation that is being rejuvenated will burst the confines of this shell.

INSTABILITY OR IMMOBILITY?

French Cabinet crises make a great impression abroad. The fact that the average length of a ministry is about eight months under the Fourth Republic, as under the Third, creates an impression of considerable political instability. The impression is false. Frenchmen have a much clearer view of their institutions in this respect, and they have long ceased to attach much importance to Cabinet crises. French crises are something like waves on the sea, nothing more than a surface agitation which leaves the depths untroubled. As we have already noted, the fall of a government does not bring great change: first, because most of the defeated ministers generally reappear in the succeeding Cabinet, second, because the senior civil service is remarkably stable, and, third, because the new ministry generally executes the same policy as its predecessor.

In reality, the fundamental defect of French politics is exactly the opposite of what superficial observers diagnose. France suffers not from excessive instability but from excessive stability, from what has been called since 1953–54 "immobility." It is extremely difficult, not to say impossible, to effect any real change in particular institutions, although almost everyone is agreed on their defects. French political life is thus strewn with a series of unresolved problems—church schools, taxation, the alcohol industry, and so on—which are regularly discussed without any progress being made toward their solution. A nineteenth-century observer noted even then that in France revolutions can be made but not reforms. The statement is accurate. The main important reforms of the last fifty years owe their accomplishment to semirevolutionary situations, namely, World War I, the Popular Front of 1936, and the Liberation of 1944.

The causes of this immobility are not easy to define. No doubt one factor to be taken into account is the structure of public opinion itself. Division into five or six factions makes it very difficult to unite a majority in favor of reform. Two or three parties may reach an agreement on the maintenance of the status quo; they find it much more difficult to agree on a change. For the status quo is generally the result of an arduously achieved compromise between different factions of public opinion and has the force of habit. Definition of a new compromise is more often than not impossible.

No doubt, too, certain features of the French temperament have something to do with this immobility. The concept "national temperament" is extremely vague and extremely controversial, so that we introduce it here with some misgivings. Nonetheless, all observers, from Ernst-Robert Curtius to Herbert Lüthy, have remarked on the fundamental conservatism of the French and have rightly attributed it to the peasant ancestry of the majority of the population. The superiority of peasant life—and of peasant life in its most traditional form—still remains one of the fundamental myths for many Frenchmen even if they have never lived in the country and if their way of life is completely urbanized. The French revolutions of the nineteenth century were the work of the towns and of Paris in particular; as soon as universal suffrage gave the countryside the majority, it disavowed the disturbances of Paris in the Second Empire.

There is, however, a tendency to exaggerate the influence of these factors, particularly the second. Actually, one of the prime causes of immobility lies in the aging of the population and of politicians since 1920. Indeed, until 1914 the republic did not give the impression of instability; important reforms were accomplished with an extraordinary continuity of principle. Political sclerosis coincides with demographic sclerosis—with a decrease in the birth rate, with the disappearance of a generation wiped out by war, with a rise in the average age of the population.

Nor should there be any exaggeration of the extent of immobility in France. It has proved possible to carry out important reforms even at times other than those of semirevolutionary upheaval. They were effected slowly, however, by stages, in more or less indirect ways, and with a certain amount of camouflage in order not to arouse the opposition of political parties and public opinion. Consequently, they have been the less noticeable, with the result that often the benefits of the shock produced by change have been lost.

RELATIVE INEFFICIENCY

The efficiency of a regime is measured by its capacity to solve the problems posed by the march of events, by its capacity, that is, to meet "the challenge of history." How has the French political system met the problems that have faced it since the end of World War II? On the whole badly, in spite of some brilliant successes.

The failures are numerous and obvious. The failure to reform the system itself is perhaps the most serious. In the years 1944 to 1946 France missed the opportunity of effecting the political revolution which she needed so badly. After two constituent assemblies and three referendums, the entire apparatus of Third Republic institutions was restored, though for a quarter of a century they had been obviously ill adapted to modern needs. After the departure of General de Gaulle, the return of the old politicians aggravated the initial mistake. The 1954 pseudo-revision of the Constitution erred in the same sense, failing to deal with any of the fundamental problems. There is perpetual talk of institutional reform. The need is recognized. Nothing is done.

The church-school question has fared little better. The Barangé Law revived the old anticlerical dispute by giving private schools barely enough financial help to prevent them from disappearing. The state could do no more in view of the fact that its own schools are becoming increasingly less capable of admitting an ever-increasing number of children, as a result of the rise in the birth rate. No one has the courage to tackle wholeheartedly a problem that would be technically easy to solve. Nor does anyone dare to face the inescapable need for changes in syllabuses and methods of teaching to adapt them to the requirements of the twentieth century and to remedy the lack of scientists. Educational reforms which have been under discussion for ten years are continually being wrecked on parliamentary rocks.

The question of taxation fares no better. The peasants continue not to pay direct taxes and, in all good faith, to consider themselves ground down by taxation. Small traders and artisans are subjected to harassment by the administration but enjoy fiscal privileges of which they too are no longer conscious. Ultimately, the real weight of income tax falls upon the salaried classes, that is, the technical experts, and upon big business. This hampers economic progress. It is true, however, that an important reform has been achieved by the introduction of a progressive income tax and a capital gains tax.

The housing problem has not been settled either. An absurd rent law gradually brought private building to a stop between 1919 and 1939. After World War II the state had to intervene with a system of bonuses and subsidies to make up for the inadequacy of private enterprise. This considerable financial effort primarily favored the construction of luxury and semiluxury homes for the middle classes. The poorer classes, who are most affected by the shortage, received much less help.

All these problems may seem unimportant in comparison with the fundamental problem that has faced France for the last ten years: the colonial problem. The war in Indo-China tragically illustrated the incapacity of the regime. The best specialists and the best officers in the army were sacrificed in a bloody war that lasted eight years and could not be won. The man who had the courage to bring to an end a venture that he had always deplored, Pierre Mendès-France, found himself held responsible by a large section of French public opinion for the loss of French influence in Indo-China. The war in Algeria has revealed the same military courage and the same political incapacity.

Nonetheless, there is a credit side to "decolonization." After the grant of independence to Tunisia and Morocco, the relations of those countries with France improved, although recent incidents in the Algerian war have caused hard feelings. The 1956 *loi-cadre*, in particular, has opened the way for developments which permit the simultaneous emergence of local nationalism and a kind of French "Commonwealth." That the nationalist parties in French Africa should today be united in agreement on the principle of union with France is evidence of their realism; but it is also evidence of the realism of France and of the efficiency in this respect of her institutions. This is a considerable victory.

The reconstruction of the railways and roads as well as the rebuilding of industry after the war is another victory. In spite of pressure from a public hungry for consumer goods after the privations of war and occupation, the government succeeded in maintaining priority for productive investments and for the reconstruction of industry, thanks to a moderate policy of economic planning. It thus laid the foundations for economic expansion.

The expansion itself may be considered one of the achievements of the regime. Less spectacular than German expansion, it faced different obstacles. Between 1919 and 1939 the French economy had become static and regressive. The postwar efforts made by the government in investment and in the encouragement and aiding of private enterprise changed the situation. There are no doubt many backward sectors in the French economy—especially agriculture and retail trading—and the state does often give protection to these backward sectors under the pressure of private interests. Nonetheless, it has exercised a beneficial and powerful influence on the economy as a whole.

Successes can be noted also in matters apparently of minor though really of major importance. Examples include the achievement in 1956 of a reform in budgetary procedure which effected a radical cure for the delays and disorders that had been the rule for half a century and the development in national finance of what are probably the most up-to-date methods of accountancy in the world. These examples show that French political institutions are not so inefficient as is thought. Nonetheless, the over-all balance of domestic matters remains largely in deficit.

The inefficiency of French institutions in diplomatic matters has been just as great. The "Great Power" policy of 1944–46 was as uncertain in aims as it was fumbling in methods. Within the NATO organization, France has never yet succeeded in defining her position clearly; the veiled reluctance of public opinion to accept United States leadership goes hand in hand with the docility of statesmen beset by financial needs. On the question of European union, incoherence reached new heights; France invented the European Defense Community, then rejected it, only to adopt immediately thereafter the principle of western European union. In relation to the Middle East, where French cultural influence is so great, no realistic policy has yet been formulated. There, however, the structure of political institutions is not the only factor: a country's decline from the status of first-class power to the status of second-class power raises extremely difficult questions of adjustment.

THE DEMOGRAPHIC REVOLUTION

No fundamental reform of French institutions appears imminent. Although some bold spirits are beginning to climb out of the rut, and although the press campaign conducted in the spring of 1956 on the merits of the presidential regime, by university teachers of such different views as Georges Vedel and the author, created some stir in political circles, there is no real chance of seeing Parliament adopt a major reform of the Constitution. Yet it is becoming increasingly doubtful whether the French political regime can continue to function very much longer on its traditional lines. For a ground swell is causing an upheaval in French society and must inevitably have its effect on French institutions. This is the demographic revolution.

On the eve of World War II France had entered on a demographic decline. The birth rate, falling regularly since 1900, had slumped from 1930 onward to such an extent that the falling death rate was inadequate to compensate for it. After 1934 the number of deaths was regularly higher than the number of births. Since 1946, on the contrary, the population of France has maintained a uniform rate of increase of approximately 0.6 per cent per year, that is, from 250,000 to 300,000 persons annually. This results less from a fall in the death rate, which has remained steady, than to a marked increase in the birth rate. The age ratios are changing: the proportion of young people is increasing and that of the old diminishing. The direct effects of this change will not be felt in politics for another ten years. Already, however, the rush of children is creating all kinds of material problems which must be solved and is making it necessary to think more definitely in terms of the future.

In addition to the postwar demographic revolution, another phenomenon is already having some effect. This is the arrival in positions of responsibility of the post-1914 generations. The most profound cause for the decline of France between the wars lay undoubtedly in the monstrous "blood-letting" of 1914–18: one and a half million dead, several million wounded, and all in the flower of their youth. Practically a whole generation was sacrificed, the generation that should have governed between the wars. This explains the scarcity of good leaders in every walk of life during that critical period.

It explains too the cleavage between the pre-1914 and later generations. The division of France into static and dynamic is not only geographical; it is also, and perhaps more, a question of age. In politics, in the senior civil service, in the army, in the university, in the fields of technology, management, and even agriculture, the fact strikes the eye. It is not a question, as in ordinary circumstances, of the natural replacement of the old by the young. The new generation which is now taking over the reins of power rejects the habits, the style, and the myths of the earlier generation.

It is not yet possible to say what direction this transformation of political institutions will take, but it is difficult to believe that none will take place. Different though they were in trend, the Mendès-France episode of 1954–55 and the wave of nationalism of 1956–57 may well, in some respects, be viewed as the first political consequences of the demographic upheaval. Both represent a reaction against parliamentary delays, against traditional methods. Different though it may be from that of Mendès-France, the style of Mollet and Lacoste is equally different from the style of the Third Republic, to which the Fourth Republic had remained faithful.

This means that the foreseeable political changes will have their risks: some indications, slight as yet, of a movement toward dictatorship have been observed as a result of the war in Algeria. The mass of French people, however, remains deeply attached to freedom and democracy. The new generations now assuming responsibility remember the Nazi Occupation and the Resistance movement.

APPENDIXES

LOCAL ELECTIONS AND REFERENDUMS

LOCAL ELECTIONS

Different electoral systems are used for the department, the commune, and the overseas territories. Every *department* elects a General Council by the single-member, simple-majority system with second ballot, each canton in the department sending one member to the Council. An absolute majority is required to win the first ballot; if no candidate obtains such a majority and therefore a second ballot must be cast, a plurality is sufficient to win.

Every *commune* elects a Municipal Council. Under the Third Republic the electoral system was simple-majority list-voting with second ballot and unrestricted cross-voting. On the first ballot, all candidates obtaining an absolute majority were elected regardless of the list to which they belonged. On the second ballot, candidates with the highest number of votes, whether they obtained an absolute majority or not, were elected regardless of the list to which they belonged.

The law of September 5, 1947, changed this traditional system in the large communes. The old system continues to operate in communes of not more than 9,000 inhabitants. But in communes with more than 9,000 inhabitants and in all communes in the Department of the Seine except Paris, elections are held on a system of proportional representation with list-voting and distribution of remainders by highest average. Theoretically, cross-voting and preferential voting are possible, but, as in national elections, the privilege is little used.

In view of their political importance as well as their part in the revolutions of the eighteenth and nineteenth centuries, a special system has been accorded to Paris and Seine. The Municipal Council of Paris is made up of ninety members elected by proportional representation with distribution of remainders according to the highest average. There are nine electoral districts which vote separately. The General Council of Seine is made up of the ninety municipal councillors together with sixty councillors elected by the cantons in the Seine suburbs under the same conditions as the municipal councillors.

Territorial Assemblies

The decrees of 1957 increasing the powers of the assemblies in overseas territories and turning them into minor local parliaments unified the electoral system. Henceforth, all *territorial assemblies* are to be elected on the simple-majority, single-ballot, fixed-list system without cross-voting or preferential voting. This electoral system, which is comparatively rare, operates in Turkey. It has the disadvantage of allowing one list to be elected in its entirety if it heads the poll although the total votes cast for all other lists may be greatly superior. In the long run the system has the advantage of preventing the multiplication of parties. It tends to create a few large and well-organized parties and in practice leads to the two-party system. Its adoption in the overseas territories was designed to foster the development of strong political parties as a mainstay of local institutions.

REFERENDUMS

There has never been any considerable development in France of direct democracy such as exists, for example, in Switzerland. French political tradition holds that Parliament is the repository of national sovereignty, and the tradition does not favor the direct participation of citizens in affairs by means of referendums or popular action. Moreover, the Bonapartes developed the so-called theory of the "appeal to the nation," which provided that the head of state might directly address the country, thus bypassing Parliament. This theory turned the referendum into a weapon against Parliament, and it contributed to the discrediting of the referendum in the eyes of French democrats. The referendum does, however, play a part in constitution-making.

The Constituent Referendum

Several French constitutions have been submitted by referendum to the people before being applied, as, for example, the Constitution of 1791 and that of 1852 with its subsequent modifications. The Constitution of 1946 was also submitted to a referendum. Furthermore, it was drawn up according to a method that had previously been approved by a referendum of the electorate.

In October, 1945, while the General Election was being held, the voters were asked to declare themselves on two questions. First, was the Constitution of 1875 (suspended during the German occupation and the Vichy regime) to be restored, or should a new constitution be drawn up? In the former case, the National Assembly that was then being elected would be the Chamber of Deputies as specified in the Constitution of 1875; in the latter, it would become a Constituent Assembly. Second, if the electorate wanted a new constitution, was the Constituent Assembly charged with drafting it to have unlimited powers and duration in accordance with tradition, or were its duration and its powers to be regulated on the basis of the draft bill that was printed on the back of the voting card? The voters decided in favor of a Constituent Assembly with restricted powers.

The Assembly, regulated by the referendum, drafted a constitutional bill which was itself submitted to a referendum on May 5, 1946. For the first time in French history, the people rejected the draft constitution submitted to them (for, 9,454,034; against, 10,584,359; abstained, 5,262,043). A second Constituent Assembly was therefore elected. It drafted the Constitution of 1946, which, submitted to a referendum on October 13, was adopted by a very narrow majority (for, 9,297,470; against, 8,165,459; abstained, 8,519,635).

This Constitution itself gives some place to the referendum in the machinery of constitutional revision. However, there was no desire to extend its use, which is an indication of the distrust of the referendum already referred to. The distrust was increased by the fact that the referendum raises difficult questions concerning the part to be played by the overseas territories. In theory, any proposal for revision voted by Parliament should be submitted to referendum; but there is no need for a referendum if the proposal for revision has been adopted by a three-fifths majority in each of the houses or if it has been adopted by a two-thirds majority of the National Assembly alone on second reading. At the time of the 1954 revision, efforts were made to achieve these majorities in order to avoid a referendum; they were successful. A referendum is compulsory if the revision concerns the existence of the Council of the Republic; it was not thought fit that the upper house could be suppressed by the lower house without the nation being consulted.

The "Consultative" Referendum

The Constitution makes no provision for the use of a referendum in matters of legislation or general policy. It has sometimes been suggested that the referendum might be employed to decide such difficult issues as the European Defense Community or the problem of subsidies for church schools. Such proposals have never come to anything and have little chance of doing so in view of Parliament's suspicion of any procedure tending to weaken its powers.

In any case, this kind of procedure could be no more than a "consultative" referendum, inviting the people to express an opinion but not to make a decision. The results of the referendum would help to enlighten Parliament but could not impose any direction upon its policy. The Constitution in fact states that national sovereignty resides in Parliament alone. The example of the 1950 referendum in Belgium on the question of the throne and the use of the referendum in Australia show that such referendums are not impossible.

THE ORGANIZATION OF THE JUDICIARY

The main lines of the French judicial system were laid down by Napoleon I. The Revolution of 1789 had first instituted the election of judges, but the system did not produce good results and could not do so in such troubled times. Napoleon preferred nominated judges, whom he sought, however, to render independent of the government by making them irremovable. At the same time, he attempted to protect the administration from the interference of the judiciary, while safeguarding the interests of the administered.

COURTS

A fundamental feature of the French system is that there are two kinds of courts dealing with different kinds of cases. If the case concerns two private individuals or concerns a criminal prosecution, it is heard by a judicial court. The judicial courts are as follows: *Juges de paix* (justices of the peace) for minor matters; *Tribunaux civils de première instance* (civil courts of first instance) for more serious questions; and *Cours d'appel* (courts of appeal) for reviewing decisions of the lower courts. In penal cases, the *Juge de paix* deals with misdemeanors, the *Tribunaux correctionnels* (criminal courts) with more serious cases, and the *Cours d'assises* (superior courts) with grave breaches of the law. In the superior courts the verdict is given by a jury of citizens chosen by lot. Above all judicial courts there is the *Cour de cassation* (supreme court of appeal) to which appeal may be made from the judgment of any lower court on a point of law. The *Cour de cassation* does not reconsider the substance of the case. There also exist commercial courts and courts dealing with professional matters: *Conseils des prud'hommes* (courts of conciliation) for disputes between employers and employees. *Tribunaux des baux ruraux* (land tenure courts) for rent and tenancy questions.

When the parties to a lawsuit are a private individual and a branch of the administration (state, department, commune, and so on), the case falls outside the province of the judicial courts and is heard by the *Tribunaux administratifs de première instance* (administrative courts of first instance), which were known until the reform of 1954 as *Conseils de préfecture* (prefectural courts), and over them the Council of State. The existence of these courts is explained historically by the fact that before 1789 judicial courts were always intervening in administrative matters and upsetting the operation of the system. To avoid this, special courts were created to deal with litigation involving the administration. This system could have endangered the rights of citizens, which the administrative courts mght have failed to recognize. But in practice the Council of State, which deals directly with the more important cases and hears others on appeal, has, as already noted, proved most independent. The system of administrative courts has given to the individual greater guaranties than he would have had from judicial courts, because judges there are sometimes less independent of authority.

It is to be noted that the administrative courts usually try cases in the absence of precise rules, of which there are very few. Consequently, they apply legal principles with great flexibility. The administrative courts of first instance were, however, long open to criticism with regard to the professional competence and independence of their members. This was not serious, since the majority of their judgments were taken on appeal to the Council of State. It was to relieve the Council of State that the reform of 1954 extended the jurisdiction of the administrative courts and attempted to improve their organization.

The existence of the Council of State is, as we have seen, a feature peculiar to the French system. It is a curious body in that its members are not only administrative judges and senior civil servants advising the government on the drafting of decrees but also form a kind of nursery from which are recruited the highest officials in the administrative services.

JUDGES

The judges of administrative courts are civil servants in status; the only officially designated judges are those of the judiciary, and to them we shall confine our remarks.

Judges are recruited by a special competitive system in which the panel is made up by the judges themselves, and the procedure guarantees impartiality. Napoleon sought to give judges independence by the additional guaranty of life tenure. The significance of this is that judges may not be dismissed, suspended, or transferred by a decision of the government. Discipline was in the hands of the *Cour de cassation*. In practice, this safeguard proved less effective than might be expected. Because there are very many grades in the hierarchy and thus possibly a great difference in situation between the judge rapidly promoted and the judge who slowly moves up on seniority, there were considerable incentives to be in favor with the authorities.

The Constitution of 1946, however, confirmed the Napoleonic principle of life tenure and created the Supreme Council of the Judiciary. This step has partially remedied the situation. Only the Supreme Council can now dismiss, suspend, or transfer magistrates. Moreover, responsibility for the promotion of judges now rests with the Supreme Council, which is composed of elected delegates. And, as we have seen, the Supreme Council is in favor of the independence of the judiciary. In spite of this, the multiple ranks in the hierarchy and the low initial salaries produce considerable competition for promotion, and such a situation is always prejudicial to true independence. Furthermore, the magistrates attached to the Public Prosecutor's office still depend for their promotion on the Minister of Justice—a political figure.

TEXT OF THE CONSTITUTION

CONSTITUTION

OF THE

FRENCH REPUBLIC

As amended on December 7, 1954

PREAMBLE

On the morrow of the victory gained by the free peoples over the regimes which have attempted to enslave and degrade the human person, the French people proclaim anew that every human being, without distinction of race, religion, or belief, possesses inalienable and sacred rights. They solemnly reaffirm the rights and freedoms of man and citizen as enshrined in the Declaration of Rights of 1789 and the fundamental principles recognized by the laws of the Republic.

In addition, they proclaim as particularly necessary in our time the following political, economic, and social principles:

The law guarantees to women, in all spheres, rights equal to those of men.

Any person persecuted by reason of his activity in furtherance of freedom has the right of asylum on the territories of the Republic.

It is the duty of all to work and the right of all to obtain employment. None shall be allowed to suffer wrong in his work or employment by reason of his origin, opinions, or beliefs.

Every man may protect his rights and interests by trade-union action and belong to the union of his choice.

The right to strike is exercised within the framework of the laws which govern it.

Each worker participates, through his delegates, in the collective settlement of working conditions as well as in the management of enterprises.

Any property, any undertaking, which possesses or acquires the character of a public service or of a *de facto* monopoly must come under collective ownership.

The nation guarantees to the individual and to the family conditions necessary to their development.

It guarantees to all—especially to children, mothers, and elderly workers

—the safeguarding of their health, material security, rest, and leisure. Every human being who is unable to work because of his age, of his physical or mental condition, or of his economic situation is entitled to obtain from the community the appropriate means of existence.

The nation proclaims the solidarity and equality of all Frenchmen in respect of the burdens imposed by national disasters.

The nation guarantees to children and adults alike equality of access to education, to professional training, and to general culture. It is the duty of the state to organize free and secular public education at all levels.

The French Republic, faithful to its traditions, conforms to the rules of public international law. It will undertake no war for the object of conquest and will never employ its forces against the liberty of any people.

On condition of reciprocity, France will accept those limitations of her sovereignty which are necessary for the organization and defense of peace.

France, together with the overseas peoples, forms a Union founded upon equality of rights and of duties, without distinction of race or religion.

The French Union is composed of nations and peoples who pool or coordinate their resources and their efforts to develop their respective civilizations, to increase their well-being, and to insure their security.

Faithful to her traditional mission, France proposes to lead the peoples of whom she has assumed charge to a state of freedom in which they administer themselves and conduct their own affairs democratically; rejecting any form of colonial rule based upon arbitrary power, she guarantees to all equal access to the public service and the individual or collective exercise of the rights and liberties proclaimed or confirmed above.

THE INSTITUTIONS OF THE REPUBLIC

Section I

SOVEREIGNTY

Article 1

France is a republic, indivisible, secular, democratic, and social.

Article 2

The national emblem is the tricolor flag—blue, white, and red, in three vertical stripes of equal size.

The national anthem is the "Marseillaise."

The motto of the Republic is: "Liberty, Equality, Fraternity."

Its principle is: government of the people, for the people, by the people.

Article 3

National sovereignty belongs to the French people.

No section of the people or any individual may assume the exercise thereof.

In constitutional matters, it is exercised by the people through their representatives and by way of referendum.

In all other matters, it is exercised by the people through their deputies to the National Assembly, elected by universal suffrage, equal, direct, and secret.

Article 4

Within the conditions laid down by law, all French citizens and nationals of both sexes, who have attained their majority and enjoy civil and political rights, have the right to vote.

Section II

PARLIAMENT

Article 5

Parliament consists of the National Assembly and of the Council of the Republic.

Article 6

The duration of the mandate of each Assembly, its mode of election, the conditions of eligibility, and those governing ineligibility and incompatibility are fixed by law.

However, both chambers are elected on a territorial basis, the National Assembly by direct universal suffrage, the Council of the Republic by communal and departmental collectivities by indirect universal suffrage. The Council of the Republic is renewable by halves.

Nevertheless, the National Assembly can itself, by proportional representation, elect councillors the number of whom may not exceed a sixth of the total number of the members of the Council of the Republic.

The number of the members of the Council of the Republic may not be less than 250, or more than 320.

Article 7

War cannot be declared without a vote of the National Assembly and the previous advice of the Council of the Republic.

The law lays down the conditions under which a state of siege is proclaimed.

Article 8

Each of the two chambers is the arbiter of the eligibility of its members and of the validity of their election; the chamber alone can accept their resignation.

Article 9

The National Assembly meets, of right, in ordinary session on the first Tuesday in October.

When this session has lasted at least seven months, the President of the Council of Ministers can close it by means of a decree issued in accord with the Council of Ministers. This period of seven months does not include interruptions of the session. Adjournments of more than eight "clear" days are considered as interruptions of the session.[1]

The Council of the Republic sits at the same time as the National Assembly.

[1] [The 1946 text read as follows: "The National Assembly meets in annual session, in full exercise of its rights, on the second Tuesday in January.

"The total length of interruptions of the session cannot exceed four months. Adjournments of meetings lasting more than ten days are considered as interruptions of the session."]

Article 10

The meetings of the two chambers are public. Verbatim reports of debates and parliamentary documents are published in the *Journal Officiel*. Each chamber may meet in secret session.

Article 11

Both chambers elect their *bureaux* every year at the beginning of the ordinary session and in accordance with the conditions laid down in their rules of procedure.

When the two chambers assemble to elect the President of the Republic, their *bureau* is that of the National Assembly.

Article 12

When the National Assembly is not sitting, its *bureau* may convene Parliament for an extraordinary session; the President of the National Assembly must do so when requested by the President of the Council of Ministers or by the majority of the members of the National Assembly.

The President of the Council closes an extraordinary session in the manner prescribed by Article 9.

When an extraordinary session is held at the request of the majority of the National Assembly or of its *bureau*, the decree of closure cannot be issued until Parliament has completed its discussion of the specific agenda for which it has been convened.[2]

Article 13

The National Assembly alone has the right to legislate. It cannot delegate this right.

Article 14

The President of the Council of Ministers and the members of Parliament have the right to initiate legislation.

Government bills are laid before the *bureau* of the National Assembly or of the Council of the Republic. However, bills relating to the ratification of treaties covered by Article 27, budgetary or finance bills, and bills involving reduction in revenue or the initiation of expenditure must be laid before the *bureau* of the National Assembly.

Bills introduced by members of Parliament are laid before the *bureau* of the chamber to which they belong and, after adoption, are transmitted to the other chamber. If bills introduced by members of the Council of the Republic entail a reduction in revenue or the initiation of expenditure, they are not admissible.[3]

[2] [The 1946 text read: "When the Assembly is not sitting, the *bureau*, controlling the acts of the Cabinet, can convene Parliament; it must do so at the request of a third of the deputies or of the President of the Council of Ministers."]

[3] [The 1946 text read: "Government bills and bills drawn up by members of the National Assembly are laid before the latter's *bureau*.

"Bills drawn up by members of the Council of the Republic are laid before the latter's *bureau* and forwarded without discussion to the *bureau* of the National Assembly."]

Article 15

The National Assembly examines government bills and members' bills, which are submitted to it, through committees of which it fixes the number, the composition, and the powers.

Article 16

The draft budget is submitted to the National Assembly. The draft may contain only financial provisions. An organic law shall fix the mode of presentation of the budget.

Article 17

The deputies to the National Assembly have the right to initiate expenditure.

However, no proposal entailing an increase in the expenditure forecast or additional expenditure may be submitted during the discussion of the budget or of anticipated and supplementary credits.

Article 18

The National Assembly settles the nation's accounts. In this matter, it is assisted by the *Cour des Comptes*. The National Assembly can intrust the *Cour des Comptes* with the carrying out of any investigation or inquiry relating to the revenue and expenditure of the state or to the administration of the treasury.

Article 19

Amnesty can be granted only by a law.

Article 20

All government or members' bills are examined by both chambers in turn, in order to secure the adoption of an identical text.

Unless the Council of the Republic has given a government or member's bill a first reading, it must give its decision at the latest within two months from the forwarding of the text adopted, at its first reading, by the National Assembly.

With regard to budgetary texts and the finance bill, the time taken by the Council of the Republic must not exceed the time previously taken by the National Assembly to examine the bill and to vote upon it. When the National Assembly states that the procedure of urgent discussion is to be applied, the time limit is twice that laid down for the debates of the National Assembly by the latter's rules.

If the Council of the Republic has not given its decision within the time limits fixed by the preceding paragraphs, the bill can be promulgated as voted by the National Assembly.

If agreement has not been reached, both chambers continue to study the bill. After two readings by the Council of the Republic, each chamber has at its disposal, for that purpose, the period of time taken by the other chamber for the previous reading, and this period of time may not be less than seven days, or one day for the texts covered by paragraph three.

When no agreement has been reached within a time limit of a hundred days from the forwarding of the bill to the Council of the Republic for its second reading—the time limit being reduced to one month in the case of budgetary texts and the finance bill, and to fifteen days in cases where the procedure relating to matters of urgency is applicable—the National Assembly can take a final decision by adopting the latest text it has itself voted or by altering it to include one or several of the amendments proposed by the Council of the Republic.

If the National Assembly exceeds or extends the time at its disposal for the examination of a bill, the time limit for the agreement of both chambers is correspondingly increased.

The time limits provided for under the present article are suspended during interruptions of the session. They may be extended by decision of the National Assembly.[4]

Article 21

No member of Parliament can be prosecuted, sought out, arrested, detained, or brought to trial by reason of opinions expressed or votes cast by him in the exercise of his functions.

Article 22

No member of Parliament can, during session, be prosecuted or arrested for a crime or a misdemeanor without the permission of the chamber to which he belongs, unless he is caught in the act. Any member of Parliament arrested when Parliament is not in session can vote by proxy for such time as the chamber to which he belongs has not taken a decision regarding the suspension of his parliamentary immunity. If it has not taken any decision within thirty days from the opening of the session, the arrested member of Parliament will be freed, of right. When Parliament is not in session, no member of Parliament can be arrested without the authorization of the *bureau* of the chamber to which he belongs, unless he has been caught in the act, unless his prosecution has been authorized, or unless he has been

---

[4] [The 1946 text read: "The Council of the Republic examines and gives its opinion upon government or members' bills voted after a first reading by the National Assembly.

"It gives its opinion at the latest two months after the law has been forwarded by the National Assembly. When the budget is under discussion, this time limit may, if necessary, be shortened, so as not to exceed the time used by the National Assembly for its examination and vote. When the National Assembly has decided upon a procedure of urgency, the Council of the Republic gives its opinion in the same time limit as that laid down for the debates of the National Assembly in the latter's rules. The time limits mentioned here are not applied during interruptions of the session. They may be lengthened by decision of the National Assembly.

"If the opinion of the Council of the Republic is favorable, or if it has not been given within the time limits set forth in the preceding paragraph, the law is passed as voted by the National Assembly.

"If the opinion of the Council is not favorable, the government bill or member's bill is given a second reading by the National Assembly. It decides finally, and in all sovereignty, upon the amendments proposed by the Council of the Republic, accepting or rejecting them, in whole or in part. In the case of total or partial rejection of these amendments, the vote following the second reading of the bill is decided by public ballot, by an absolute majority of the members of the National Assembly, when the vote on the whole has been taken under the same conditions by the Council of the Republic."]

finally convicted. The detention or prosecution of a member of Parliament is suspended if the chamber to which he belongs so demands.

Article 23

Members of Parliament receive an indemnity fixed in relation to the remuneration of a category of civil servants.

Article 24

No one can belong both to the National Assembly and to the Council of the Republic.

Members of Parliament can belong neither to the Economic Council nor to the Assembly of the French Union.

Section III

THE ECONOMIC COUNCIL

Article 25

An Economic Council, whose status is fixed by law, examines, in an advisory capacity, government and members' bills which are within its province. These bills are submitted to it by the National Assembly before the latter debates them.

In addition, the Economic Council can be consulted by the Council of Ministers. It must be consulted on the establishment of a national economic plan, the object of which is the full employment of men and the rational use of material resources.

Section IV

DIPLOMATIC TREATIES

Article 26

Diplomatic treaties regularly ratified and published have force of law, even in cases where they might be contrary to certain internal French laws, and their implementation calls for no legislative measures other than those required for their ratification.

Article 27

Treaties relating to international organizations, peace treaties, commercial treaties, and treaties which involve the finances of the state, those which concern the personal status and the property rights of French citizens abroad, those which affect internal French laws, and those which carry with them the cession, exchange, or acquisition of territory are final only after having been ratified by a law.

No cession, exchange, or acquisition of territory is valid without the consent of the population concerned.

Article 28

Diplomatic treaties which have been ratified and published and have priority over internal laws can be neither abrogated nor amended nor suspended without a regular repudiation through diplomatic channels. When it is one of the treaties covered by Article 27, its repudiation must be authorized by the National Assembly, an exception being made in the case of commercial treaties.

Section V

THE PRESIDENT OF THE REPUBLIC

Article 29

The President of the Republic is elected by Parliament. He is elected for seven years. He is re-eligible once only.

Article 30

The President of the Republic appoints, in the Council of Ministers, the members of the Council of State, the Grand Chancellor of the Legion of Honor, ambassadors and envoys extraordinary, the members of the Higher Council and of the Committee of National Defense, rectors of universities, prefects, the directors of the civil service, generals, and the representatives of the government in overseas territories.

Article 31

The President of the Republic is kept informed of international negotiations. He signs and ratifies treaties.

The President of the Republic accredits ambassadors and envoys extraordinary to foreign powers; foreign ambassadors and envoys extraordinary are accredited to him.

Article 32

The President of the Republic presides over the Council of Ministers. He sees that minutes of the meetings are kept and is responsible for their preservation.

Article 33

The President of the Republic presides over, with the same powers, the Higher Council and the Committee of National Defense, and assumes the title Head of the Armies.

Article 34

The President of the Republic presides over the Supreme Council of the Judiciary.

Article 35

The President of the Republic exercises in the Supreme Council of the Judiciary the right of reprieve.

Article 36

The President of the Republic promulgates laws within ten days of their transmission to the government after their final adoption. This time limit is reduced to five days in cases of urgency declared by the National Assembly.

Within the time limit fixed for promulgation, the President of the Republic can, in a message stating his grounds, ask the two chambers for another debate, which cannot be refused.

Failing the promulgation of laws by the President of the Republic within the time limits prescribed by this Constitution, promulgation is effected by the President of the National Assembly.

Article 37

The President of the Republic communicates with Parliament by means of messages to the National Assembly.

Article 38

All the acts of the President of the Republic must be countersigned by the President of the Council of Ministers and by a Minister.

Article 39

Not more than thirty days and not less than fifteen days before the expiration of the term of the President of the Republic, Parliament proceeds to elect a new President.

Article 40

If, in application of the preceding article, the election has to take place during a period when the National Assembly is dissolved in conformity with Article 51, the powers of the President of the Republic are extended until the election of the new President. Parliament proceeds to elect this new President within ten days of the election of the new National Assembly.

In this case, the appointment of the President of the Council of Ministers takes place within the fifteen days following the election of the new President of the Republic.

Article 41

If circumstances duly recognized by a vote of Parliament prevent the President from exercising his office, if the Presidency is vacated by death, resignation, or any other reason, the President of the National Assembly assumes temporarily the functions of the President of the Republic. He himself is replaced by a Vice-President.

The new President of the Republic is elected within ten days except in cases where the provisions of the preceding article apply.

Article 42

The President of the Republic is answerable only to a charge of high treason. He can be impeached by the National Assembly and sent before the High Court of Justice under the conditions set forth in Article 57 hereunder.

Article 43

The duties of the President of the Republic are incompatible with any other public office.

Article 44

Members of families which have reigned over France are ineligible for the Presidency of the Republic.

Section VI

THE COUNCIL OF MINISTERS

Article 45

At the beginning of each legislature, the President of the Republic, after the usual consultations, appoints the President of the Council.

The latter selects the members of his Cabinet and sends a list of them to the National Assembly, before which he presents himself in order to obtain its confidence with regard to the program and to the policy which he intends to adopt, except when the National Assembly is prevented from meeting by circumstances beyond its control.

The vote is taken by open ballot and on a simple majority.

The same applies, in the course of the legislature, if the office of the President of the Council of Ministers is vacant, except in the cases described in Article 52.

Article 51 does not apply in the case of a Cabinet crisis occurring within fifteen days of the appointment of the Ministers.[5]

Article 46

The President of the Council and the Ministers chosen by him are appointed by a decree of the President of the Republic.

Article 47

The President of the Council of Ministers insures the carrying out of laws.

He makes appointments to all civilian and military posts except those mentioned in Articles 30, 46, and 84.

The President of the Council controls the armed forces and co-ordinates the work of national defense.

The acts of the President of the Council of Ministers provided for in this article are countersigned by the Ministers concerned.

Article 48

The Ministers are collectively responsible to the National Assembly for the general policy of the Cabinet, and individually for their personal actions.

They are not responsible to the Council of the Republic.

Article 49

The question of confidence cannot be raised except after a discussion by the Council of Ministers; it can be raised only by the President of the Council.

A vote on a question of confidence cannot take place less than twenty-four hours after the question has been put to the Assembly.[6] It is taken by open ballot.

Confidence is withheld from the Cabinet by an absolute majority of the deputies to the Assembly. Refusal entails the collective resignation of the Cabinet.

[5] [The 1946 text read: "At the beginning of each legislature, the President of the Republic, after the usual consultations, appoints the President of the Council.

"The latter submits to the National Assembly the program and policy of the Cabinet which he intends to form.

"The President of the Council and the Ministers can be appointed only after the President of the Council has been granted the confidence of the Assembly by public vote and an absolute majority of the deputies, except when the National Assembly is prevented from meeting by circumstances beyond its control."]

[6] [The effect of the 1954 revision was to substitute "twenty-four hours" for "one clear day."]

Article 50

A vote of censure by the National Assembly entails the collective resignation of the Cabinet.

A vote on a motion of censure takes place in the same conditions and in the same manner as a vote on a question of confidence.

A vote of censure can be adopted only by an absolute majority of the deputies to the Assembly.

Article 51

If, within a period of eighteen months, two Cabinet crises occur under the conditions set forth in Articles 49 and 50, the dissolution of the National Assembly may be decided upon by the Council of Ministers, after consultation with the President of the Assembly. The dissolution will be pronounced, in conformity with this decision, by a decree of the President of the Republic.

The provisions of the above paragraph are applicable only after the expiration of the first eighteen months of the legislature.

Article 52

In case of dissolution, the Cabinet remains in office.

However, if dissolution has been preceded by the adoption of a motion of censure, the President of the Republic appoints the President of the National Assembly as President of the Council and Minister of the Interior.

General elections take place at least twenty days and at most thirty days after the dissolution.

The National Assembly convenes, of right, on the third Thursday following its election.[7]

Article 53

The Ministers have access to both chambers and to their committees. They must be heard when they so request.

They may be assisted in debates before the chambers by commissioners appointed by decree.

Article 54

The President of the Council of Ministers may delegate his powers to a Minister.

Article 55

If the Presidency of the Council of Ministers is vacated by death or by any other cause, the Council of Ministers appoints one of its members to assume provisionally the Presidency of the Council.

[7] [The 1946 text read: "In case of dissolution, the Cabinet, with the exception of the President of the Council and of the Minister of the Interior, remains in office to attend to current affairs.

"The President of the Republic appoints the President of the National Assembly as President of the Council. The latter appoints a new Minister of the Interior in agreement with the *bureau* of the National Assembly. He appoints as Ministers of State members of political groups not represented in the government."]

Section VII

The Responsibility of Ministers under the Penal Code

Article 56

Ministers are responsible under the penal code for the crimes and offenses committed by them in the exercise of their functions.

Article 57

Ministers can be impeached by the National Assembly and sent before the High Court of Justice.

The National Assembly decides by secret vote and by an absolute majority of its members, excluding those who might be called upon to take part in the prosecution, on the investigation or the prosecution of the case.

Article 58

The High Court of Justice is elected by the National Assembly at the beginning of each legislature.

Article 59

The organization of the High Court of Justice and its rules of procedure are fixed by a special law.

Section VIII

The French Union

I. Principles

Article 60

The French Union consists, on the one hand, of the French Republic, which comprises metropolitan France and the overseas departments and territories, and, on the other hand, of the associated territories and states.

Article 61

The position of the associated states within the French Union is settled for each of them by the act which defines their relations with France.

Article 62

The members of the French Union pool all the means at their disposal to guarantee the defense of the whole of the Union. The government of the Republic is charged with the co-ordination of these means and with control of the policy appropriate for preparing and insuring this defense.

II. Organization

Article 63

The central organisms of the French Union are: the Presidency, the High Council, and the Assembly.

Article 64

The President of the French Republic is the President of the French Union, of which he represents the permanent interests.

Article 65

The High Council of the French Union is composed—under the presidency of the President of the Union—of a delegation of the French government and of the representation which each of the associated states has power to accredit to the President of the Union.

Its function is to assist the government in the general management of the Union.

Article 66

The Assembly of the French Union consists of members one half of whom represent metropolitan France, the other half representing the overseas departments and territories and the associated states.

An organic law will determine under what conditions the different sections of the population can be represented.

Article 67

The members of the Assembly of the Union are elected by the territorial assemblies as far as the overseas departments and territories are concerned; they are elected, as far as metropolitan France is concerned, two-thirds by the members of the National Assembly representing metropolitan France and one-third by the members of the Council of the Republic representing metropolitan France.

Article 68

The associated states can appoint delegates to the Assembly of the Union within limits and conditions defined by a law and an internal act of each state.

Article 69

The President of the French Union convenes the Assembly of the French Union and closes its sessions. He must convene it when so requested by half its members.

The Assembly of the French Union cannot sit during an interruption of the sessions of Parliament.[8]

Article 70

The rules in Articles 8, 10, 21, 22, and 23 apply to the Assembly of the French Union under the same conditions as to the Council of the Republic.

Article 71

The Assembly of the French Union takes cognizance of the proposals which are submitted to it, for advice, by the National Assembly, or the government of the French Republic, or the governments of the associated states.

The Assembly is qualified to pronounce itself on draft proposals submitted by one of its members and to instruct its *bureau* to forward them to the National Assembly. It can make proposals to the French government and the High Council of the French Union.

To be admissible, the draft proposals mentioned in the preceding paragraph must relate to legislation concerning overseas territories.

[8] [Cf. Article 9.]

Article 72

In the overseas territories, legislative power belongs to Parliament in matters of criminal law, the organization of public freedoms, and political and administrative organization.

In all other matters, French law is applicable in overseas territories only under special provisions or if it has been extended by decree to overseas territories after consultation with the Assembly of the Union.

In addition, by derogation from Article 13, special provisions for each territory can be decreed by the President of the Republic in the Council of Ministers after previous consultation with the Assembly of the Union.

III. Overseas Departments and Territories

Article 73

The legislative system of the overseas departments is the same as that of the metropolitan departments, except in certain cases defined by law.

Article 74

The overseas territories are endowed with individual status which takes into account their particular interests within the over-all interests of the Republic.

This status and the internal organization of each overseas territory or of each group of territories are determined by law after advice of the Assembly of the French Union and consultation with the territorial assemblies.

Article 75

The respective status of the members of the Republic and of the French Union is subject to development.

Statutory amendments and the passage from one category to another within the framework set forth in Article 60 can be brought about only by a law voted by Parliament, following consultation with the territorial assemblies and with the Assembly of the Union.

Article 76

The representative of the government in each territory or group of territories is intrusted with the powers of the Republic. He is the head of the administration of the territory.

He is responsible for his acts to the government.

Article 77

An elected assembly is instituted in each territory. The electoral procedure, the composition, and the mandate of this assembly are fixed by law.

Article 78

In groups of territories, the management of common interests is intrusted to an assembly consisting of members elected by the territorial assemblies. Its composition and its mandate are fixed by law.

Article 79

The overseas territories elect representatives to the National Assembly and to the Council of the Republic under conditions fixed by law.

Article 80

All nationals of overseas territories are citizens, on the same basis as French citizens of the mother country or of overseas territories. Special laws shall determine the conditions under which they are to exercise their rights as citizens.

Article 81

All French citizens and nationals of the French Union are citizens of the French Union, a title which entitles them to the enjoyment of the rights and freedoms guaranteed by the Preamble to the present Constitution.

Article 82

Citizens who do not enjoy French civilian status preserve their personal status so long as they do not renounce it.

This status cannot, in any case, constitute a ground for refusing or restricting the rights and liberties attached to French citizenship.

Section IX

THE SUPREME COUNCIL OF THE JUDICIARY

Article 83

The Supreme Council of the Judiciary is composed of fourteen members:
The President of the Republic, Chairman;
The Minister of Justice, Vice-President and Keeper of the Seals;
Six persons elected for six years by the National Assembly by a two-thirds majority, from outside its ranks, six deputy members being elected under the same conditions;
Six persons appointed as follows: four members of the judiciary elected for six years as prescribed by law and representing each category of the judiciary, with four deputies elected under the same conditions; two members appointed for six years by the President of the Republic outside Parliament and the judiciary but within the legal profession, two deputies being appointed under the same conditions.

The decisions of the Supreme Council of the Judiciary are made by a majority vote. When votes are equally divided, the President casts a vote.

Article 84

The President of the Republic appoints the judges, with the exception of the public prosecutors, on the nomination of the Supreme Council of the Judiciary.

The Supreme Council of the Judiciary insures, in accordance with law, the discipline of these judges, their independence, and the administration of the courts of law.

These judges are irremovable.

Section X

TERRITORIAL COLLECTIVITIES

Article 85

The French Republic, one and indivisible, recognizes the existence of territorial collectivities.

These collectivities are the communes and departments and the overseas territories.

Article 86

The framework, the area, the possible regrouping, and the organization of the communes and departments and overseas territories are fixed by law.

Article 87

The territorial collectivities are freely self-administering by councils elected by universal suffrage.

The carrying out of the decisions of these councils is insured by their mayor or their president.

Article 88

The co-ordination of the activity of civil servants, the representation of the national interests, and the administrative supervision of the territorial collectivities are assured on the departmental level by government delegates appointed by the Council of Ministers.

Article 89

Organic laws shall extend departmental and communal freedoms; they may provide for certain large towns administrative rules and structures different from those of small communes and include special provisions for certain departments; they shall fix the conditions of implementation of Articles 85 to 88 above.

Laws shall also fix the conditions in which shall function the local branches of the central administration, in order to bring closer together the administration and the administered.

Section XI

THE REVISION OF THE CONSTITUTION

Article 90

Revision takes place on the following condition: it must be decided upon by a resolution adopted by an absolute majority of the members of the National Assembly.

The resolution defines the object of the revision.

It is submitted, after a minimum delay of three months, for a second reading which must take place under the same conditions as for the first, unless the Council of the Republic has adopted the same resolution by an absolute majority, the matter having been referred to it by the National Assembly.

After this second reading, the National Assembly draws up a draft bill for the amendment of the Constitution. This draft is submitted to Parliament and voted by a majority in the manner laid down for an ordinary law.

It is submitted to a referendum unless it has been adopted at a second reading by the National Assembly by a two-thirds majority or has been voted by a three-fifths majority in each of the chambers.

The bill is promulgated by the President of the Republic as constitutional law within eight days of its adoption.

No constitutional amendment concerning the existence of the Council of the Republic may be effected without the agreement of this Council or without recourse to a referendum.

Article 91

The Constitutional Committee is presided over by the President of the Republic.

It is composed of the President of the National Assembly, the President of the Council of the Republic, seven members elected from outside its ranks by the National Assembly at the beginning of each annual session by proportional representation of the political groups, and three members elected under the same conditions by the Council of the Republic.

The Constitutional Committee examines whether the laws voted by the National Assembly entail a revision of the Constitution.

Article 92

Laws are referred to the Committee, within the period prescribed for promulgation of the law, by a joint request from the President of the Republic and the President of the Council of the Republic, the Council of the Republic having reached a decision by an absolute majority of its members.

The Committee examines the law, endeavors to bring about an agreement between the National Assembly and the Council of the Republic, and if it does not succeed, it makes a decision within five days of being called upon to act. In cases of urgency, this period is reduced to two days.

It is empowered to decide only on matters relating to the possibility of revision of Sections I to X of the present Constitution.

Article 93

Any law which, in the opinion of the Committee, entails a revision of the Constitution, is returned to the National Assembly for another reading.

If Parliament confirms its first decision, the law cannot be promulgated before the Constitution has been revised in the manner laid down in Article 90.

If the law is considered to be in conformity with the provisions of Chapters I to X of the present Constitution, it is promulgated within the time limit fixed by Article 36, to which is added such delays as are provided for in Article 92 above.

Article 94

If the whole of metropolitan France or part of it be occupied by foreign troops, no procedure for revision may be initiated or pursued.

Article 95

The republican form of government cannot be the object of a proposed revision.

APPENDIX *D*

COMPOSITION OF THE NATIONAL ASSEMBLY*

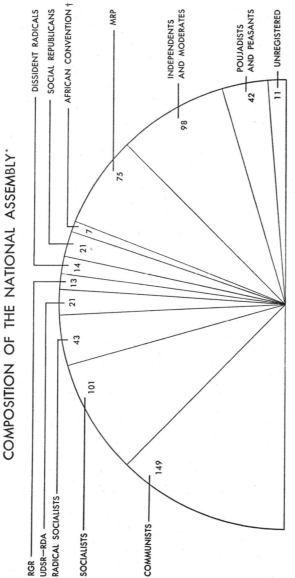

RGR ————————————— 13

UDSR—RDA ————————— 14

RADICAL SOCIALISTS ————— 21

DISSIDENT RADICALS ————— 7

SOCIAL REPUBLICANS ———— 21

AFRICAN CONVENTION † ———

SOCIALISTS —————————— 101

MRP —————————————— 75

INDEPENDENTS AND MODERATES —— 98

COMMUNISTS ———————— 149

POUJADISTS AND PEASANTS —— 42

UNREGISTERED ——————— 11

43

* Number of seats in October, 1957.

† Affiliated with the MRP.

217

NATIONAL ASSEMBLY ELECTION RESULTS

	1946	1951	1956
Communists ⎱ Progressives ⎰	5,489,288	5,057,305	5,514,403
Left-wing groups		38,393	393,219
Socialists	3,431,954	2,744,842	3,247,431
Radical Socialists ⎱ RGR-UDSR ⎰	2,831,834	1,887,583	2,834,265
MRP	5,058,307	2,369,778	2,366,321
Gaullists		4,125,492	842,351
Moderates	2,565,526	2,656,995	3,257,782
Poujadists			2,483,813
Extreme Right			260,749
Other parties	63,976	87,346	98,600
Votes cast	19,203,070	19,129,064	21,298,934
Number of registered voters	25,052,233	24,530,523	26,774,899

PREMIERS OF THE FOURTH REPUBLIC

Date	Premier	Party
12–16–46	Blum	Socialist
1–22–47	Ramadier	Socialist
11–24–47	Schuman	MRP
7–27–48	Marie	Radical
9–11–48	Queuille	Radical
10–28–49	Bidault	MRP
7–12–50	Pleven	UDSR
3–10–51	Queuille	Radical
8–8–51	Pleven	UDSR
1–20–52	Faure	Radical
3–8–52	Pinay	Moderate
1–8–53	Mayer	Radical
6–28–53	Laniel	Moderate
6–18–54	Mendès-France	Radical
2–20–55	Faure	Radical
1–7–56	Mollet	Socialist
6–20–57	Bourgès-Maunoury	Radical
11–7–57	Gaillard	Radical

INDEX

INDEX

African Socialist Movement, 111
Agriculture
 and alcohol, 119–20
 and farmer pressure groups, 118–20
 and French diversity, 6–7
 overrepresented, 70
Algeria, 176, 177, 182
Auriol, Vincent, 40, 41, 42, 53, 179–80

Barangé Law, 93, 110, 121–22, 136, 188
Blum, Léon, 24, 43, 50, 105
Boulanger incident, 94–95
Bourgès-Maunoury, Maurice, 48, 99, 100
Briand Aristide, 43, 102
Bureau, 20–21, 27
Bureau d'âge, 20–21
Bureaux, 20
Business; *see* Industry

Cabinet (or Council of Ministers)
 and African parties, 111
 appointment and dismissal of, 45–46
 compared to Anglo-American counterparts, 49, 50, 185
 decree laws by, 57–58
 and Economic Council, 75
 hierarchy in, 46–47
 and instability, 186
 kinds of meetings of, 47–48
 powers of Parliament over, 39, 51–54, 138–40
 powers of, over Parliament, 54–56
 secretariats for, 47
 solidarity of, 48–50
Cadre law, 57–58
Cadre party, 100–101, 102
Catholic Church; *see* Barangé Law; Clericalism
Centralization, 143, 164–70
Charles X, 10, 85
Charter of 1814, 10
Charter of 1830, 10, 86
Church schools; *see* Barangé Law; Clericalism

Civil rights
 and arrest and arraignment procedures, 149–50
 and freedom
  of association, 154–55
  of domicile, 150–51
  of education, 152–53
  of employment, 156
  of expression, 153
  of religion, 152
  to travel, 151
 and Freemasonry, 123
 French tradition of, 143, 145 ff.
 and intellectuals, 163
 and the judiciary, 150–51, 160–61
 and League for the Rights of Man, 123
 and regulation of private enterprise, 157–58
 and right of asylum, 151
 and social diversity, 161–63
 and Teachers' League, 123
 and trade unions, 156–57
Civil service
 and business, 128, 173–74
 and centralization, 169
 and education, 152
 increasing influence of, 59, 127–28
 independence of, 171–73
 recruitment for, 169–70
 technicians in, 128
Clemenceau, Georges, 43, 50
Clericalism; *see also* Barangé Law
 and Catholic Church, 120–22
 and French diversity, 5
 and MRP, 65, 93, 109
 and religious orders, 155
 and the Right, 85, 91–93, 120–21, 133
Committees; *see* National Assembly; Parliament
Communes
 colonial, 175
 metropolitan, 164–66, 195
Communist party, 5, 22, 67, 105–8, 135, 137